A SEARCH FOR SYNTHESIS:

CONTEMPORARY RE-INTERPRETATIONS OF CLASSICISM, THE
"NEOCLASSICAL SYNTHESIS," AND POST-KEYNESIAN ECONOMICS

by

Ching-Yao Hsieh

Stephen L. Mangum

George Washington University

With a Foreword by James R. Barth

OLYMPUS PUBLISHING COMPANY
Salt Lake City, Utah

To

Courtney Ann and Robert Paul

Stephen James and Jonathan Garth

ACKNOWLEDGEMENTS

We express our thanks to James R. Barth for numerous suggestions, constant encouragement and for having consented to compose a foreword to this volume. A special debt of gratitude is owed to Gwen Luke who expertly typed the entire manuscript. Finally, our thanks to the staff of Olympus Publishing Compay for speedily turning the completed manuscript into its published form.

FOREWORD

Despite the increased mathematical sophistication of macroeconomic models and the widespread use of electronic computers to test these models, there is still considerable controversy over the appropriate role of the government in the U.S. economy. This controversy concerns not only the extent to which the fiscal and monetary authorities can and should smooth cyclical movements in output but also exactly what share of output should be absorbed by the government. At present, unfortunately, a successful resolution to this controversy still remains a goal rather than an accomplishment.

An important aspect of the controversy essentially reduces to whether or not markets clear. Presumably, if markets clear and externalities are absent, then no transactions could be made that would make somebody better off without making someone else worse off. In other words, when markets clear (i.e., excess demand is identically equal to zero in each and every market), then everyone is in equilibrium in the sense of optimizing or maximizing utility. Under such circumstances, there is clearly no compelling reason for the government to intervene in the market place. More specifically, this means that attempts to "fine-tune" the economy would be inappropriate.

Not all markets may clear, however, If this is the case, then it is possible for transactions to take place that could make some individuals better off while not making others worse off. Stated another way, not all individuals are optimizing or maximizing utility when some markets are in disequilibrium. It is this type of situation that is typically used to justify government intervention, including attempts at "fine-tuning."

These ideas may become clearer with the aid of an illustration. Consider a labor market in which the nominal wage rate is either fixed or moves sluggishly relative to the price level (due to the existence of an exogenously determined multi-period contract or the fact that wages are dependent solely upon some weighted average of past prices.) In such a situation it may be possible for the fiscal and monetary authorities to pursue aggregate demand policies that raise prices and thus, given our assumption, reduce real wages which, in turn, stimulate employment or decrease unemployment. Rising unemployment rates may therefore be counteracted by stimulative aggregate demand policies. On the other hand, when prices begin to rise too rapidly the process may simply be reversed (i.e., "tight" monetary and fiscal policies can be implemented). In short, fine-tuning may be used to reduce, if not completely eliminate, business cycles.

If, however, wages and prices are sufficiently flexible so that the labor market is always cleared, then monetary and fiscal policies may not be able to systematically affect unemployment. But this may not be particularly troublesome, since any unemployment that exists when the labor market is cleared is presumably voluntary. The only qualification is that there may be longer-term or natural unemployment (as opposed to cyclical unemployment) largely due to changes in labor force growth and composition, technological factors and reversals in the competitiveness of important U.S. industries vis-a-vis foreign industries. Dealing with this type of un- employment, however, is likely to involve more consistent and predictable (and thus more permanent) government policies for money growth, tax rates, spending and regulation than what are commonly referred to as "stop-go" policies.

Although the market-clearing issue is quite important, there are other aspects to the controversy over the most appropriate way to model a macroeconomy. These include the appropriate concept of equilibrium in the presence of historical time and uncertainty, whether the assumption of profit maximization is still tenable, the extent to which general equilibrium analysis should be de-emphasized in favor of more selective or special analyses and whether institutional factors are adequately taken into account in existing macroeconomic theories. Needless to say, before the various aspects of the controversy can be resolved, they must be understood. And this is the great virtue of Ching-Yao Hsieh and Stephen L. Mangum's book, for all the major aspects of the controversy over the workings of the macroeconomy are fully discussed. Equally important, the authors place all of the issues into historical perspective. This book should therefore appeal not only to those persons interested in current controversies in macroeconomics but also those interested in the history of economic thought.

It is certainly true that there are already numerous books in the areas of macroeconomics and the history of economic thought. For this reason it is important to emphasize that this book is unique in that it completely integrates both of these areas. To be more explicit, it contains a comprehensive treatment of the major alternative approaches to macroeconomics, including classical, supply-side, Keynesian, monetarist, Austrian, rational expectation-ist, Marxian and Post-Keynesian. The authors have specif-ically succeeded in providing in one place an impressive re-interpretation of the classical, neo-classical and post-Keynesian approaches in the context of contemporary develop-ments in macroeconomics. They also provide, moreover, an insightful discussion of the key elements that any successful synthesis of the competing approaches is likely to contain as well as provide some evidence that such a synthesis may already be beginning to take place. All in all, this book will be a valuable sourcebook to all those interested in better understanding the past, present and potential future major themes in macroeconomics. On this score, C.Y. Hsieh and Steve Mangum are to be applauded for their efforts.

James R. Barth
Washington, D.C.
December 1982

TABLE OF CONTENTS

FIGURES

INTRODUCTION

Since the late 1960s the seeming inability of traditional monetary and fiscal policies to combat "stagflation" has accelerated the erosion of confidence in the prevailing economic paradigm, the "Neoclassical Synthesis."[1] Dissensions among the members of the economics profession on both sides of the Atlantic have grown in number. By the 1970s, a majority of economists had recognized a "crisis" in economic theory. The clarion call was given by Joan Robinson in her Richard T. Ely Lecture entitled: "The Second Crisis of Economic Theory" in 1971.[2] In 1974, Sir John Hicks delivered his Jahnsson Lecture on THE CRISIS IN KEYNESIAN ECONOMICS.[3] More recently, Daniel Bell and Irving Kristol have edited a collection of essays entitled, THE CRISIS IN ECONOMIC THEORY.[4]

Parallel to this development, a crisis has also emerged in the Marxian camp. The failure of Marxian theory to

---

[1] The phrase was coined by Paul Anthony Samuelson. See THE COLLECTED SCIENTIFIC PAPERS OF PAUL ANTHONY SAMUELSON, Vol.2 (Mass: M.I.T. Press, 1966), pp. 111 and 1271. Also see Paul A. Samuelson, ECONOMICS, 6th Edition (New York: McGraw-Hill, 1964), pp. 360-361.

[2] Joan Robinson's Ely Lecture, delivered to the American Economic Association Annual Meeting at New Orleans, December 27, 1971 with J.K. Galbraith being Chairperson.

[3] Sir John Hicks, THE CRISIS IN KEYNESIAN ECONOMICS, Yrjo Jahnsson Lectures (New York: Basic Books, Inc., Publishers, 1974).

[4] THE CRISIS IN ECONOMIC THEORY edited by Daniel Bell and Irving Kristol (New York: Basic Books, Inc., Publishers, 1981).

explain the durability of capitalism and the slow growth of the socialist economies has caused deep soul-searching and disillusionment among Marxian economists. This prevailing sentiment is reflected in the famous quip of the Maoist Michel le Bris: "God is dead; Marx is dead; and I don't feel too well myself." Among the revisionist movements in socialist countries, the most complete theoretical criticisms of Marxian theory have been stated by Antony Cutler, Barry Hindess, Paul Hirst and Athar Hussain in their book, MARX'S CAPITAL AND CAPITALISM TODAY (1977).[5]

One salient and common cause for these two "crises" may be traced to the neglect, by both camps, of institutional and social changes in the monetary economy of industrial capitalism. In the case of Marxian economics, the four authors of MARX'S CAPITAL AND CAPITALISM TODAY point out:

> Marxism currently has no adequate theory of modern monetary forms, of financial capitalist institutions and their different modes of articulation into the financial systems of capitalist national economies, and of the forms of organizations of large-scale industrial capitalist enterprises and the types of economic calculation they undertake. These deficiencies are real and salient ones...The theorisation in CAPITAL of, for example, money, credit, capitalist organization and calculation are all seriously inadequate.[6]

---

[5] Antony Cutler, Barry Hindess, Paul Hirst and Athar Hussain, MARX'S CAPITAL AND CAPITALISM TODAY (London: Routledge & Kegan Paul, 1977). Two volumes. Evidence of revisionist economic movements in Socialist countries are common in the daily press. See, for instance, Dan Morgan's article "East Europe Tries Modified Capitalism: Hungary's Economy Sets the Pace," THE WASHINGTON POST, May 24, 1982, p.A1.

[6] Cutler, Hindess, Hirst and Hussain, op.cit., p. 2.

In the opinion of the four authors, capitalism is far more complex and resilient than the traditional Marxists had realized. The labor theory of value is obsolete in explaining pricing decisions of modern corporations.

As for the "Neoclassical Synthesis," much of past analyses in macro and microeconomics were based upon the foundation of Walrasian general equilibrium. They have failed to consider historical time and the emergence of various uncertainty-reducing institutions in a monetary economy. As observed by Paul Davidson, "the main characteristics of a real world monetary economy are: Uncertainty, Fallibility, Covenants, Institutions, Commerce, Finance and Trust. These are the Seven Wonders on which the Modern World is based."[7]

The Neo-Walrasians have been very resilient. F.H. Hahn admitted in 1970: "the Walrasian economy that we have been considering, although one where the auctioneer regulates the terms at which goods shall exchange, is essentially one of barter."[8] K.J. Arrow and F.H. Hahn in 1971 wrote:

> The terms in which contracts are made matters. In particular, if money is the good in terms of which contracts are made, then the prices of goods in terms of money are of special significance. This is not the case if we consider an economy without a past and without a future. Keynes wrote that 'the importance of money essentially flows from it being a link between the present and the future' to which we add that it is important also because it is a link between the past and the present. If a serious monetary theory comes to be written, the fact that contracts are indeed made in terms of

---

[7] Paul Davidson, MONEY IN THE REAL WORLD (New York: John Wiley & Sons, 1972, 1978), 2nd edition, p. 147.

[8] F.H. Hahn, "Some Adjustment Problems," ECONOMETRICA, 38 (1970), p. 3.

3

money will be of considerable importance.[9]

In the economics profession, we are indeed living in a very exciting age of reconstruction in economic theory. The winter of despair is fading; the spring of hope is now emerging. We are witnessing the search for a "New Synthesis" which will be built on the foundations of the more lasting insights of Classicism, Neoclassicism and Post-Keynesianism. It is this perception that provides the rationale for the title of this book: A SEARCH FOR SYNTHESIS: CONTEMPORARY RE-INTREPRETATIONS OF CLASSICISM, THE "NEOCLASSICAL SYNTHESIS" AND POST-KEYNESIAN ECONOMICS.

This book consists of four parts. The major tenets of Classicism are considered in Part I. The discussion is confined to three representative writers; namely, Adam Smith, David Ricardo and Robert Thomas Malthus. No attempt is made to give a chronological survey of the development of classical political economy from Quesnay to John Stuart Mill and Marx. That is the task of traditional textbooks on the history of economic thought. Our objective is to highlight the links between classical theory and modern economics. The similarities and crucial differences between the writings of Adam Smith and contemporary "supply-side" economics are discussed first. Next, the influence of Ricardian economics on post-Keynesian economics as well as on the "new classical macroeconomics" are considered.[10] The link between Ricardo

---

[9]K.J. Arrow and F.H. Hahn, GENERAL COMPETITIVE ANALYSIS (San Francisco: Holden-Day, Inc., 1971), pp. 356-357.

[10]The leading writers of the "new classical macroeconomics" are Robert Lucas, Thomas Sargent, Neil Wallace and Robert Barro. The leading writers of post-Keynesian economics are Joan Robinson, N. Kaldor, J.A. Kregel, L. Pasinetti, D.M. Nuti, Piero Sraffa, J. Eatwell and others in England; P. Garegnani, A.Roncaglia and others in Italy; A.Asimakopoulos and G.C. Harcourt in Australia; K.R.Bharadwaj and A.Bhaduri in India; T.K. Rymes in Canada; E.J.Nell, Paul Davidson, S.Weintraub, A.S.Eichner, B.J.Moore and others in the U.S.

and contemporary "supply-side" economics is also under the purview of Part I. In surveying the lasting influences of Ricardo, Piero Sraffa's prelude to a critique of neoclassical price theory is highlighted.[11] The closing chapter of Part I deals with causality in classical theory. The discussion is presented in the light of Sir John Hicks' 1979 exposition.[12]

The "Neoclassical Synthesis" and its critiques are the subject of Part II. A macroeconomic model is first introduced to illustrate the basic tenets of this paradigm. The model uses the IS-LM framework originally introduced by Sir John Hicks. Its microfoundations are Walrasian general equilibrium theory. The equilibriating mechanism is limited to prices. Next, the theoretical heritage of the "Neoclassical Synthesis" is traced, followed by a brief survey of some of the important criticisms of the "Neoclassical Synthesis" from three sources: (1) the theorists of "disequilibrium macroeconomics,"[13] (2) the exponents of "Rational Expectations" (the "new classical macroeconomics") and (3) the Austrian School. Part II concludes with a discussion of causality in the "Neoclassical Synthesis."

The post-Keynesian approach to micro- and macroeconomics is highlighted in Part III. The explicit role played by investment emerges as a common thread tying the various theories together. For instance, as pointed out by Alfred S. Eichner, "Post-Keynesian theory offers an explanation of economic growth and income distribution--with the two viewed

----

[11] Piero Sraffa, PRODUCTION OF COMMODITIES BY MEANS OF COMMODITIES: PRELUDE TO A CRITIQUE OF ECONOMIC THEORY (London: Cambridge University Press, 1960).

[12] Sir John Hicks, CAUSALITY IN ECONOMICS (New York: Basic Books, Inc., Publishers, 1979).

[13] The leading writers of "disequilibrium macroeconomics" are A. Leijonhufvud, R. Clower, R. Barro and H. Grossman.

5

as being directly linked to one another. The key determinant
is the same for both. This is the rate of investment,
whether measured against total national income or viewed as
the percentage change over time."[14] In microeconomics, the
post-Keynesian theory of prices is dynamic. Pricing
decisions are viewed as dominated by a long-term perspective
reflecting the overriding goal of the large corporation:
continuous and accelerating growth. Expansion requires
investment; investment needs financing. Hence a target rate
of profit is incorporated into the cost-determined prices.
Here again the central role of investment is made explicit.
Following a brief discussion of the neo-Austrian and other
criticisms of post-Keynesian economics, Part III closes with
a discussion on causality centered on the work of Sir John
Hicks.

Part IV considers the harbingers of the emerging "New
Synthesis." For example, in the area of general equilibrium
analysis Frank Hahn has observed: "...there are good grounds
for believing that we shall soon have satisfactory theories
of non-Walrasian equilibria and these are highly likely to
leave scope for government macro-policy to be effective."[15]
In the area of labor economics, the challenge of segmented
labor market theories to orthodox theory will also make
modifications and additions to orthodox labor economics. The
main contributions of these various segmented labor market
theories, as observed by Glen G. Cain, "are (1) the idea of
endogenous determination of attitudinal variables among
workers and (2) the historical and institutional dimensions
of internal labor markets—which enrich our understanding of

---

[14] See Alfred S. Eichner's Introduction to A GUIDE TO POST-
KEYNESIAN ECONOMICS (White Plains, New York: M.E. Sharp,
Inc., 1978, 1979), pp. 11-12.

[15] See Frank Hahn's essay, "General Equilibrium Theory" in THE
CRISIS IN ECONOMIC THEORY, edited by Daniel Bell and Irving
Kristol, 1981, p. 137.

the economics of bureaucratic organization."[16] Another optimistic signal of the narrowing gap among the opposing theories is that the post-Keynesians seem to have toned down their criticisms of quantitative techniques. More and more econometric based studies of post-Keynesian theories are being published. The Leonard Forman and Alfred S. Eichner paper, "A Post-Keynesian Short-Period Model: Some Preliminary Econometric Results" is just one of the many manifestations of movement in this direction.[17] An even stronger indication of the coming of the "New Synthesis" is a survey of economists cited by Cicarelli and Stuck which produced the following list of "breakthroughs" and developments likely to occur in economics within the next 20 years or so:[18]

-- synthesis of prevailing monetarist and neo-Keynesian economics

-- widespread professional acceptance of the post-Keynesian paradigm, its emphasis on the determination of aggregate supply as well as aggregate demand

-- expanded study of the interrelationships between economic variables and technological variables, with greater awareness of energy as a production input equal to labor and capital

---

[16] See Glen G. Cain, "The Challenge of Segmented Labor Market Theories to Orthodox Theory: A Survey" in JOURNAL OF ECONOMIC LITERATURE, Vol. XIV, No. 4, December 1976, pp. 1215-1257. Quote from page 1248.

[17] See Leonard Forman and Alfred S. Eichner, "A Post Keynesian Short-Period Model: Some Preliminary Econometric Results" in JOURNAL OF POST KEYNESIAN ECONOMICS, Vol. IV, No. 1, Fall 1981, pp. 117-135.

[18] See James Cicarelli and John Stuck, "Economics: The Next Twenty Years" in JOURNAL OF POST KEYNESIAN ECONOMICS, Vol. III, No. 1, Fall 1980, pp. 116-122.

-- a comprehensive understanding of inflation and its determinants

-- greater emphasis on disequilibrium analysis in micro and macro theory and less on equilibrium analysis

-- a new theoretical framework in international economics capable of analyzing both growing world interdependency and international reactions to supranational events.

This book is designed for graduate and advanced undergraduate students in economics. The objective is to assist such students to have a better perspective and understanding of the alternative paradigms in their field, and the historical development of these paradigms. Secondly, this approach will help them to integrate their studies of micro- and macroeconomics into an understandable whole in preparation for comprehensive examinations in macroeconomics and any further work in the field. By presenting the history of economic thought in the context of lessons for today and the future, we believe that this book will be a useful organizing device for any student of economics, and a useful text in courses such as macroeconomics and the history of economic analysis.

PART I

CONTEMPORARY RE-INTERPRETATIONS OF CLASSICISM

CHAPTER I

THE SUPPLY SIDE ECONOMICS OF ADAM SMITH

Classical Economics and Contemporary "Supply-Side Economics"

Contemporary "supply-side economics" is essentially a response to the vexing stagflation and other economic problems of our time.[1] It is basically a reaffirmation of traditional policies to increase the wealth of nations and to achieve an efficient allocation of resources. The policy concern of contemporary supply-siders is to redress what they consider to be the destructive effects of demand management and excessive regulatory policies since the 1960s. As aptly stated by James R. Barth, the specifics of today's supply-side program are "reductions in marginal tax rates, cuts in

---

[1] For lucid discussions of supply-side economics see: James R. Barth, "The Reagan Program for Economic Recovery: Economic Rationale (A Primer on Supply-Side Economics)", ECONOMIC REVIEW, Federal Reserve Bank of Atlanta, September 1981; John A. Tatom, "We Are All Supply-Siders Now!" REVIEW, Federal Reserve Bank of St. Louis, May 1981, Vol. 63, No. 5, pp. 18-30; Robert E. Keleher and William P. Orzechowski, "Supply-Side Effects of Fiscal Policy: Some Historical Perspectives," reviewed in the Federal Reserve Bank of Atlanta, ECONOMIC REVIEW (February 1981), pp. 26-28; Thomas J. Hailstones, A GUIDE TO SUPPLY-SIDE ECONOMICS (Richmond, Virginia: Robert F. Dame, Inc., 1982); James T. Laney, "The Other Adam Smith," ECONOMIC REVIEW, Federal Reserve Bank of Atlanta, October, 1981, pp. 26-29; Robert M. Dunn, Jr., ECONOMIC GROWTH AMONG INDUSTRIALIZED COUNTRIES: WHY THE UNITED STATES LAGS (Washington, D.C.: National Planning Association, 1980); and Arthur B. Laffer and R. David Ranson, "A Formal Model of the Economy", mimeographed (Washington, D.C." Office of Management and Budget, 1970).

the growth in government spending, a slow and steady growth in the money supply and regulatory reform."[2] By now, practically all economists have perceived that the so-called "supply-side economics" is not a revolutionary doctrine, nor is it an innovation of the Reagan administration. It should be recalled that long before the rise of contemporary supply-siders, the general equilibrium models constructed by Patinkin, Hicks, Solow and others under the paradigm of the "grand neoclassical synthesis" had implicit "supply-side" tenets.[3] Such models generally highlight the price system as the equilibriating mechanism and relegate the demand management arguments of the Keynesians to the background.

The classical economists from Adam Smith to John Stuart Mill, just like the Reagan administration, tried very hard to sell the exciting promises of "supply-side economics." They, too, encountered severe criticisms and stubborn forces of resistance. They were labelled as "philosophic radicals" by their opponents[4] in that they agitated for political and economic reforms to redress the destructive effects of mercantilist policies and to implement the self regulating market mechanism both domestically and internationally.

The classical economists did not conceive the market mechanism and the system of economic freedom as arising in a

---

[2] James R. Barth, op.cit., p. 4.

[3] See Don Patinkin, MONEY, INTEREST AND PRICES, 2nd edition (Evanston, Ill.: Harper & Row, 1965); R.M. Solow, "A Contribution to the Theory of Economic Growth," QUARTERLY JOURNAL OF ECONOMICS, Vol. 70, Feb., 1956; and T.W. Swan, "Economic Growth and Capital Accumulation," ECONOMIC RECORD, Vol. XXXLL, Nov. 1956.

[4] See Elie Halevy, THE GROWTH OF PHILOSOPHIC RADICALISM, trans. Mary Morris (London, 1928) (Boston: The Beacon Press, 1955).

vacuum. There is a tendency, when discussing the emphasis of classical economics on economic freedom and the laissez faire approach to economic policy, to minimize, in fact ignore, any real role for government. However, the classicists did define a significant role for government. Government was to determine and enforce the legal framework necessary for the exercise of economic freedom.[5] Lionel Robbins observes:

> The invisible hand which guides men to promote ends which were no part of their intention, is not the hand of some god or some natural agency independent of human effort; it is the hand of the law giver, the hand which withdraws from the sphere of the pursuit of self interest those possibilities which do not harmonize with the public good. There is absolutely no suggestion that the market can furnish everything; on the contrary, it can only furnish anything when a host of other things have been furnished another way.[6]

Even the acrimonious critic of the market mechanism, Karl Polanyi, asserts that "laissez faire was planned;

---

[5]Ricardo expressed this idea well:
"To keep men good you must as much as possible withdraw from them all temptations to be otherwise. The sanctions of religion, of public opinion, and of law, all proceed on this principle, and that State is perfect in which all these sanctions concur to make it in the interest of all men to be virtuous, which is the same thing as to say, to use their best endeavor to promote the general happiness." J.R. McCulloch, editor, THE WORKS OF DAVID RICARDO (London: John Murray, 1881), p. 554.

[6]Lionel Robbins, THE THEORY OF ECONOMIC POLICY IN ENGLISH CLASSICAL POLITICAL ECONOMY (London: Macmillan & Co. Ltd., 1952), pp. 56-57.

planning was not."[7] Polanyi points out that, although the idea of the self regulating market mechanism was conceived during the Enlightenment, it was only by the 1820s that the liberal creed began to assume its evangelical fervor. The three basic tenets of this militant liberal creed were: (1) the establishment of a competitive labor market which was brought into existence for the first time by the Poor Law Amendment Act of 1834, (2) the restoration of the automatic gold standard which was accomplished by Peel's Bank Act of 1844 and (3) the enforcement of international free trade which became a reality after passage of the Anti-Corn Law Bill of 1846.[8]

A simplistic explanation of the invisible hand concept often implies a degree of social harmony that seems most unbelievable in reality. But to believe such harmony was inevitable was not what the classicists were saying. Indeed, they argued that such harmony, a very limited kind of harmony, would have to be created by a system of social control. The classicists envisioned such social control as being established through government and what Warren Samuels has termed "the nonlegal or nondeliberative forces of social control" such as morals, religion, customs and education. As

---

[7] See Karl Polanyi, THE GREAT TRANSFORMATION (Boston: Beacon Press, 1957), Chapter 12, p. 141.

[8] See Karl Polanyi, ibid., Chapter 12. Polanyi argues that these pieces of legislation, passed under the pressure of the philosophic radicals, established laissez faire. Laissez faire is therefore man-made, rather than incumbent in the workings of natural law. In fact, Polanyi asserts that laissez faire is most unnatural. Just as the human body develops sytems to protect itself from disease, so do economic systems and economic agents. Economic protection-ism is natural in Polanyi's view; unions are a natural response to worker uncertainty. Laissez faire and the legislation by which it was spawned tore apart what was natural. Laissez faire in his view is therefore unnatural.

Samuels states:

> ...not only did the classicists recognize the created character of the social order...but also they were cognizant of the roles of both the legal and nonlegal or nondeliberative forces of social control...moreover, and this fact is of great importance, the classicists' case for the relative de-emphasis of the legal forces, i.e. the role of the government in the economy, was in effect premised on the effective operation of the non-deliberative forces of social control.[9]

The major focus and interests of the classical writers were the viability of the economy and the process of economic

---

[9] Warren J. Samuels, THE CLASSICAL THEORY OF ECONOMIC POLICY (Cleveland: The World Publishing Company, 1966) p. 23. Samuels does a superb job of reviewing the classical writers such as Smith, Ricardo, Bentham, J.S. Mill, et al. for reference to nonlegal sanctions. His book is worthwhile reading. In Chapter 2 Samuels presents strong evidence, through quotations, that Smith viewed religion as a force "restricting and channelling behavior" (p. 34); Ricardo mentioning religion as "one of the forces directing behavior to the virtues promotive of the general happiness" (p. 39); and Mill's "inculcation of morals as a constraint upon behavior" (p. 51). In THE THEORY OF MORAL SENTIMENTS Smith writes "when custom and fashion coincide with the natural principles of right and wrong, they heighten the delicacy of our sentiments, and increase our abhorrance for everything which approaches to evil" (p. 60-61). Samuels presents evidence that the main body of classicists viewed education to be "a social contract operating through the inculcation of individuals in the prevailing moral code, training individuals for a plce in the status quo, and impressing upon individuals the existent cosmology within the constraints of which private thought takes place" (p.66).

growth. Viability requires the equality of inputs and outputs. Otherwise, the economy will not be self-sustaining. Growth depends upon the surplus of outputs over inputs and upon the best utilization of the surplus or net product. These ideas are best stated by Vivian Walsh and Harvey Gram:

> (In the classical model) inputs are produced commodities which are treated as variables, and not as parameters. Commodities are produced by means of commodities so that time enters essentially into the economic problem. (The simplest way to illustrate the classical theory is in the context of a one-sector corn model. The economic question would then be:) will the corn produced this year be enough to provide the necessary inputs for next year's production? Here the fundamental concepts are viability and surplus, and the problem of allocating the surplus between the accumulation of capital and luxury consumption over and above subsistence come to the fore.[10]

As Walsh and Gram document, the classical writers show that for an economy to be capable of growth, the technology of production must yield a net output over and above inputs. Hence, technology of production emerges as the central concept in classical analysis. It determines not only viability and surplus, but also the natural price[11] and the natural rate of profit in the spirit of von Neumann. Their basic models implicitly assume that the production function is a linear process. If constant returns to scale are

_____

[10] See Vivian Walsh and Harvey Gram, CLASSICAL AND NEOCLASSICAL THEORIES OF GENERAL EQUILIBRIUM (New York: Oxford University Press, 1980), p. 5. The words in brackets are ours.

[11] See J. von Neumann, "A Model of General Economic Equilibrium," REVIEW OF ECONOMIC STUDIES, 13, 1945-46, 1-9.

assumed, "it is then possible to present the technology for producing corn by a single 'coefficient:' the fraction of a unit of corn needed to produce a unit of corn a_{cc} ."[12] In the Ricardian subsistence-wage model, workers' consumption is included as part of the means of production, hidden within the technical coefficient, a_{cc} . The one-sector corn model may be stated as follows:[13]

Let Y_c stand for the gross output of corn and $a_{cc}Y_c$ denote the input of corn required for the production of Y_c units of corn. A viable corn economy in which surplus is positive may be characterized by the following equations:

(a) $a_{cc}Y_c < Y_c$, or, $1 - a_{cc} > 0.$

(b) $Y_c = a_{cc}Y_c + g\,a_{cc}Y_c + \lambda_c Y_c$, or, $a_{cc}Y_c + g\,a_{cc}Y_c = Y_c - \lambda_c Y_c.$

where $a_{cc}Y_c$ represents replacement investment; $g\,a_{cc}Y_c$ represents net investment; and $\lambda_c Y_c$ defines consumption of corn over and above subsistence. The symbol λ_c denotes the fraction of gross output of corn allocated for luxury consumption. Equation (b) is simply the familiar identity equation, $Y = C + I$, or $I = Y - C$.

Dividing both sides by Y_c , Equation (b) is transformed into:

(c) $a_{cc} + g\,a_{cc} = 1 - \lambda_c$, or, $\lambda_c = -a_{cc}g + (1 - a_{cc}).$

This equation describes the consumption-growth trade-off in the corn model which is illustrated by Figure 1.1 below.

_____

[12] See Walsh and Gram, op.cit., p. 13.

[13] It should be noted that the classical corn model is the prototype of one-sector growth models, such as the Harrod-Domar model and Solow and Swan's neoclassical growth models.

FIGURE 1.1

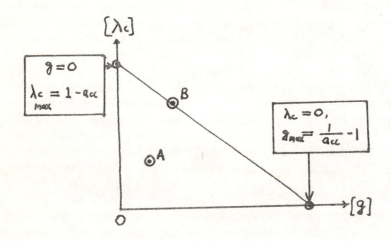

Maximum luxury consumption, $\lambda_{c_{max}} = 1 - a_{cc}$, (if g = 0) is indicated by the limiting point on the vertical axis which measures λ_c. The maximum growth rate of output, $g_{max} = \frac{1}{a_{cc}} - 1$, (if λ_c = 0) is represented by the limiting point on the horizontal axis which measures the growth rate, g. The mercantilist misuse of surplus may be represented by a point such as A inside the trade-off line. A high consumption economy may be depicted by point B on the trade-off line.

The corn model clearly demonstrates that viability and the rate of growth of output depend entirely on the technology of production,   . In what follows it will be shown that, in the classical world, natural prices and the natural rate of profit also are technologically determined.

The Main Theme of the Wealth of Nations

Adam Smith was truly a "supply-sider" in economic analysis. His major work, THE WEALTH OF NATIONS, is a theoretical attack on mercantilism, showing that mercantilism's incumbent misallocation of economic surplus is harmful to economic growth and must be replaced by a policy of laissez faire. The main theme of the book is economic growth and a subsidiary theme is the efficient allocation of given resources. Contrary to popular belief, Smith discusses the competitive market mechanism and optimal allocation of given resources according to consumer wants in only two chapters, Chapters VII and IX in Book I. Even these microeconomic writings are growth oriented. The main theme is aptly reinterpreted by Hla Myint as follows:

> The central principle, which successfully unifies the various classical economic doctrines from Adam Smith to J.S. Mill, embodies the following fundamental proposition: viz. the economic welfare of society can be more effectively promoted by (i) increasing the physical productivity of labour, and (ii) increasing the total volume of economic activity, rather than tamely accepting the given quantity of productive resources and making refined adjustments in allocating them among different industries. From this follow the two major canons of classical economic policy, (i) free trade which extends the scope of the division of labour and brings fresh resources into the productive framework, and (ii) capital accumulation which enables society to maintain a greater quantity of labour."[14]

---

[14] Hla Myint, THEORIES OF WELFARE ECONOMICS (New York: Augustus M. Kelley, 1948), p. 12.

The fundamental Smithian theme may be illustrated by the following simplified version of Irma Adelman's growth model.[15]

(1) $Y = F(K, L, N)$.

Equation (1) is the aggregate production function. Smith recognized the existence of three factors of production: capital or "stock" which is designated by the symbol K, labor which is represented by the symbol L and land designated by the symbol N. The symbol Y stands for aggregate output. It should be noted that behind the symbol L is the Smithian doctrine of productive labor. The wealth of nations (Y) is treated as a product of labor productivity and the employment of productive labor. As pointed out by John Hicks, "there is no fixed capital in Smith's (formal) model; but he does have something that corresponds to gross investment...The labour which is employed in this "gross investment" he calls "productive labour." Thus it is productive labour that plays the same part in his system as gross investment does in ours.[16]

Smith saw the productivity of labor as depending on the division of labor which is limited by the extent or size of the market. A liberal economic policy and an end to mercantilism were viewed as the means of widening the market, promoting the division of labor and spurring capital accumulation.

---

[15] See Irma Adelman, THEORIES OF ECONOMIC GROWTH AND DEVELOPMENT (Stanford, California: Stanford University Press, 1961), Chapter 3.

[16] See John Hicks, CAPITAL AND GROWTH (New York: Oxford University Press, 1965), p. 37. Productive labor is that which is investment oriented, increasing future output. In contrast, unproductive labor according to Smith can be thought of as that employed in production of consumption goods.

It should be noted that the Smithian production function is not subject to the restriction of diminishing marginal returns. Smith was not a "dismal scientist." He optimistically assumed that there was an automatic flow of technological progress that permits continued growth in output and productivity. However, Smith did share with his successors the view of the eventual coming of the stationary state.[17]

The Smithian aggregate production function nevertheless has two restrictions:

---

[17] Irma Adelman selects the following passage from Smith's WEALTH OF NATIONS on the stationary state:

In a country which has acquired the full complement of riches which the nature of its soil and climate, and its situation with respect to other countries, allowed it to require; which could, therefore, advance no further, and which was not going backwards, both the wages of labour and the profits of stock would probably be very low. In a country fully peopled in proportion to what either its territory could maintain or its stock employ, the competition for employment would necessarily be so great as to reduce the wages of labour to what was barely sufficient to keep up the number of labourers, and, the country being already fully peopled, that number could not be augmented. In a country fully stocked in proportion to all the business it had to transact, as great a quantity of stock would be employed in every particular branch as the nature and extent of trade would admit. The competition, therefore, would everywhere be as great, and consequently the ordinary profit as low as possible." From Adam Smith, THE WEALTH OF NATIONS (New York: Random House, 1937), p. 53.

21

$$(2) \quad \frac{\partial F}{\partial K} = g(K, U), \text{ and}$$

$$(3) \quad \frac{\partial F}{\partial L} = h(K, U).$$

Equation (2) states that the marginal productivity of capital, $\frac{\partial F}{\partial K}$, depends upon the quantity of capital employed and upon the institutional framework of the economy which is depicted by the symbol U. Equation (3) refers to the functional relationship between the marginal productivity of labor, $\frac{\partial F}{\partial L}$, and the same two independent variables.

Smith believed that the institutional framework was given exogenously. It is an autonomous policy variable which can shift the production function upward. Thus, we may write:

$$(4) \quad U = \overline{U}.$$

The justification for this equation is that the classical writers believed in the positive role of the state. As pointed out by Lionel Robbins, there were two different strands of thought in the great liberal movement of the 18th and 19th centuries.[18] The Physiocrats and Bastiat represent one strand which has its origin in the tradition of natural law and natural right. The philosophy of natural law stresses that the rational order of nature is the embodiment of justice and that it is eternal, unchanging and independent of man's private reason. Hence, it is ascertainable by reason.[19] According to Mercier de la Riviere and Bastiat, the criterion of economic policy should be conformity with the natural order at all times and in all places. In this

---

[18] See Lionel Robbins, op. cit., pp. 46-47.

[19] See Peter J. Stanlis, EDMUND BURKE AND THE NATURAL LAW (Ann Arbor: The University of Michigan Press, 1965); and NATURAL LAW AND MODERN SOCIETY (Cleveland, Ohio: The World Publishing Company, 1966).

view the functions of the state should be minimal. The
English classical economists, on the other hand, followed the
Utilitarian tradition founded by Hume and Bentham, "according
to which all laws and rights were to be regarded as essentially man-made and to be evaluated according to their
effects on the general happiness, long term and short.
Smith, frequently uses the terminology of NATURERECHT, but
his arguments are consistently utilitarian in character."[20]

(5) $\dfrac{dN}{dt} = 0.$

This equation states that land is fixed in quantity
which is implied by Smith in his statement that land rent is
a monopoly price. Therefore the aggregate production
function may be written more simply as:

(6) $Y = F(K, L).$

The growth rate of the annual flow of output may be obtained
by differentiating equation (6). Doing so one obtains:

(7) $\dfrac{dY}{dt} = \dfrac{\partial F}{\partial K} \dfrac{dK}{dt} + \dfrac{\partial F}{\partial L} \dfrac{dL}{dt}.$

By substituting equations (2), (3) and (4) into (7), the
following expression is derived:

(8) $\dfrac{dY}{dt} = g(K, \bar{u}) \dfrac{dK}{dt} + h(K, \bar{u}) \dfrac{dL}{dt}.$

The term $\dfrac{dK}{dt}$ (capital accumulation) is determined by the
rate of savings, or parsimony. Smith believed that under
normal conditions savings would always be invested and that
savings rather than consumption promotes growth. It should
be noted that the Smithian theory of savings and investment
together with his real sector analysis (his basic model did
not make money a causative factor in the economic process)

---

[20]See Lionel Robbins, op. cit., p. 47.

23

represent three important features of Say's Law.[21]

As to the allocation of aggregate output between savings and consumption, Smith argued that the rate of saving depends crucially upon the rate of profit. As long as there is a positive rate of profit, savings and capital accumulation would continue. This doctrine may be stated symbolically as:

$$(9) \quad \frac{dK}{dt} = k\left[r - \bar{r}, Y\right].$$

where the symbol r represents the rate of profit at time t, $\bar{r}$ symbolizes the minimum value of the rate of profit which covers compensation for risks, and Y represents aggregate output, the source of savings. Now, what determines the rate of profit? Here, Smith brought in his view of the positive function of the state. The rate of profit, he contends, is regulated by the institutional environment; i.e., the degree of monopoly or competition, the extent of regulation of business, the control of international trade, taxation and so forth. Being an optimist, Smith asserted that liberal economic policy (U) could always ensure a positive rate of profit. The Smithian view is summarized as follows:

$$(10) \quad r - \bar{r} = m(K, \bar{u}),$$

where $\frac{\partial M}{\partial K} < 0$.

Smith explains the term signifying the rate of growth of the labor force, dl/dt , by his theory of population which anticipates that of Malthus.

$$(11) \quad \frac{dL_s}{dt} = q(\omega - \bar{w}).$$

---

[21] See Thomas Sowell, SAY'S LAW (Princeton: The Princeton University Press, 1972), pp. 15-17.

Equation (11) depicts the Smithian theory of population. The symbol $\frac{dls}{dt}$ designates the rate of growth of the labor supply which varies with the difference between the market wage rate, w, and the subsistence wage rate, $\bar{w}$. If the market wage rate exceeds the subsistence wage rate, the supply of labor will increase and vice versa. The subsistence wage rate is that wage rate which will keep the existing labor supply constant, neither increasing or decreasing.

The rate of increase in the demand for labor in Smithian population theory is represented by the following equation:

$$(12) \quad \frac{dld}{dt} = a \, \frac{dK}{dt} + b \, \frac{dY}{dt}$$

The term $\frac{dld}{dt}$ represents the rate of growth of the demand for labor. The symbols a and b represent the contributions to the rate of growth of the demand for labor by capital accumulation, and by the rate of growth of output which is the source of the rate of increase in saving. Behind the demand for labor function is the well known wages fund doctrine, which is an integral part of the classical economists' concept of capital. Robert V. Eagly observes:

> Following Quesnay's lead, classical economists defined capital quite comprehensively to include command of all the reproducible inputs used in production, i.e., machinery, raw materials, and labor. The degree of abstraction in the capital concept was considerable. To consider the initial allocation process, the total capital stock was conceptualized to consist not of use specific commodities but of abstract commodities 'in general,' a malleable putty-like commodity unit that could be allocated either to the wages fund or to the stock of machinery. Such an abstraction

permitted classical analysis to concentrate on the problem of capital allocation.[22]

Let us assume that the homogeneous output in the Smithian model is corn. Capital stock then consists of bushels of corn kept in storage which are saved from the previous production period. This capital stock is divided into two components during the production period: (a) the means of production (seeds) and (b) the means of subsistence for the laborers employed in the production of corn. This second component is the wages fund. Given implicitly the fixed capital-labor ratio which is determined exogenously by technology, capital and labor are jointly demanded. It is in this way that the demand for labor becomes a function of capital accumulation. The allocation of capital stock in classical theory is depicted schematically in Figure 1.2.

$$(13) \quad \frac{dL_s}{dt} = \frac{dL_d}{dt}.$$

Equation (13) is based on the Smithian assumption that in the long run the supply of labor will be in proportion with the demand for labor. Hence, Equation (12) may be used to describe the forces determining the rate of growth of the

---

[22] See Robert V. Eagly, THE STRUCTURE OF CLASSICAL ECONOMIC THEORY (New York: Oxford University Press, 1974), p. 34. Samuel Hollander points out that the British economy of Smith's day was not basically 'agricultural.' "The agricultural sector itself was actually one of the most capital intensive sectors, and structural change within the manufacturing sector was transforming the nature of the economy. It is clear from Smith's account both of the industry structure and technological change that he was aware of the beginnings of a transition; and it is the trend which matters." See Hollander's THE ECONOMICS OF ADAM SMITH (Toronto and Buffalo: University of Toronto Press, 1973), pp. 311-312.

Figure 1.2

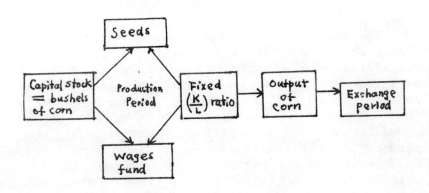

labor force. We may rewrite the growth rate of labor in the following form:

$$(14) \quad \frac{dL}{dt} = a\,\frac{dk}{dt} + b\,\frac{dY}{dt}.$$

If we substitute Equation (14) into the equation for the annual flow of output (Equation 8), the following expression is derived:

$$(15) \quad \frac{dY}{dt} = g(k,\bar{u})\,\frac{dk}{dt} + h(k,\bar{u})\left(a\,\frac{dk}{dt} + b\,\frac{dY}{dt}\right).$$

By collecting the $\frac{dY}{dt}$ terms on the left hand side of Equation (15) and factoring out the terms in $\frac{dk}{dt}$ on the right hand side, the solution of the model is obtained:

$$(16) \quad \frac{dy}{dt} = \frac{dk}{dt} \left\{ \frac{g(K,\overline{u}) + ah(K,\overline{u})}{1 - bh(K,\overline{u})} \right\}.$$

The solution succinctly summarizes the main theme of THE WEALTH OF NATIONS. It points out that the rate of growth of output crucially depends upon two elements: (a) capital accumulation and (b) liberal economic policies. Equation (16) not only brings forth the "supply-side economics" of Adam Smith in bold relief, but also clearly demonstrates that capital accumulation is the unifying principle tying together the various specific doctrines (viz. the theory of savings and investment, population theory, the wages fund doctrine, the principle of free trade, the theory of value, monetary theory, public finance and the concept of economic welfare) in one "magnificient dynamics."[23] Some of the growth oriented doctrines will be considered in the following section.

Growth-Oriented Specific Doctrines

Microeconomics

Smithian microeconomics, like his macroeconomics, reflects a preoccupation with the issues of viability and growth. The problem of price determination is divided by Smith (and other classical economists) into two parts: (a) the natural price and (b) the market price. The natural price is inherent in the production process itself. In the modern terminology of linear programming it is the dual of the primal problem of output maximization. This concept may be explained in the context of the corn model.

---

[23] The expression, "magnificient dynamics" is coined by William J. Baumol. See his ECONOMIC DYNAMICS (New York: The Macmillan Company, 1951), Part I.

TABLE 1.1

The Primal	The Dual
(i) $\lambda_c = (1 - a_{cc}) - a_{cc}g$.	(iii) $P_c a_{cc} + r P_c a_{cc} = P_c$.
(ii) $\lambda_c = 0$, $g_{max} = \frac{1}{a_{cc}} - 1$.	(iv) $a_{cc}(1+r) = 1$.
	(v) $r = \frac{1}{a_{cc}} - 1$.

Equation (i) states the trade-off between luxury consumption and growth. Equation (ii) defines the maximum
growth rate of output. Turning to the dual problem, equation
(iii) describes the production price of corn. The symbol P_c
stands for the price of corn; $P_c a_{cc}$ represents the money cost
of replacing the means of production; and r is the rate of
profit on the value of the capital investment, viz. $P_c a_{cc}$.
It should be noted that, in any one-sector model, there is no
problem of determining relative prices for the price of corn
in terms of itself is unity. Therefore, after dividing
through by P_c and factoring out a_{cc} Equation (iii) is
transformed into Equation (iv). Equation (v) is obtained by
rearranging terms in (iv).

Equation (iii) depicts the natural (production) price of
corn independent of market exchange. The natural price is
embedded in the technology of production and reflects the
viability and surplus of the system of production as a whole.
It is analogous to the shadow price (accounting price) in
linear programming. The dual relationship is shown by the
equality of the maximum rate of growth of output $\left(g_{max} = \frac{1}{a_{cc}} - 1 \right)$

and the natural rate of profit $\left(r = \frac{1}{a_{cc}} - 1 \right)$. The reason for this equality is simply that the rate of increase of output will exactly suffice to cover the interest cost of investment in inputs. The same theorem was derived by von Neumann in his seminal paper, "A Model of General Economic Equilibrium." In both the classical corn model and the disaggregated capital (multicommodity) model of von Neumann, both the maximum rate of growth of output and the corresponding rate of profit are determined by the technology of production. In the corn model, the technology of production is denoted by the coefficient a_{cc} .

The classical exchange process (including that of Smith) is best illustrated by a heterogeneous commodity model. As in the corn model, the capitalists own the entire capital stock (the means of production) at the beginning of the production period. The existing technology of production determines the allocation of the capital stock. The capitalists also own all of the commodities produced at the end of the production period. The market exchange period then begins. The market exchange is envisioned as the exchange of produced goods among the capitalists. The purpose of the exchange process is to obtain the inputs required by the next production period (remember that commodities are produced by means of commodities). The prices involved in this process are market prices. There need not be immediate conformity with the natural price. When market prices deviate from natural prices, it is a manifestation that the conditions of viability and growth of the economy have not been fulfilled.

Competition among the capitalists eventually will bring the market prices in conformity with natural prices. As observed by David P. Levine, "the market acts exclusively to 'execute' the laws of the production system as those laws are expressed in the production price."[24] The equilibrating

---

[24] See David P. Levine, "Aspects of the Classical Theory of Markets," AUSTRALIAN ECONOMIC PAPERS, June 1980, p. 4.

mechanism in the classical system is the movement of capital among the industries, seeking the highest rate of return. As a result of such movements market prices will change; consequently the rate of profit will change also. The optimal set of relative prices (those that are in conformity with natural prices) is reached when the rate of profit is uniform in all sectors of the economy. Robert V. Eagly observes: "The uniform profit criterion thus makes relative prices dependent upon the size, productivity and distribution of the economy's total capital stock-evidence once again of the all-pervasive importance of capital in classical theory."[25] This is also evidence of the growth oriented microeconomics of Smith and the classical economists.

Welfare Economics

The welfare economics of Adam Smith is as preoccupied with capital accumulation and economic growth as is his microeconomics. The classical index of economic welfare was stated by Smith in the WEALTH OF NATIONS, Book I, Chapter V. Although the title of the chapter is "Of The Real And Nominal Price Of Commodities, Or Of The Price In Labour, Or Their Price In Money," it "is not concerned with value theory but with welfare economics, and, in particular, with the problem of index numbers of welfare."[26]

Smith first pointed out that labor "is the real measure of exchangeable value of all commodities."[27] He then elaborated further:

[25]Robert V. Eagly, op. cit., p. 49.

[26]Mark Blaug, ECONOMIC THEORY IN RETROSPECT, Revised Edition (Homewood, Illinois: Richard D. Irwin, Inc., 1968), p. 51.

[27]Adam Smith, op. cit., p. 30.

The real price that every thing costs to the man who wants to acquire it, is the toil and trouble of acquiring it. What every thing is really worth to the man who has acquired it, and who wants to dispose of it or exchange it for something else, is the toil and trouble which it can save to himself, and which it can impose upon other people.[28]

In the above passage, Smith considered subjective utility (or the disutility of the "toil and trouble" of labor) as the index of economic welfare. Thus Hla Myint observes: "this passage would suggest that Smith considered the essence of man's struggle against nature as consisting in the outlay of subjective disutility rather than, as Ricardo would say, in the physical unit of labour. Since outlay and return must be comparable, the statement implies that Smith was trying to arrive at a subjective concept of income as distinct from Ricardo's concept of objective physical output."[29]

However, Smith's focus of attention soon shifted from the subjective utility approach to the objective approach of physical output. The reason for this shift was his pre-occupation with capital accumulation and economic growth. In the words of John Hicks: "There can be little doubt that Smith intended this chapter (Book II, Chapter III, "Of The Nature, Accumulation, And Employment of Stock") to be regarded as the center-piece of his whole work. Book I and the earlier chapters of Book II lead up to it; the rest of the work consists, in large, of the application of it."[30] In order to rationalize this change of focus, Smith seems to assume that subjective satisfaction is roughly proportional

---

[28]Adam Smith, op. cit., p. 30.

[29]Hla Myint, op. cit., pp. 19-20.

[30]John Hicks, op. cit., p. 36.

to the quantity of physical output. His classical successors generally accepted this assumption without further modification.

It has generally been taken for granted that the fundamental assumption of classical welfare economics is that consumer sovereignty guided by the "invisible hand" would teleogically achieve a social optimum. However, the main textual evidence of the classical discussion of perfect competition as the efficient allocator of given resources was confined to Book I, Chapters 7 and 10 of the WEALTH OF NATIONS. The competitive equilibrium in output markets was considered by Smith in Chapter 7; the competitive factor market equilibrium was discussed in Chapter 10. The only other textual evidence for efficient allocation of given resources is the familiar Ricardian comparative cost doctrine in the theory of international trade. From these scanty sources, one would conclude that the allocative concept of perfect competition is a subsidiary theme in classical economics.

The Role of Money

The role of money was also seen by Adam Smith within a growth related framework. This is evidenced by his treatment of the nominal quantity of money as an endogenous variable. Smith wrote:

> The quantity of money...must in every country naturally increase as the value of the annual produce increases. The value of the consumable goods annually circulated within the society being greater, will require a greater quantity of money to circulate them. A part of the increased produce, therefore, will naturally be employed in purchasing, wherever it is to be had, the additional quantity of gold and silver necessary for circulating the rest. The increase of those

metals will in this case be the effect, not the cause, of the public prosperity.[31]

A cursory reading of the above mentioned passage gives the impression that Smith sounded like the nineteenth century anti-bullionists. This impression is reinforced by his "real bills doctrine." However, as pointed out by David Laidler:

> Smith was a proponent of banking and paper money, and was in no sense an adherent of any type of 'money does not matter' doctrine. His advocacy here hinged on supply-side considerations of a type analyzed in the 1960s literature dealing with the influence of money and growth and economic welfare. The issues involved here are clearly long run in nature...Smith's treatment of banking was an integral part of his treatment of the process of economic growth.[32]

As to the Smithian "real bills doctrine," Laidler argues:

> ...although there can be no doubt that Smith espoused the Real Bills Doctrine, he was not led to argue, as were many later adherents of the fallacy, that the banking system could safely be left to its own devices, even in the absence of specie convertibility. It was not, therefore, a fundamental component of his analysis of banking policy in the same sense as his insistence upon the importance of convertibility. Nothing illustrates this point more clearly than the fact that it was specie

---

[31] Adam Smith, op. cit., pp. 323-324.

[32] David Laidler, "Adam Smith as a Monetary Economist," THE CANADIAN JOURNAL OF ECONOMICS, XIV, NO. 2, May, 1981, p. 193. The underline is ours.

convertibility, not any limitation on the type of loans that banks might make, that Smith wished to see written into law.[33]

Fiscal Policy

Adam Smith's pervasive concern for economic growth also dominated his discussions of taxation and public debt. In the "Introduction and Plan" to the WEALTH OF NATIONS, Smith laid down two major determinants of the aggregate supply of output: (1) "the skill, dexterity and judgement with which its labour is generally applied," and (2) "the proportion between the number of those who are employed in useful labor and those who are not so employed." Smith argued that high taxes on wages would hurt these determinants. He wrote:

> If direct taxes upon the wages of labour have not always occasioned a proportionable rise in those wages, it is because they have generally occasioned a considerable fall in the demand for labour. The declension of industry, the decrease in employment for the poor, the diminution of the annual produce of the land and labour of the country, have generally been the effects of such taxes. In consequence of them, however, the price of labour must always be higher than it otherwise would have been in the actual state of the demand; and the enhancement of price, together with the profit of those who advance it, must always be finally paid by the landlords and the consumers...
>
> Absurd and destructive as such taxes are, however, they take place in many countries.[34]

---

[33] David Laidler, ibid., pp. 198-199.

[34] Adam Smith, op. cit., p. 817. The underlines are ours.

Smith stressed that taxes on capital and profits would hurt savings and investment and that high import duties would encourage smuggling. He wrote:

> High taxes, sometimes by diminishing the consumption of the taxed commodities, and sometimes by encouraging smuggling, frequently afford a smaller revenue to government than what might be drawn from more moderate taxes. When the diminution of the revenue is the effect of the diminution of consumption, there can be but one remedy, and that is the lowering of the tax. When the diminution of the revenue is the effect of the encouragement given to smuggling, it may perhaps be remedied in two ways; either by diminishing the temptation to smuggle, or by increasing the difficulty of smuggling.[35]

As observed by Robert E. Keleher,[36] the inverse relationship between high tax rates and tax revenue stated by Adam Smith in the preceding passage clearly anticipated the "Laffer Curve" of our time.

Adam Smith and his successors generally opposed deficit spending and advocated paying off the national debt. He wrote:

> In the payment of the interest of the public debt, it has been said, it is the right hand which pays the left. The money does not go out of the country. It is only a part of the revenue of one set of the inhabitants which is transferred to

---

[35] Adam Smith, op. cit., p. 835. The underlines are ours.

[36] Robert E. Keleher, "Historical Origins of Supply-Side Economics," ECONOMIC REVIEW, Federal Reserve Bank of Atlanta, January, 1982, pp. 12-19.

another; and the nation is not a farthing the poorer. This apology is founded altogether in the sophistry of the mercantile system...[37]

Smith further pointed out that the existence of a huge public debt required higher taxes to pay the interest on the debt. From the standpoint of his "Laffer view," such fiscal policy would be detrimental to economic growth. Is it safe to pressume that Smith would endorse the major elements of today's supply-side economics? The "supply-siders" would like to think so. This is evidenced by the vogue of "Adam Smith" ties worn by some of the faithfuls at the early stage of the Reagan administration.

Perspective

The exciting promises of the classical "supply-side economics" were, to a large extent realized, especially for Great Britain. The United Kingdom was able to monopolize the Industrial Revolution for 100 years. Unquestionably, some of the material improvements did "trickle down" to other parts of the world. What is the explanation for this phenomenal success? The answer lies partially in the institutional environment of the time. James T. Laney perceptively observes that the moral basis of capitalism depends upon disciplined, public spirited citizens who are willing to postpone immediate reward for the sake of future productivity. He writes: "it is important for us to recognize that the basic condition for the emergence of capitalism was the postponement of gratification for the sake of investment and enterprise, in other words, for the sake of future productivity."[38] That these virtues were widely

---

[37] Adam Smith, op. cit., p. 879.

[38] See James T. Laney, op. cit., p. 27.

upheld during the classical period is documented by Ralph H. Tawney in his RELIGION AND THE RISE OF CAPITALISM and by Max Weber in his PROTESTANT ETHIC AND THE SPIRIT OF CAPITALISM.[39] Even during the 1930s the puritan work ethic was still the basic ethos of the western free enterprise market economy.

In the past 50 years or so, the perception of a dramatic change in the basic ethos of capitalism has grown. Many commentators point to a decline in the work ethic and the rise of consumerism as having greatly undermined the moral and psychological foundations of the free enterprise market economy. The increased labor force participation rates of the past decades may at first blush seem at odds with a decline in the work ethic. However, a strong moral compulsion for work may be differentiated from the desire for the financial and intrinsic rewards that employment brings.[40] Accompanying the rise of consumerism and hedonism, the growth of the welfare state, decades of prosperity and other factors have contributed to the emergence of "the entitlements mentality."[41] This mentality manifests itself in legislated price floors, the institution of cost of living allowances (COLAs) in contracts, import quotas, agricultural subsidies and powerful lobby groups. Perhaps more individuals than ever before in our history feel that the government or the

---

[39] Richard H. Tawney, RELIGION AND THE RISE OF CAPITALISM (New York: Harcourt, Brace & Co., 1926) and Max Weber, PROTESTANT ETHIC AND THE SPIRIT OF CAPITALISM (London: G. Allen and Unwin Ltd., 1930).

[40] A thoughtful and entertaining discussion of past and future trends in work can be found in Sar A. Levitan, WORK IS HERE TO STAY, ALAS! (Salt Lake City: Olympus Publishing Co.; 1973).

[41] Uwe E. Reinhardt, "Diagnosing The Great American Belly-ache," PRINCETON ALUMNI WEEKLY, February 22, 1982, pp. 19-26.

collective owes them their sustinence in times of difficulty and increasingly at all other times as well.

Secondly, the costly tradeoff between efficiency and equity has been overlooked by ardent advocates of more egalitarian income distribution. Third, the rise of single issue politics has drastically changed the institutional environment of traditional "supply-side economics." Under these conditions, the exciting promises of contemporary supply-siders could easily appear to be oversold. The extent of success of modern "supply-side economics" may depend, to a large extent, upon the ability of the Reagan administration to restore the traditional moral and psychological foundation of the society. If this preconditon could be met, the supply-siders would have a much easier task in initiating a "new beginning."

CHAPTER 2

THE "SUPPLY-SIDE" ECONOMICS OF DAVID RICARDO

Ricardo and A Theory of Secular Distribution

In the preface of his THE PRINCIPLES OF POLITICAL
ECONOMY AND TAXATION, Ricardo states his main theme:

> The produce of the earth--all that is derived
> from its surface by the united application of
> labour, machinery and capital, is divided among
> three classes of the community, namely the propri-
> etor of the land, the owner of the stock or capital
> necessary for its cultivation, and the labourers by
> whose industry it is cultivated.

> But in different stages of society, the propor-
> tions of the whole produce of the earth which will
> be allotted to each of these classes, under the
> names of rent, profit, and wages will be essen-
> tially different...To determine the laws which re-
> gulate this distribution is the principal problem
> of Political Economy: much as the science has been
> improved by the writings of Turgot, Stuart, Smith,
> Say, Sismondi, and others, they afford very little
> satisfactory information respecting the natural
> courses of rent, profit, and wages.[1]

The reason for Smith's neglect in developing a rigorous
theory of distribution was that his interest was focused on
the two main factors responsible for increasing the wealth of
nations, i.e. (a) technology; and (b) the employment of

---

[1] David Ricardo, THE PRINCIPLES OF POLITICAL ECONOMY AND
TAXATION, Everyman's Library (London: J.M. Dent & Sons Ltd.,
1955), p. 1.

productive labor. Hence Smith adopted the "labor commanded" measure of value as a "cast-iron argument to show that the economic welfare of society could invariably be increased by increasing the amount of savings."[2]

As a subsidiary theme of his analysis, Smith thought that the distribution of income could be explained through the theory of production prices. Smith maintained that the production prices of every commodity, including the supply price of the means of production, could be reduced to wages, profits and rent. Thus Maurice Dobb refers to the Smithian doctrine as an "adding up theory,"[3] which Harry G. Johnson

---

[2] Hla Myint explains the Smithian "labor commanded" measure of value by the following arithmetic example: "Let us say that the current social output is made up of 1000 units of wage goods and that out of this 1000 units, 600 units are paid out as wages and 200 units each are paid out as rents and profits. Then according to Smith this state of affairs means that: (i) the current social output of 1000 wage units is the product of only 600 units of labor 'embodied' in its production. (Given the money wage rate of one unit per man, the 1000 units divided by the given money wage rate can command 1000 units of labor); (ii) if the entire amount of the 1000 units have been saved and reinvested or 'embodied' in the next year's production, the social output of that year would be raised very appreciably. Thus, assuming labor yields a constant return, if 600 units of labor can produce 1000 units of wage goods, then 1000 units of labour can produce 1666 units. Assuming the supply of labour remains elastic at the wage of one wage unit per man, then this would give society a command over 1666 units of labour." op. cit., p. 21.

[3] Maurice Dobb, THEORIES OF VALUE AND DISTRIBUTION SINCE ADAM SMITH (London: Cambridge University Press, 1973), p. 46.

considers to be "no theory of distribution at all."[4] In the opinion of Alessandro Roncaglia, total decomposition of price into wages, profits and rent is impossible. He says:

> In fact, whenever there is at least one commodity directly or indirectly necessary for the production of all commodities in the economy (a 'basic product' in Sraffa's terminology), the cost of production of each commodity will include a residual, and no matter how many times the process of reduction is repeated this residual cannot be eliminated, even as the process of reduction tends to infinity.[5]

Ricardo criticized Smith for mixing up production price with the problem of distribution. He also objected to the Smithian treatment of wages, profits and rents in the "total decomposibility theorem" as being independent of one another. Since Ricardo's objective was to examine the laws which regulate the distribution of net product (surplus) among the three classes of society, and since he considered the capitalist class to be the engine of growth, it was important to him to be able to determine whether the capitalists were indeed receiving additional resources when distribution changed. Thus Smith's "labor commanded" measure of value was not suitable for Ricardo's purpose, for the quantities expressed by the "labor commanded" measure were not independent of relative prices and the money wage rate. What Ricardo sought was an invariant measure of value which would be independent of distribution.

---

[4] Harry G. Johnson, THE THEORY OF INCOME DISTRIBUTION (London: Gray-Mills Publishing Ltd., 1973), p. 12.

[5] Alessandro Roncaglia, SRAFFA AND THE THEORY OF PRICES (Chichester, New York: John Wiley & Sons, 1978), Translation from Italian by J.A. Kregel, p. 9.

The main thrust of the Ricardian theory can be summarized in the following flow diagram (Figure 2.1). We shall proceed by considering each component. We shall then discuss some of the lasting influences of the Ricardian analysis.

Ricardo expounded the "labour embodied" theory both as an invariable measures and as the source of value. He asserted:

> The value of a commodity, or the quantity of any commodity for which it will exchange, depends on the relative quantity of labour which is necessary for its production, and not on the greater or lesser compensation which is paid for that labour.[6]

The introduction of capital does not invalidate the "embodied labour" theory in Ricardo's view. He maintained that the same principle would still hold true.

> Not only (does) labour applied immediately to commodities affect their value, but the labour also which is bestowed on the implements, tools, and buildings with which such labour is assisted.[7]

In other words, Ricardo treated capital as "labour embodied" in the capital goods produced in the previous periods.

However, Ricardo was not a diehard "labour embodied" theorist. As observed by George J. Stigler, Ricardo's emphasis on the quantitative importance of labor was an empirical, rather than an analytical proposition. "An analytical statement concerns functional relations; an empirical statement takes account of the quantitative

---

[6] David Ricardo, op. cit., p. 5.

[7] David Ricardo, op. cit., p. 13.

FIGURE 2.1

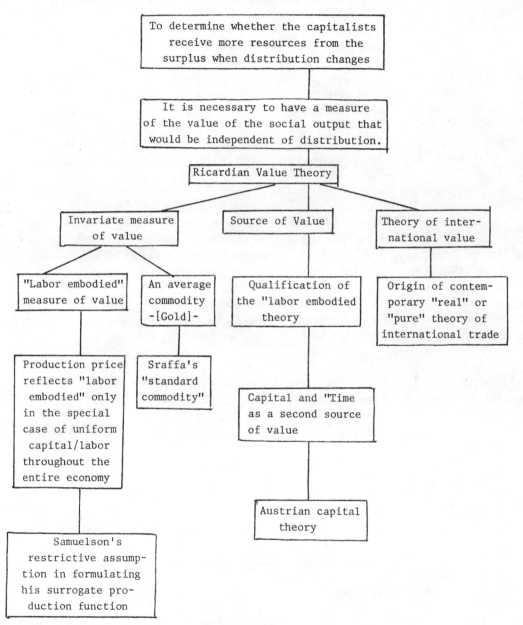

significance of the relationships."[8] Stigler further points
out:

> McCulloch, Bailey, and Malthus correctly understood
> Ricardo's theory to be a cost-production theory
> excluding rent, and De Quincey should probably be
> added to this group. The theory was understood as
> a simple labor-quantity theory by Say and Mill, and
> also by Torrens. It is worth repeating that
> Ricardo accepted Malthus' analysis and rejected
> Mill's. The theory was more widely understood in
> its correct sense in Ricardo's time than later
> times.[9]

The same view was expressed by John M. Cassels in his
article, "A Re-Interpretation of Ricardo on Value." Cassels
emphasized that "Ricardo's famous chapter on value was never
intended as an exposition of any theory of value in the
accepted sense of the term but was written for the special
purpose of providing him a particular logical link that was
required in his elaborate chain of reasoning about the
dynamics of distribution."[10]

----

[8] George J. Stigler, "Ricardo and the 93 Per Cent Labor Theory
of Value," reprinted from the AMERICAN ECONOMIC REVIEW, Vol.
XLVIII (June, 1958) in his ESSAYS IN THE HISTORY OF ECONOM-
ICS (Chicago: The University of Chicago Press, 1965), p.
341.

[9] George J. Stigler, ibid., pp. 339-340.

[10] John M. Cassels, "A Re-Interpretation of Ricardo on Value"
reprinted from THE QUARTERLY JOURNAL OF ECONOMICS, Vol.
XLIX (May, 1935) in READINGS IN THE HISTORY OF ECONOMIC
THEORY, edited by Ingrid H. Rima (New York: Holt, Rinehart
and Winston, Inc., 1970), p. 86.

The special purpose Ricardo envisioned was to use the "labour embodied" theory to clinch his arguments against the corn laws.[11] In order to simplify the analysis, Ricardo formulated a simple corn model to present his case. Its policy orientation and Ricardo's non-Walrasian methodology prompted Joseph A. Schumpeter to call it "the Ricardian vice."[12]

The Ricardian Corn Model

The Ricardian corn model consists of four building blocks: (i) the West-Malthus-Ricardo theory of differential rent; (ii) the wages fund doctrine; (iii) the subsistence theory of wages; and (iv) the "embodied labor" theory of value. The first two building blocks were contained in his ESSAY ON THE INFLUENCE OF A LOW PRICE OF CORN ON THE PROFIT OF STOCK (1815); and the last two were expounded in his THE PRINCIPLES OF POLITICAL ECONOMY AND TAXATION (1817).

Ricardo's wages fund theory is similar to that of Adam Smith. The subsistence wage theory is derived from the Malthusian theory of population. The main idea of the theory of rent is that land is variable in quality and fixed in supply. When a country is sparsely populated, only the best quality land would be cultivated. As the population grows, it would become necessary to cultivate land of inferior quality. Thus, there would be diminishing returns in agriculture. Should the corn laws be enacted, England would

---

[11]The term "corn" was used sometimes to mean not only grain but all agricultural wage goods. The purpose of the "corn laws" was to protect British wheat farmers by prohibiting foreign wheat import.

[12]Joseph A. Schumpeter, HISTORY OF ECONOMIC ANALYSIS (New York: Oxford University Press, 1954), p. 473.

be condemned to raise her required food from her fixed supply of land. As the population grew and the margin of cultivation was extended, the landlords of better quality land would receive rent. Rent per acre represents the difference between the net profit per acre on the better quality land and that on the inferior land. If no rent were charged on the better quality land, there would be no incentive for farmers to extend the margin of cultivation to inferior land. At the extensive margin of cultivation, there would be zero rent. The better quality land would be intensively cultivated. However, the principle of diminishing marginal returns would also apply to the intramarginal land, with the intensive margin of cultivation reached when the net profit per acre disappears.[13]

As a master model builder, Ricardo demonstrated his superior skill by eliminating rent as a component of the production costs of the homogeneous wage good, corn. He pointed out that rent "is never a new creation of value but always a part of the revenue already created." Ricardo wrote:

> The value of corn is regulated by the quantity of labor bestowed on its production on that quality of land, or with that portion of capital, which pays no rent. Corn is not high because a rent is paid, but a rent is paid because corn is high; and it has been justly observed that no reduction would take place in the price of corn although landlords should forego the whole of their rent.[14]

---

[13] For a detailed discussion of the West-Malthus-Ricardo rent theory, see Ingrid H. Rima, DEVELOPMENT OF ECONOMIC ANALYSIS (Homewood, Illinois: Richard D. Irwin, Inc., 1927), Third edition, chapters 6 and 7.

[14] David Ricardo, op. cit., p. 38.

The reasoning behind this famous passage was perceptively explained by Mark Blaug as follows: "In the Ricardian system, resources are viewed as shifting between land and industry, never between different uses of land. Since land has no alternative uses, rental payments do not affect the supply price of agricultural produce. 'Pure rents' are transfer costs and involve no using up of resources."[15]

Ricardo further asserted that the interests of the landlords are always opposed to the interest of every other class in the community. When the price of corn increases owing to increased difficulty in production, "the landlord is doubly benefited...First, he obtains a greater share, and, secondly, the commodity in which he is paid is of greater value."[16]

The Ricardian corn model can be described by two alternative graphical presentations. We shall consider the Kaldorian formulation first,[17] and then summarize Baumol's formulation.[18] The agricultural sector of the economy may be depicted by the following Kaldorian diagram:

---

[15] Mark Blaug, RICARDIAN ECONOMICS (New Haven: Yale University Press, 1958), p. 13.

[16] David Ricardo, op. cit., p. 45.

[17] Nicholas Kaldor, "Alternative Theories of Distribution: reprinted from REVIEW OF ECONOMIC STUDIES, Vol. XXIII, No. 2 (1955-6) in his ESSAYS ON VALUE AND DISTRIBUTION (Illinois: The Free Press of Glencoe, 1969).

[18] William J. Baumol, ECONOMIC DYNAMICS (New York: The Macmillan Co., 1951), Chapter 2.

FIGURE 2.2

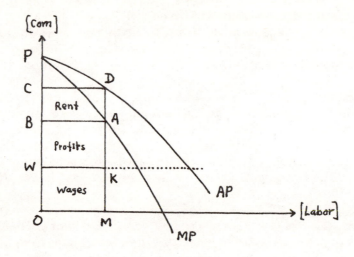

The vertical axis of Figure 2.2 measures the quantity of the homogeneous wage-good, corn, while the horizontal axis measures the amount of labor employed in agriculture. The curve Ap represents the average product of labor and the curve Mp denotes labor's marginal product. The downward sloping shape of the two curves reflects the assumption of diminishing marginal returns in agriculture. Given the demand for food, the quantity of labor employed is determined by the distance OM on the horizontal axis in Figure 2.2. Given OM units of labor, total output of corn is represented by the rectangle OCDM. Rent is the difference between the average and marginal products of labor. The average product of labor is indicated by the vertical distance DM (=CO) and the marginal product of labor is denoted by the vertical distance AM (=BO). Total rent is represented by the rectangle BCDA. Note that the marginal product of labor is not equal to the wage rate. It is the sum of wages and profits. OW (=KM) depicts the long-run subsistence wage rate determined by the Malthusian theory of population which is assumed to be constant over time. In modern parlance, the Ricardian hypothesis implies an infinitely elastic supply curve of labor indicated by the horizontal line WK. What is the demand for labor in this model? It is the agricultural wages fund indicated by the rectangle OWKM, which shows the total quantity of labor employed at the subsistence-wage rate OW.

What about the rate of profit? It is represented by the ratio, r = profits/wages. In Figure 2.2, r = ((AK - KM)/KM) x 100% = ((AK/KM)-1) x 100%. In as much as KM is assumed to be constant, it follows that the rate of profit varies with AK. As capital accumulates, the quantity of labor employed will grow, so that any addition to the total wages fund will tend to be a horizontal addition pushing the vertical line KM to the right.

Ricardo was able to draw precise predictions about the secular changes in the distributive shares from his corn model. These predictions are demonstrated by Figure 2.3. The initial equilibrium situation is represented by the rectangle OCDM. The distributive shares are: Rent (BCDA), Profits (WBAK) and Wages (OWKM). Over the course of capital accumulation and population growth, the margin of cultivation is extended. As a result of diminishing marginal productivity of labor at the margin, the secular distributive share of the landlords will rise at the expense of the capitalists' share. This tendency of increasing rent and a failing rate of profit is represented in Figure 2.3 by the rectangle OBEN, which is the total corn output resulting from the employment of ON units of labor. Total rent is now GFEH, which is greater than the original rectangle BCDA. Total profits are indicated by the rectangle WGHL, which is smaller than the original rectangle WBAK. Total wages also rise from OWKM to

51

Figure 2.3

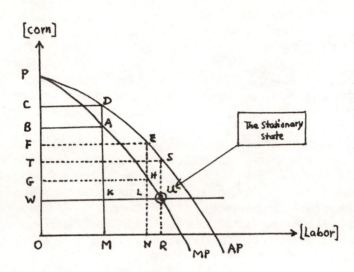

OWLN. Since the subsistence-wage rate remains unchanged at OW, the rate of profit consequently falls.

The "stationary state" eventually will arrive. The "doomsday" is indicated by the point U where total corn output is represented by the rectangle OTSR; total rent is denoted by the rectangle WTSU; and the total subsistence-wage bill is the rectangle OWUR. Thus, the total output of corn is entirely eaten up by rent and wages. Profits are entirely wiped out. This is Ricardo's indictment of the corn laws.

The model implies that should England follow the law of comparative labor costs and acquire additional corn through free trade, the "doomsday" would be postponed. Alternatively, technical progress in agriculture could put off the

52

"doomsday" for some time. Free trade or technical progress would be reflected in an upward shift of the Ap and Mp curves in Figure 2.3. However, unless the two curves could be shifted up continuously, the inevitability of the "doomsday" would not be eliminated.

An alternative description of Ricardo's predictions has been suggested by William J. Baumol (Figure 2.4). The horizontal axis measures the size of the working population, while the vertical axis measures total product and total wage payments after deducting rent. Since the subsistence wage rate is constant, total wage payments are given by the straight line OS through the origin. The slope of OS indicates the subsistence wage rate. OP represents the total product of corn after deducting rent. The shape of the production function reflects the assumption of diminishing returns in agriculture. It also conveys the idea that rent payments will grow simultaneously with the increase in the working population.

The prediction of a falling rate of profit and the arrival of the "stationary state" are explained as follows: Suppose that we start with a working population of OR_1. Total subsistence-wage payments will be R_1S_1 and an amount S_1P_1 will be left over for profits. This will induce capital accumulation which, in turn, will drive market-wage payments up to R_1P_1. Once the disparity between the market-wage payments and the subsistence-wage payments takes place, capital accumulation will cease. In the meantime, following the Malthusian theory, population will increase. As the resulting supply of labor will be greater than the demand for labor, competition among laborers for employment will drive the market-wage rate down to the subsistence level again. Consequently, population growth will be checked at the point OR_2. Once more a profit margin will appear (the distance S_2P_2), and capital accumulation will again take place. Market-wage payments are soon driven up to R_2P_2, population grows to OR_3, and so on, in a series of steps represented by the stepped line S_1P_1 S_2P_2 S_3P_3 ..., gradually approaching

53

Figure 2.4

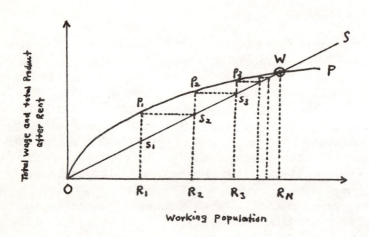

the point W where the two curves intersect. At W, total output is completely exhausted by rent and subsistence-wage payments. The rate of profit is zero and the "stationary state" has arrived.

Ricardo's Standard Commodity

To generalize the simple corn model, Ricardo sought to find the link between distribution in the agricultural sector and distribution in the community as a whole. He found the introduction of fixed capital to greatly complicate the problem, for an element of "time" was thus introduced into the production process. The ratio of fixed capital to the circulating capital paid to labor (the capital-labor ratio) may differ among occupations, fixed capital may differ in durability and the rates of turnover of circulating capital may differ. Ricardo wrote:

> It appears, then, that the division of capital into different proportions of fixed and circulating capital, employed in different trades, introduces a considerable modification to the rule, which is of universal application when labour is almost exclu-[19] sively employed in production...

In section IV of Chapter I "On Value," Ricardo gave two arithmetic examples to illustrate the necessary qualifications of the "labor embodied" theory.

CASE I: The introduction of fixed capital into the production of the more expensive commodity. Suppose that two men each employ 100 laborers each year, but one in the second year uses machines produced in the first year. In the second year, the machine-user must make not only the regular return on the circulating capital used to employ labor, but a rate of profit on the circulating capital invested must be included in the production price of the commodity.

Year (1)--One man employs 100 laborers at the wage rate of £ 50 per man to construct a machine. So the total wage bill is £ 5000. The other man also employs 100 laborers at the wage rate of £ 50 per man to grow corn. His total wage bill is £ 5000. At the end of the year, the value of the machine = the value of the corn = £ 5000 plus 10 percent profit = £ 5500.

Year (2)--One employs 100 men = £ 5000 to grow corn, as before; the value of the corn = £ 5000 plus £ 500 = £ 5500. The other employs 100 = £ 5000 plus capital worth £ 5500 to

---

[19] David Ricardo, op. cit., p. 23.

produce cloth; the value of the cloth = £ 5000 plus £ 500 plus 10 percent of £ 5500 = £ 6050.

Ricardo points out:

> Here, then, are capitalists employing precisely the
> same quantity of labour annually on the production
> of their commodities, and yet the goods they
> produce differ in value on account of the different
> quantities of fixed capital.[20]

CASE II: Variations in the period of production. Suppose that two commodities each require 40 man-years to produce; in one case, 20 men are employed for two years, and in the other 40 men for one year.

Commodity (1)--In the first year 20 laborers are employed to produce the commodity at the wage rate of £ 50 per man. The total wage bill equals £ 1000. The value of the output is £1000 plus 0.1 (£ 1000) or £ 1100. In the second year, the same number of men are employed at the same wage rate. The total wage bill is £ 1000. But 10 percent must be earned also on the investment made in the first year. The total value of output for the two years is £ 1100 plus £ 1100 plus 0.1(£ 1100) = £ 2310.

Commodity (2)--To produce the second good, the capitalist employs the entire 40 men in one year at the wage rate of £ 50 per man. His total wage bill = £ 2000; the value of his output = £ 2000 plus 0.1(£ 2000) = £ 2200.

Ricardo observes:

---

[20] David Ricardo, op. cit., p. 23.

This case appears to differ from the last, but is, in fact, the same. In both cases the superior price of one commodity is owing to the greater length of time which must elapse before it can be brought to market.[21]

Ricardo thus included the remuneration of capital in production costs and admitted that "waiting" (or time) was also a source of value. This implies that any change in money wage rates or in the rate of profit will alter the structure of relative prices and therefore the valuation of the output to be distributed. Since Ricardo's theory of value is subsidiary to his theory of distribution, another invariant measure had to be found. Ricardo believed that a "standard commodity" would provide an "invariable measure of value." Ricardo wrote:

> Neither gold, then, nor any other commodity, can ever be a perfect measure of value for all things; but I have already remarked that the effect on the relative prices of things, from a variation in profits, is comparatively slight; that by far the most important effects are produced by the varying quantities of labour required for production; and, therefore, if we suppose this important cause of variation removed from the production of gold, we shall probably possess as near an approximation to the standard measure of value as can be theoretically conceived. May not gold be considered as a commodity produced with such proportions of the two kinds of capital as approach nearest to the average quantity employed in the production of most commodities? May not these proportions be so nearly equally distant from the two extremes, the one

---

[21] David Ricardo, op. cit., p. 23.

where little fixed capital is used, the other where little labour is employed, as to form a just mean between them?[22]

Ricardo then pointed out that, "if, then, I may suppose myself to be possessed of a standard so nearly approaching to an invariable one, the advantage is that I shall be able to speak of the variations of other things without embarrassing myself on every occasion with the consideration of the possible alteration in the value of the medium in which price and value are estimated."[23]

Although the choice of metallic money as the invariable measure was just a hypothesis, Ricardo intended to show that a rise in wages would raise the price of all commodities produced largely with embodied labor or with capital of less than average durability and that a rise in wages would lower

_____

[22] David Ricardo, op. cit., pp. 28-29. It is interesting to note that Ricardo considered that the effect on relative prices of a change in the total wage bill and in the rate of profit "could not exceed 6 or 7 percent" (op.cit., p. 22). Hence George J. Stigler refers to the Ricardian theory as the "93 percent labor theory of value." Stigler observes: "I can find no basis for the belief that Ricardo had an analytical labor theory of value, for quantities of labor are not the only determinants of relative values. Such a theory would have to reduce all obstacles of production to expenditures of labor or assert the irrelevance of non-existence of non-labor obstacles, and Ricardo does not embrace that view. On the other hand, there is no doubt that he held what may be called an empirical labor theory of value, that is, a theory that the relative quantities of labor required in production are the dominant determinants of relative values." op. cit., p. 333.

[23] David Ricardo, op. cit., p. 29.

the relative prices of goods produced with fixed capital of more than average durability.

Ricardo's idea of using a "standard commodity" as the invariable measure of value has been demonstrated by Piero Sraffa. Sraffa showed how such a commodity might be formed as a composite good. His analysis will be discussed in the following section.

The Lasting Influences of Ricardo

The "Sraffian Revolution"

The "Ricardian problem" was solved by Piero Sraffa[24] in his PRODUCTION OF COMMODITIES BY MEANS OF COMMODITIES (1960).[25] The main objective of this book was to provide an alternative to the modern marginal theory of relative prices.

---

[24]The label "Sraffian Revolution" was given by Alessandro Roncaglia. See his essay "The Sraffian Revolution" in MODERN ECONOMIC THOUGHT, edited by Sidney Weintraub (University of Pennsylvania Press, 1977), pp. 163-177. In his examination of the Marxian "transformation problem," Paul A. Samuelson made passing reference to what he called "this age of Leontief and Sraffa." See Samuelson's essay, "Understanding the Marxian Notion of Exploitation: A Summary of the So-Called Transformation Problem Between Marxian Values and Competitive Prices" in the JOURNAL OF ECONOMIC LITERATURE, Vol. IX, No. 2 (June 1971). Subsequently, A.L. Levine wrote an article entitled, "This Age of Leontief...And Who? An Interpretation" in the same journal, Vol. XII, No. 3 (September, 1974).

[25]Piero Sraffa, PRODUCTION OF COMMODITIES BY MEANS OF COMMODITIES-PRELUDE TO A CRITIQUE OF ECONOMIC THEORY (London, Cambridge University Press, 1960).

An integral part of the Sraffian analysis is the "standard commodity," which serves as the invariable measure of value to distinguish changes in relative prices caused by changes in distribution from those relative price changes resulting from changes in the technique of production. There are several by-products of the terse Sraffian theory. One of these is the possibility of capital reversal and reswitching which caused the post-Keynesians to question neoclassical capital theory. The so-called "Cambridge controversies in the theory of capital" will be considered in Part III of this book. Another important by-product of the Sraffian theory is the purging of Say's Law from the classical concepts. As observed by Alessandro Roncaglia:

> In the conception of the economy implicit in Sraffa's analysis, the decisions of the entrepreneurs are independent because they are assumed to be logically antecedent to, and not concomitant with, the decisions of the consumers. The elements of uncertainty that characterize entrepreneurial decision making are thus placed in the forefront of the analysis. This uncertainty should be considered as 'structural' in nature, for it stems directly from the very organization of the economic system around several diversified decision-making centres.[26]

In this respect, Roncaglia asserts that "Sraffa's research on relative prices also provides the opportunity to purify the Keynesian theory of any marginal residuals.[27]

The chain of reasoning leading to Sraffa's solution to the "Ricardian problem" may be depicted as in Figure 2.5. In the preface of his book, Sraffa emphasizes:

---

[26] Alessandro Roncaglia, op. cit., p. 24.

[27] Alessandro Roncaglia, op. cit., p. xviii.

Figure 2.5
Sraffa's "Invariable Measure of Value"

Determinants of Relative Prices

In a system of subsistence production without surplus, relative
prices are determined by production
conditions alone.

In a system of production
with a surplus, relative
prices are determined by:

The manner in which the
surplus is distributed
between wages and profits

Production conditions

The "Standard Commodity" required to distinguish
changes in relative prices resulting from
changes in distribution from those caused by
changes in production techniques.

The "Standard Commodity" is derived from the "Standard System
of Production." The price of the total output of the standard
system is used as the numeraire. Hence, its price is unity.
The rate of profit (r) in the "standard system" is a ratio
between quantities of the "standard commodity" (just like the
Ricardian corn rate of profit). Given the technique of
production, the relation between w and r is given by the
equation: $r = R(1-W)$ where R is the maximum amount of profit.
The "trade off" between r and W is depicted by the following diagram:

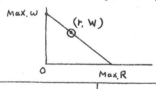

Assuming uniform rate of profit under competitive conditions,
a change in distribution, such as a reduction of the share of wages,
the price of the "standard commodity" will remain unchanged. But
prices of commodities produced with high ($\frac{k}{L}$) ratio will fall;
prices of commodities produced with low ($\frac{k}{L}$) ratio will rise.

61

"This investigation is concerned exclusively with such properties of an economic system as do not depend on changes in the scale of production or in the proportions of 'factors'....The marginal approach requires attention to be focused on change, for without change either in the scale of an industry or in the 'proportions of the factors of production' there can be neither marginal product nor marginal cost."[28]

Since Sraffa considers the case where there are no changes in output and no changes in the proportions in which different means of production are used, the question of variation or constancy of returns simply does not arise.

The main theme of the book is the analysis of relative prices. Sraffa observes that in the case of an extremely simple society which produces just enough to maintain itself (production for subsistence), relative prices are determined by production conditions alone. Sraffa writes:

There is a unique set of exchange-values which if adopted by the market restores the original distribution of the products and makes it possible for the process to be repeated; such values spring directly from the methods of production.[29]

In other words, this is the Sraffian version of the classical natural prices considered in Chapter 1 of this book.

If the economy's production system generates a surplus (over and above the minimum necessary for replacement and subsistence), the problem of distributing the surplus appears. In this case, the determinants of relative prices

---

[28] Piero Sraffa, op. cit., p. v.

[29] Piero Sraffa, op. cit., p. 3.

are: (a) conditions of production and (b) the manner in which the surplus is distributed between wages and profits. Surplus may be considered the national income which will be exhausted by the payments of wages and profits. It follows that variations in the distribution between wages and profits will cause relative prices to change. In the extreme case where the whole national income goes to wages, the relative prices of the commodities produced would conform to the "labor embodied" theory of value. The other extreme case would be where profits exhaust the entire surplus. What concerns Sraffa is the problem of determining changes in relative prices caused by changes in the wage share between the two limiting cases. It should be noted that in adopting variable wages, Sraffa departs from the classical subsistence–wage model of Ricardo. In doing so, Sraffa points out: "The quantity of labour employed in each industry has now been represented explicitly, taking the place of the corresponding quantities of subsistence."[30]

An arithmetic illustration of the actual system with surplus is given by Sraffa as follows:[31]

T. Iron		T. Coal		QR. Wheat		Labour		
90	+	120	+	60	+	3/16	=	180 t. iron
50	+	125	+	150	+	5/16	=	450 t. coal
40	+	40	+	200	+	8/16	=	480 qr. wheat
180		285		410		1		

"where, since iron happens to be produced in a quantity just sufficient for replacement (180 t.), the national income (surplus) includes only coal and wheat and consists of 165 t. of the former and 70 qr. of the latter."[32] All three industries are defined to be basic industries. A basic good (in a system without joint products) is defined as one which

---

[30]Piero Sraffa, op. cit., p. 10.

[31]Piero Sraffa, op. cit., p. 19.

63

enters as an input in the production of all commodities directly or indirectly. A non-basic good is one that does not enter as an input into a basic good. Non-basic goods have no part in the determination of the system of prices.

Sraffa takes the value of the national income as a numeraire. Its price, therefore, is unity. "It thus becomes the standard in terms of which the wages and prices are expressed."[33] Once a numeraire is arbitrarily chosen, Sraffa points out that the study of price movements following a change in distribution becomes complicated:

> It is impossible to tell (for) any particular price fluctuation whether it arises from the peculiarities of the commodity which is being measured or from those of the measuring standard. The relative peculiarities...can only consist in the inequality in the proportions of labour to means of production in the successive 'layers' in to which a commodity and the aggregate of its means of production can be analysed; for it is such an inequality that makes it necessary for the commodity to change in value relative to its means of production as the wage changes.[34]

To obtain an "invariable measure of value," Sraffa sought a "standard commodity" which would be invariate in price with respect to the aggregate means of production. This condition is only met by an industry that produces a "standard commodity" using inputs (means of production) which are physically homogeneous with the output produced. The

[32]Piero Sraffa, op. cit., p. 19.

[33]Piero Sraffa, op. cit., p. 19

[34]Piero Sraffa, op. cit., p. 18.

derivation of the [35] "standard commodity" is illustrated by Sraffa as follows:

First, the "standard system" is obtained by reducing the production equations for iron and coal in the actual system by a certain percentage. A fraction of 3/5 is extracted from the means of production and the output of the coal industry. The reduced production equation for the coal industry is:

30 iron + 75 coal + 90 wheat + 3/16 labour = 270 t. coal [36]

A fraction of 3/4 is extracted uniformly from the means of production and the output of the wheat industry. The reduced production equation for the wheat industry is:

30 iron + 30 coal + 150 wheat + 6/16 labour = 360 gr. wheat

The reduced-scale system is the "standard system," which consists of the following three equations:

90 iron + 120 coal + 60 wheat + 3/16 labour = 180 t. iron

30 iron + 75 coal + 90 wheat + 3/16 labour − 270 t. coal

30 iron + 30 coal + 150 wheat + 6/16 labour = 360 gr. wheat

———   ———   ———   ———

150   225   300   12/16

"The proportions in which the three commodities are produced in the new system (180 : 270 : 360) are equal to those in which they enter its aggregate means of production (150 : 225 : 300)." [37] The "standard commodity" sought is

——————————

[35] Piero Sraffa, op. cit., p. 18.

[36] 3/5(50) = 30; 3/5(125) = 75; 3/5(150) = 90; 3/5(3/16) = 3/16; and 3/5 (400) = 270.

[37] Piero Sraffa, op. cit., p. 20.

accordingly made up in the proportions: (150/150 : 225/150 : 300/150) = (180/180 : 270/180 : 360/180) = (1 t. iron: 1.5 t. coal: 2 gr. wheat).

Next, Sraffa derives the "standard ratio" from the "standard system." Since in the "standard system" the three commodities are produced in the same proportion as they enter the aggregate means of production, it implies that the rate by which the quantity produced exceeds the quantity used up in production is the same for each of them. In the above example the rate of surplus for each commodity is 20 percent:

(90 + 30 + 30) (1 + 0.20) = 180 t. iron

(120 + 75 + 30) (1 + 0.20) = 270 t. coal

(60 + 90 + 150) (1 + 0.20) = 360 gr. wheat

The 20/100 ratio is what Sraffa calls the "standard ratio."

The "standard ratio," R, is the maximum technically determined rate of surplus for the "standard system." J.A. Kregel observes:

> As the rate of surplus is the same for all processes there is no problem of aggregation. Thus the standard ratio may be determined irrespective of the prices of the goods and the ratio is invariant even when all the commodities are multiplied by their prices. Because of the nature of the standard system, the proportions of the component commodities of the ratio of aggregate net product to the aggregate means of production will be unchanged when the net product is divided in any proportions between wages and profits (despite the necessary concomitant changes in prices). Thus the rate of surplus is the same in both physical and

value terms when the division of the surplus between wages and profits changes.[38]

With the aid of the "standard commodity," Sraffa makes a general statement about the relationship between the proportion of the surplus paid as wages and the rate of profit, r, in the "standard system." This relationship is depicted by the straight line wage-profit frontier in Figure 2.6.

Figure 2.6

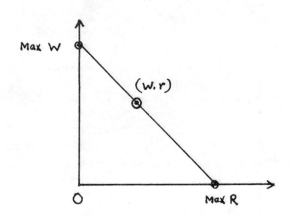

[38] J.A. Kregel, RATE OF PROFIT, DISTRIBUTION AND GROWTH: TWO VIEWS (Chicago: Aldine-Atherton, 1971), p. 24.

The equation for Sraffa's wage-profit frontier is: r = R(1-W) where W is the proportion of the surplus (net product) of the "standard system" that goes to wages and R is the maximum rate of profit. The actual rate of profit is represented by the symbol r. The derivation of the wage-profit equation is as follows:

(1) r = profits/means of production = P/M

(2) R = surplus/means of production = S/M

(3) $r/R = P/S$

(4) $S = 1 = W + P$, or $P = 1-W$

(5) $r/R = 1-W$, or $r = R(1-W)$.

One of the important by-products of Sraffian theory is that it provided a stepping stone in the "Cambridge controversies" in capital theory. In the opinion of J.A. Kregel:

> Sraffa reaches his most forceful conclusions concerning the effect of the rate of profits and distribution on the valuation problem by extending the results of the dated labour and fixed capital approaches to the problem of the choice of techniques of production. It is in this exposition that Sraffa's 'critique' of existing economic theory (as suggested by the subtitle of his book) is most explicit.[39]

The neoclassical theory of the choice of techniques assumes that the costs of each of the existing techniques is known and invariant to different wage rates and profit rates. The orthodox neoclassical proposition is that high capital intensity (a high capital-labor ratio) is always

_____

[39] J.A. Kregel, op. cit., p. 35.

68

associated with a low rate of profit and a high wage rate. Behind this neoclassical theorem is the principle of factor substitution. A low rate of profit means capital is the abundant factor; the high wage rate indicates that labor is the scarce factor. In order to maximize profits and minimize costs, entrepreneurs will choose the technique of production that uses the cheaper factor more than the expensive factor. The neoclassical capital deepening theorem may be represented by the following familiar diagram.

If the assumption of invariant costs is replaced by the assertion that the costs of constructing different techniques vary when the rates of wages and profit change, then the

Figure 2.7

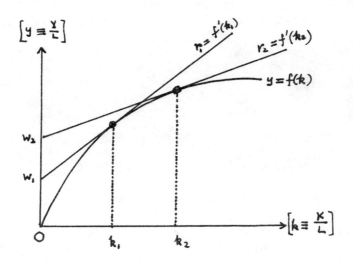

neoclassical theorem is invalidated. This is what Sraffa does in employing an operation of "reduction to dated quantities of labor." This operation is one "by which, in the equation of a commodity, the different means of production used are replaced with a series of quantities of labour, each with its appropriate date."[40]

Following Sraffa, take the equation which represents the production of a commodity "a," where the wage rate, both the input prices, and the output price, P_a, are expressed in terms of the "standard commodity:"

$$(A_a P_a + B_a P_b + \ldots + K_a P_k)(1 + r) + L_a w = A P_a$$

where "a," "b," ..."k" represent commodities, each produced by a separate industry. Sraffa calls A the quantity annually produced of "a;" B the similar quantity of "b;" and so on. A_a, B_a, ..., K_a represent the quantities of "a," "b," ..., "k" annually used by the industry which produces the output A.

By "reduction to dated quantities of labor," Sraffa asserts that the means of production of output A (i.e., A_a + B_a + ... + K_a) can be replaced by their own means of production and quantities of labor, each with appropriate "date." Thus Sraffa is able to resolve prices into a series composed of terms containing wages and rates of profit with a finite upper limit, the maximum, rate of profit, R.

Following J.A. Kregel,[41] suppose there are two techniques, each requiring 25 periods for construction and each requiring 20 units of labor but applied in different time patterns. Technique A requires that all of the 20 units

---

[40] Piero Sraffa, op. cit., p. 34.

[41] J.A. Kregel, THE RECONSTRUCTION OF POLITICAL ECONOMY: AN INTRODUCTION TO POST-KEYNESIAN ECONOMICS (New York: John Wiley & Sons, 1973), pp. 94-95.

of labor be applied during period 8; technique B spreads the application of labor, requiring 19 units at the beginning of construction and then applying one unit during the last period before completion. Thus, the construction costs of A and B will be:

$$\text{Cost of A} = w0(1 + r)^1 + \ldots + w20L(1 + r)^8 + \ldots + w0(1 + r)^{25}$$

$$\text{Cost of B} = w19L(1 + r)^1 + \ldots + w0(1 + r)^8 + \ldots + wL(1 + r)^{25}$$

If the real wage rate is equal to one, then the rate of profit is equal to zero (the maximum W on the wage-profit frontier). As the rate of profit rises, the real wage falls. Thus there will be a real wage value associated with each rate of profit above zero. R is reached when the real wage falls to zero. J.A. Kregel gives a numerical illustration of this phenomena in the following:[42]

Rate of Profit (r)	Real Wage (w)
0	1
5	4/5
10	3/5
15	2/5
20	1/5
25	0

Thus for a rate of profit of 0.05 and a real wage of 4/5 the costs of the two techniques will be:

---

[42] J.A. Kregel, op. cit., p. 95.

Cost of A = $4/5w \times 20L(1 + 0.05)^8$

Cost of B = $4/5w \times 19L(1 + 0.05)^1 + 4/5w \times 1L(1 + 0.05)^{25}$

The above illustration shows clearly that the relative costs of the two techniques change at different rates of profit. Technique B is cheaper at low rate of profit, and becomes more expensive at high rates of profit. Hence, there is the possibility of "capital reversal" and "double switching." These phenomena have been documented by G.C. Harcourt in his book, SOME CAMBRIDGE CONTROVERSIES IN THE THEORY OF CAPITAL (1972).

Ricardo and Post-Keynesian Economics

It may sound paradoxical that the "supply-sider," Ricardo, should be embraced by the post-Keynesians. However, the post-Keynesians have repeatedly stated that their work is a more or less conscious return to the method, if not the exact theorems of Ricardo. Luigi L. Pasinetti observes:

In spite of Keynes' own understandable enthusiasm for Malthus (in view of the latter's treatment of effective demand), and in spite of Keynes' frequent harsh remarks on Ricardo, it is basically the Ricardian method of analysis that Keynes has revived. The most typical indication of this is to be found in the directness with which Keynes proceeds to state his assumptions. Like Ricardo, he is always looking for fundamentals. He singles

72

out for consideration the variables he believes to be the most important.[43]

Joan Robinson thinks that "Ricardo can help Keynes out in the concepts of the normal rate of profit and the value of capital." She points out:

Sraffa's revival of the classical theory of the rate of profit provides the normal long-period analysis that the post-Keynesian theory requires. It was wrong to class Ricardo with Pigou. Keynes knocked out neoclassical equilibrium and set his argument in historical time. Here he and Ricardo are on the same side.[44]

Turning to the theory of distribution and growth, the post-Keynesians frame their theory in the tradition of Ricardo and Marx. Nicholas Kaldor's "widow's cruse" theory of distribution is an illustration of this tradition. As pointed out by Pasinetti:

---

[43] Luigi L. Pasinetti, GROWTH AND INCOME DISTRIBUTION: ESSAYS IN ECONOMIC THEORY (London: Cambridge University Press, 1974), p. 43. Pasinetti also points out that Schumpeter perceived this very clearly when he wrote: "the similarities between the aims and methods of those two eminent men, Keynes and Ricardo, is indeed striking, though it will not impress those who look primarily for the advice a writer tenders. Of course, there is a world between Keynes and Ricardo in this respect, and Keynes' views on economic policy bear much more resemblance to Malthus'. But I am speaking of Ricardo's and Keynes' methods of securing the clear-cut result. On this point they were brothers in spirit" (Schumpeter, op. cit., p. 473n).

[44] Joan Robinson's FORWARD TO A GUIDE TO POST-KEYNESIAN ECONOMICS, edited by Alfred S. Eichner (White Plains, New York: M.E. Sharpe, Inc., 1978), p.xx.

If Harrod-Domar hypotheses are inserted into Ricardo's theoretical scheme and proper account is taken of Keynes' effective demand requirements for full employment, we are led back to the old Ricardian problem of income distribution, but with an entirely new answer. Nicholas Kaldor was the first to see this clearly.[45]

The post-Keynesians also embrace the classical concept of competition in the tradition of Smith, Ricardo and Marx. Peter Kenyon observes:

> Competition in classical economic thought from Adam Smith to Karl Marx is...a process, not an end-state. As reflected in investment and growth policies, competition involves the process by which resources are allocated--and, ultimately, income distribution--between social classes over time rather than just their allocation among individuals at a point in time. This emphasis reflects the preoccupation of the classical economists (particularly Ricardo and Marx) with the concept of capital and the process of capital accumulation.[46]

Together with the rejection of the Walrasian concept of competition, the post-Keynesians' approach to the theory of prices is more or less in the classical tradition. Alfred S. Eichner points out that a distinctive post-Keynesian price theory is now emerging.[47] Essentially, it consists of two

---

[45] Luigi L. Pasinetti, op. cit., p. 97. The Kaldorian theory will be considered in Part III of this book.

[46] Peter Kenyon, "Pricing" in A GUIDE TO POST-KEYNESIAN ECONOMICS, p. 37.

[47] Alfred S. Eichner, "Introduction to the Synposium: Price Formation Theory" in JOURNAL OF POST-KEYNESIAN ECONOMICS, Vol. IV, No. 1, Fall 1981, pp. 81-84.

types of studies: (a) the study of long-period steady-state prices which build on the work of Sraffa, Leontief and von Neumann and (b) the study of historically observed changes in price level which is based on the works of M. Kalecki, J. Steindle, A.S. Eichner and D. Levine. The post-Keynesians emphasize that the essential role of prices is to assure the viability and expansion of the system. "This new theory diverges sharply from the models of pricing behavior found in economics textbooks. Since the price level depends, via the need for funds to finance investment, on the rate of economic expansion, the post-Keynesian theory of price formation is a dynamic one."[48]

Ricardo and the "New Classical Macroeconomics"

Economics, like politics, sometimes makes for strange bed fellows. Not only do the post-Keynesians in their critique of the "neoclassical synthesis" have some affinity to Ricardo's framework, but the theorists of the "new classical macroeconomics"[49] (exponents of the "rational expectations" hypothesis) also embrace some of the Ricardian propositions in their revision of the same orthodoxy. In doing so, an important controversy over the effectiveness of deficit financed compensatory fiscal policy has arisen between the "revisionists" and the Keynesians.

---

[48] Alfred S. Eichner, op. cit., p. 81. The post-Keynesian price theory will also be considered in Part III of this book.

[49] The "new classical macroeconomics: combines the assumptions of "rational expectations" and continuous market clearing. Some of the chief exponents are Robert Lucas, Thomas Sargent, Neil Wallace, Robert Barro and E. Malinvaud.

The controversy was highlighted by Robert J. Barro's essay, "Are Government Bonds Net Wealth?"[50]   While Barro did not mention Ricardo in his essay, James M. Buchanan points out that "the thrust of Barro's argument supports the Ricardian theorem to the effect that taxation and public debt issue exert basically equivalent effects.[51]   This proposition is referred to by Buchanan as the "Ricardian equivalence theorem."

The implications of Barro's analysis for macroeconomic theory and policy are succintly summarized by James Tobin as follows:[52]

(a) The "Ricardian equivalence theorem" denies the potency of deficit financed compensatory fiscal policy.

(b) If deficit finance is ineffective in the short run, it is also innocuous in the long run for (i) it "crowds out" neither private capital formation nor foreign investment and (ii) it does not add fuel to the flames of inflation.

(c) It denies the "Pigou effect."

(d) It denies that social security benefits stimulate consumption. The expansionary effect of such payments is viewed as completely offset by the "rational expectations" of the public who interpret benefits as suggesting a higher

---

[50] Robert J. Barro, "Are Government Bonds Net Wealth?" JOURNAL OF POLITICAL ECONOMY, Vol. 85, No. 1, Feb. 1977, pp. 1095--1117.

[51] James M. Buchanan, "Barro on the Ricardian Equivalence Theorem" JOURNAL OF POLITICAL ECONOMY, Vol. 84, No. 2, April 1976, pp. 337-342.

[52] James Tobin, ASSET, ACCUMULATION AND ECONOMIC ACTIVITY (Chicago: The University of Chicago Press, 1980), pp. 51-52.

stream of future social insurance taxes and restrain present consumption accordingly.

(e) It denies the effectiveness of open-market purchases of government securities.

(f) It denies the long-run burden of public debt, since the revived Ricardian theorem asserts that private capital formation will not be "crowded out" by government deficit finance.

Thus, Tobin observes: "The 'Ricardian equivalence theorem' is fundamental, perhaps indispensable, to monetarism."[53]

Ricardo did convey the "equivalence theorem" in the following passages from the PRINCIPLES:

> When, for the expenses of a year's war, twenty millions are raised by means of a loan, it is the twenty millions which are withdrawn from the productive capital of the nation. The million per annum which is raised by taxes to pay the interest of this loan is merely transferred from those who pay it to those who receive it, from the contributor to the tax to the national creditor. The real expense is the twenty millions, and not the interest which must be paid for it. Whether the interest be or be not paid, the country will neither be richer nor poorer.[54]

> A man who has 10,000, paying him an income of 500, out of which he has to pay 100 per annum towards the interest of the debt, is really worth only 8000, and would be equally rich, whether he con-

---

[53] James Tobin, op. cit., p. 53.

[54] David Ricardo, op. cit., p. 161.

tinued to pay 100 per annum, or at once, and for
only once, sacrificed 2000.[55]

Gerald P. O'Driscoll, Jr. points out that Ricardo wrote
an article after the PRINCIPLES concerning the "Funding
System,"[56] In that article, Ricardo made more explicit
statements on the "equivalence theorem."[57] Both Tobin and
O'Driscoll, Jr. comment that Ricardo added important qualifications to the "equivalence theorem." In the view of the
latter, "Ricardo continued his analysis in a manner that not
merely modified it but completely changed it from an "equivalence theorem" to a "non-equivalence theorem."[58]

Ricardo's defense of taxation as opposed to borrowing as
a method of financing a war is conveyed by the following
passages from his PRINCIPLES:

It is error and delusion to suppose that a real
national difficulty can be removed by shifting it
from the shoulders of one class of the community,
who justly ought to bear it, to the shoulders of
another class, who, upon every principle of equity,
ought to bear no more than their share. From what
I have said, it must not be inferred that I consider the system of borrowing as the best calculat-
ed to defray the extraordinary expenses of the

---

[55]David Ricardo, op. cit., pp. 163-164.

[56]This article appeared in the 4th, 5th and 6th editions of
the ENCYCLOPEDIA BRITANNICA.

[57]Gerald P. O'Driscoll, Jr., "The Ricardian Nonequivalence
Theorem," JOURNAL OF POLITICAL ECONOMY, Vol. 85, No. 1,
February 1977, pp. 207-210.

[58]Gerald P. O'Driscoll, Jr., op. cit., p. 208.

state. It is a system that tends to make us less
thrifty--to blind us to our real situation.[59]

A county which has accumulated a large debt is
placed in a most artificial situation;...it becomes
the interest of every contributor to withdraw his
shoulder from the burden, and shift this payment
from himself to another; and the temptation to
remove himself and his capital to another country,
where he will be exempted from such burdens,
becomes at last irresistable.[60]

Ricardo and Modern "Supply-Side" Economics

In spite of the fact that modern "supply-siders" often
cite Adam Smith and tend to neglect Ricardo, both in theory
and in policy recommendations Ricardo is not out of step with
today's "supply-side" economics. In the first place,
Ricardo, like contemporary "supply-siders," was a firm
believer in the efficacy of the market mechanism. His
attacks on the "corn laws" and his formulation of the comparative cost doctrine of international trade provide ample
evidence of this contention.

Secondly, he was opposed to excessive government spending and high burdens of taxation. On the destructive effects
of taxation, Ricardo wrote:

There are no taxes which have not a tendency to
lessen the power to accumulate. All taxes must
either fall on capital or revenue. If they
encroach on capital, they must proportionately
diminish that fund by whose extent the extent of

---

[59] David Ricardo, op. cit., pp. 162-163.

[60] David Ricardo, op. cit., p. 163.

the productive industry of the country must always be regulated; and if they fall on revenue, they must either lessen accumulation, or force the contributors to save the amount of the tax, by making a corresponding diminution of their former unproductive consumption of the necessaries and luxuries of life. Some taxes will produce these effects in a much greater degree than others; but the great evil of taxation is to be found, not so much in any selection of its objects, as in the general amount of its effects collectively.[61]

The above passage certainly has a modern ring. It could well be a contemporary "supply-sider" arguing for tax reduction. Ricardo, like Smith, opposed deficit spending. As observed by Thomas Sowell, "like Smith, he was concerned that the political advantages of deficit spending would increase the total amount spent, and increase the danger of 'wantonly' (both men used the same word) becoming engaged in war." He (Ricardo) added: "There cannot be any greater security for the continuance of peace than the imposing on the ministers the necessity of applying to the people for taxes to support a war."[62]

Turning to Ricardo's monetary policy prescriptions, it should be recalled that during the "Bullionist controversy" in the inflationary phase of the Napoleonic war,[63] Ricardo

---

[61] David Ricardo, op. cit., p. 95.

[62] Thomas Sowell, op. cit., p. 68.

[63] For a lucid and detailed account of the "Bullionist Controversy," see Jacob Viner, STUDIES IN THE THEORY OF INTERNATIONAL TRADE (New York: Harper & Brothers Publishers, 1937), Chapters 3 and 4. The "Bullionists" were Walter Boyd, Lord King, Henry Thornton, John Whaeately, Francis Horner and Ricardo. The "Anti-Bullionists" were Nicholas Vansittart, George Ross, Henry Boase, Bosanquet, Coutts Trotter and J.C. Herries.

led the "Bullionists" who argued that the main culprit of the currency depreciation was the overissue of bank notes by the Bank of England. As observed by Jacob Viner,

> Their conclusions rested on the following reasoning: The rate of exchange between two currencies depended solely or mainly on their relative purchasing power over identical transportable commodities in the two countries; on quantity theory of money grounds, prices in the two countries depended on the quantities of money circulating therein; the price of bullion in paper currency was governed by the exchange rates with metallic standard currencies; therefore, if the exchanges were below metallic parity, and if there was a premium on bullion over paper, this was evidence that prices were higher in England, and the quantity of currency in circulation greater, than would have been possible under the metallic standard, prevailing to the suspension of convertability.[64]

The policy prescription of Ricardo for this economic ill was a tight rein on the note issue of the Bank of England. Should he be transported to our time, Ricardo would recommend a slow and steady growth in the money supply.

---

[64] Jacob Viner, op. cit., p. 126. England suspended specie payments in 1797 following a general panic induced by rumors of a French landing on English soil, and accentuated by failures and suspensions on the part of the country banks, led to a general clamor for gold.

CHAPTER 3

THE "DEMAND-SIDE ECONOMICS" OF THOMAS ROBERT MALTHUS

The "supply-side economics" of Ricardo argued that capital accumulation would lead to economic growth before reaching the "stationary state." This argument was supported by Say's Law which in essence denied the possibility of prolonged insufficiency of effective demand.[1] Ricardo

---

[1] For an indepth discussion of Say's Law, see Thomas Sowell, SAY'S LAW (Princeton, New Jersey: Princeton University Press, 1972). Thomas Sowell points out: "Say's Law as it appeared in classical economics involved seven major propositions: (1) Production necessarily generates purchasing power of equal value, in the form of factor payments, so that it is always objectively possible to sell any given level of output at cost-covering prices (James Mill). (2) People's behavior patterns are such that they will not desire to save more than they desire to invest, nor do they generally desire to hold money balances beyond that needed for transactions in the immediate period (Adam Smith). (3) Investment does not reduce aggregate demand, but merely transfers it from one group of potential consumers (capitalists) to another (workers in the investment goods sector) (Adam Smith). (4) As output increases, increased quantities of some goods exchange against increased quantities of other goods; increased supply creates correspondingly increased demand (J.B. Say). (5) Each individual works only in anticipation of consumption equal to his own output, so that aggregate quantity supplied equals the aggregate quantity demanded ex ante as well as ex post (James Mill). (6) Increased savings (quantity or function not distinguished) increase the rate of growth (Adam Smith). (7) Periods of unsold goods are due to internally disproportionate production, which can be eliminated by increasing the output of some other goods which will be traded for the goods currently in excess (J.B. Say)." op. cit., pp. 32-33.

employed the method of comparative statics in his analysis of secular growth. Hence, he ignored the disturbances in the transitional process. Ricardo wrote: "I put these immediate and temporary effects quite aside, and fixed my whole attention in the permanent state of things which will result from them."[2] This orthodox classical thesis was criticized by writers on both sides of the English channel.[3] The leading critic of Ricardian economics in England was Thomas Robert Malthus.

Mark Blaug observes that "from the moment of their first meeting in 1811 Malthus and Ricardo disagreed on almost all the fundamental topics of political economy."[4] By the time of the post-Napoleonic war depression, Malthus took issue with Ricardo on the efficacy of capital accumulation in his PRINCIPLES OF POLITICAL ECONOMY (1820). The polemics has been called by students of history of economic thought "the glut controversy." In Book I of his PRINCIPLES, Malthus attacked the Ricardian embodied labor theory of value by refining and extending the Smithian labor-commanded theory. The purpose of the tortuous reasoning was to bring out the pivotal role of effective demand. While the Malthusian

---

[2] See Piero Sraffa, ed. WORKS AND CORRESPONDENCE OF DAVID RICARDO, op. cit., Vol. III, p. 120.

[3] The well-known critics were Sismondi, Malthus, William Spence, Lauderdale and Chalmers. M.F. Bleaney observes: "Two main strands of underconsumptionism are identified, whose main propositions are somewhat different. One strand--the Malthusian heritage--emphasizes the absolute level of saving, while the other--stemming from Sismondi-- emphasizes the distribution of income per se as the cause of crises." See his UNDERCONSUMPTION THEORIES: A HISTORY AND CRITICAL ANALYSIS (New York: International Publishers, 1976), p. 3.

[4] Mark Blaug, RICARDIAN ECONOMICS, A HITORICAL STUDY (New Haven: Yale University Press, 1958), p. 80.

attack is most unpalatable, his major point is clear and concise. "The unsatisfactory character of Malthus' value theory, however, is of no great moment to his basic theme. Though designed to serve as a theoretic warrant for the contention that general gluts were possible, the entire analysis of Book I of Malthus' PRINCIPLES is strictly speaking irrelevant to that proposition."[5]

Malthus--A Keynesian?

Malthus' basic theme was the examination of optimum saving in a growth context. This he expounded in Book II of his PRINCIPLES. He never really considered the determination of the static equilibrium level of income in the short run. Thus his notion of insufficient effective demand takes on a non-Keynesian meaning.[6]   The reasons why Malthus failed to

---

[5] These are the writings of Mark Blaug, op. cit., p. 82.

[6] In his ESSAYS IN BIOGRAPHY (London: Macmillan and Co., Ltd., 1933, pp. 144-145), Keynes wrote: "If only Malthus, instead of Ricardo, had been the parent stem from which nineteenth-century economics proceeded, what a much wiser and richer place the world would be today! I have long claimed Robert Malthus as the first of the Cambridge economists..." Again in THE GENERAL THEORY OF EMPLOYMENT, INTEREST AND MONEY (London: Macmillan and Co., Ltd., 1936, p. 362), Keynes praised Malthus' notion of insufficiency of effective demand as "a scientific explanation of unemployment." Closer examinations of Malthus' theory by contemporary writers, however, show that Keynes' eulogy tended to be overly generous. See Mark Blaug, op. cit., p. 87; Thomas Sowell, op. cit., Chapter 3; B.A. Corry, MONEY, SAVING, AND INVESTMENT IN ENGLISH ECONOMICS 1800-1850 (London: St. Martin's Press, 1962), Chapter 7; Michael Bleaney, op. cit., Chapter 2; and Lionel Robbins, THE THEORY OF ECONOMIC DEVELOPMENT IN THE HISTORY OF ECONOMIC THOUGHT (New York: St. Martin's Press, 1968), p. 59.

85

formulate a precise theory of income determination of the Keynesian type may best be explained with the aid of the following familiar textbook models:[7]

THE CLASSICAL SYSTEM

(1) $y = y(N)$.

(2) $N_d = D(\frac{W}{P})$.

(3) $N_s = S(\frac{W}{P})$.

(4) $M = kPy$

(5) $S = S(r)$.

(6) $I = I(r)$.

(7) $S = I$.

THE KEYNESIAN SYSTEM

(1') $y = y(N)$.

(2') $N_d = D(\frac{W}{P})$.

(3') $W = W_o$.

(4') $M = kPy + L_2(r)$, $\frac{\partial l_2}{\partial r} = \infty$.

(5') $S = S(Y)$.

(6') $I = I(r)$.

(7') $S = I$.

The classical system as expressed above is a composite model constructed by contemporary macrotheorists to sharpen our understanding of the differences between Keynesian theory and pre-Keynesian ideas. Equation (1) is the short run aggregate production function with fixed capital stock and one variable factor, labor. The symbol y stands for real output and N denotes employment of labor. Equation (2) is the demand for labor function where N_d denotes labor demanded and the real wage rate is symbolized by $\frac{W}{P}$. Equation (3) is the supply of labor function which is also dependent on the real wage rate.

The money market equilibrium condition is represented by Equation (4) where M is the supply of nominal money, determined exogenously by the monetary system. The demand for nominal money balances is represented by kPy.

---

[7] See William H. Branson, MACROECONOMIC THEORY AND POLICY, 2nd Edition (New York: Harper & Row, Publishers, 1979), Part II.

Equation (5) is the savings function and Equation (6) is the investment function. Both savings and investment are functions of the rate of interest, r. Equation (7) is the output market equilibrium condition.

The spirit of Say's Law is inherent in the system. Under the assumptions of certainty and perfect competition, the model shows that price flexibility automatically assures full employment equilibrium. The employment level is determined by the interaction of supply and demand functions in the labor market. With equilibrium employment determined, the output level is determined through the equation for the short run aggregate production function. The system is essentially supply-side determined. The demand forces represented in equations 4 through 7 exercise no influence in the determination of the output level. The nature of the system of equations virtually rules out the possibility of underemployment equilibrium due to insufficiency of effective demand.

The above Keynesian model reveals the theoretical innovations employed by Keynes to break Say's Law. There are several approaches to finding the Achilles Heel of Say's Law. One way is through the assumption of wage rigidity as represented by Equation (3'). If for some reason the labor market is unable to determine a unique equilibrium level of employment, demand forces become an ingredient in income determination. Alternatively, it would be sufficient to demonstrate the possibility of shortage of effective demand, by invoking the concept of the "liquidity trap" $\frac{\partial L_i}{\partial r} = \infty$. Another route to reach the same destination would be to highlight the fact that saving and investment are made by different groups of people with different motives. Hence, there is no guarantee that ex ante saving and investment will always be equal. This idea is conveyed by Equations (5') and (6') where savings is shown as a function of income while investment is treated as depending upon interest rates. Any one of these alternative routes is sufficient to break Say's Law. To have all of them in one model is "overkill."

87

Did Malthus follow any of the above-mentioned alternative routes in his attack on Say's Law? He did not. Not
only did he not consider wage rigidity, Malthus also ruled
out monetary causes of underemployment equilibrium. In his
arguments there was no place for hoarding, let alone a
"liquidity trap." Furthermore, he subscribed to the Smithian
saving-is-spending theorem which is one of the building
blocks of Say's Law. Thus, he failed to consider any
divergence between ex ante saving and investment. In
addition, Malthus recognized only the "capacity-creating
effect" of investment and neglected the demand generating
effects of investment (the familiar Keynesian investment
multiplier). Compounded by his muddled concept of a schedule
relating saving (or consumption) to income, Malthus had no
notion of the Keynesian investment multiplier effect. Should
he have grasped the dual effect of investment, viz. the
demand-generating and capacity-creating effects, he could[8]
have developed a growth theory in the spirit of Evsey Domar.
Malthus also neglected the role of technical progress. Thus,

---

[8] See E.D. Domar, "Capital Expansion, Rate of Growth and
Employment," ECONOMETRICA, 1964, pp. 137-147 and his
"Expansion and Employment," AMERICAN ECONOMIC REVIEW, 1947,
pp. 34-35. The Keynesian concern of insufficiency of
investment is clearly stated by Domar as follows: (i)
$\Delta Y_d = \frac{1}{s} \Delta I$ where the subscript d indicates aggregate
demand. This equation states the Keynesian investment
multiplier. Malthus failed to consider this aspect. (ii)
$\Delta Y_s = \delta I$ where the subscript s denotes potential
productive capacity and $\delta = \frac{1}{\beta} = \frac{Y}{K}$.
This equation represents the Keynesian "capacity-
creating effect" of investment which Malthus recognized.
(iii) $\Delta Y_d = \Delta Y_s$. This equation states the equilibrium
condition. By substitution, the following equation is de-
rived: (iv) $\frac{\Delta I}{I} = s\delta$. Equation (iv) states the required
rate of increase in investment to maintain equality between
aggregate demand and aggregate supply continuously over
time. Malthus did not understand this implication of
Keynesian growth theory.

he had no concept of autonomous investment. These analytical weaknesses explain the reasons why Malthus failed to break Say's Law. In spite of these limitations, we "cannot take away from him the merit of having been aware precisely of the problem of lack of effective demand, which Keynes was able to deal with, in a theoretically better and successful way, a century later."[9]

The Malthusian Theory of Optimal Savings

Let us now consider the main theme of the analysis of Thomas Malthus. The stumbling block of Malthus' dynamic analysis again appears to be the saving-is-spending theorem. Like Ricardo, Malthus assumed that only the propertied class had the capacity to save. But he differed from Ricardo by assuming that an act of saving by the propertied class had a dual effect, namely: (i) it decreased the demand for consumer goods by the savers and (ii) it simultaneously led to an increase in the productive capacity through the capacity-creating effect of investment. Although Malthus recognized that the demand for productive labor was a function of capital accumulation, he assumed that the additional demand for consumer goods following the increased employment of productive labor could hardly offset the reduced demand by savers. The overall result would be a state of "general glut." The falling rate of profit would check capital accumulation before the arrival of the "stationary state." Malthus' general conclusion was that there should be an optimal level of savings in order to keep the economy on the steady-state path. Over-saving and too much investment would lead to underconsumption and stagnation.[10]

---

[9] These are the words of Luigi L. Pasinetti. See his GROWTH AND INCOME DISTRIBUTION (London: Cambridge University Press, 1947), p. 30 note.

[10] For more detailed discussions of Malthus' optimum saving theory, see Marc Blaug, op. cit., Chapter 5.

It is interesting to note that Malthus' optimum saving theory has certain formal resemblance to Edmund Phelps' "golden rule of accumulation."[11] We emphasize the term "formal," for the two theories are different in their analytical content. The "golden rule of accumulation" is one of the theorems of neoclassical growth theory which is the antithesis of the Malthusian analysis. Yet both theories emphasize the desirability of optimum saving. The "golden rule of accumulation" is illustrated by Figure 3.1.

Figure 3.1

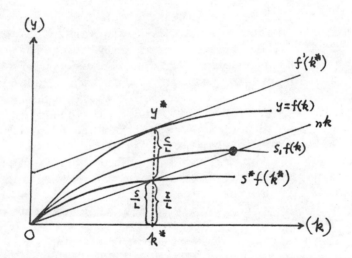

---

[11] See Edmund S. Phelps, GOLDEN RULES OF ECONOMIC GROWTH (New York: Norton, 1966). For an important discussion of optimal neoclassical growth theory, see Ching-Yao Hsieh, A SHORT INTRODUCTION TO MODERN GROWTH THEORY, with Ahmad A. Abushaikha and Anne Richards (Washington, D.C.: University Press of America, 1978), Chapter 9.

Figure 3.1 is the familiar diagram depicting a simple neoclassical growth model without technical progress such as that discussed by R.M. Solow in his seminal article, "A Contribution To The Theory Of Economic Growth" (1956).[12] The vertical axis measures per capita output, y; the horizontal axis measures the per capita capital/labor ratio, k. The curve y = f(k) is the linearly homogeneous neoclassical production function in per capita terms. The slope at any point on the production function measures the marginal productivity of capital (in per capita terms) which, in equilibrium under conditions of perfect competition, is equal to the rate of profit, viz. f'(k) = r. The curve sf(k) is the saving function, where s denotes the constant saving ratio. The curve nk may be called the "golden age line," for it is the locus of all possible "golden age" or "steady state" growth paths. By "golden age" growth path, it is meant that output, capital, and labor all grow at the same constant rate:

$$\text{(a)} \quad \frac{\Delta Y}{Y} = \frac{\Delta K}{K} = \frac{\Delta L}{L} = n.$$

where n is the constant labor force growth rate demographically determined. It follows that along any "golden age" or "balanced growth" path, $\dot{k} = 0$. The nk line is derived as follows: Rewrite Equation (a) and transform it into per capita terms:

$$\text{(b)} \quad \frac{S}{L} = \frac{I}{L} = nk.$$

Since, in the neoclassical analysis, it is assumed that saving always equals investment, equation (b) may be stated as

$$\text{(c)} \quad sf(k) = nk.$$

---

[12] See Robert M. Solow, "A Contribution To The Theory Of Economic Growth," QUARTERLY JOURNAL OF ECONOMICS, Vol. 70, Feb. 1956.

This equation is the necessary condition for the "golden age" growth path. It states the condition necessary for investment (saving) per man to keep the capital/labor ratio constant ($\dot{k} = 0$). In Figure 3.1 the "golden age output" is indicated by y* and the corresponding "golden age capital/ labor ratio" by k*.

The "golden rule of accumulation" means choosing a per-capita-consumption maximizing k* along a "golden age growth path." It is really a central planning problem. Suppose the central planner could choose among different "golden age growth paths," each characterized by a different k* and corresponding saving ratio, s*, required to keep $\dot{k} = 0$. To find the optimum s*, let us first locate k*. We begin by writing an expression for per capita consumption:

(d) $\quad c \equiv \dfrac{C}{L} = \dfrac{Y}{L} - \dfrac{I}{L} = f(k) - \dfrac{\dot{K}}{L}.$

which simply states that consumption per man equals output per man minus investment per man. If we multiply the term $\dfrac{\dot{K}}{L}$ by $\dfrac{K}{K}$ we obtain:

(e) $\quad c = f(k) - \dfrac{\dot{K}}{L}\dfrac{K}{K} = f(k) - \dfrac{\dot{K}}{K}\dfrac{K}{L}.$

Since the constrained optimization problem under consideration here refers to the "golden age growth path" and since along this growth path $\dfrac{\dot{K}}{K} = n$, Equation (e) may be rewritten as

(f) $\quad c = f(k) - nk.$

Differentiating this equation with respect to k and setting it equal to zero yields:

(g) $\quad \dfrac{dc}{dk} = f'(k) - n = 0.$

The "golden age" k* is found when the slope of the production function, f'(k), parallels the slope of the nk line, which is n. This is shown in Figure 3.1. It is interesting to note that the condition stated in (g) is

formally identical to the static profit maximization
condition of the theory of the firm.

Having located k*, let us now try to find the corresponding s*. This is done by first giving a definition to
the saving ratio:

(h) $\quad s \equiv \dfrac{S}{Y} = \dfrac{I}{Y} = \dfrac{\dot{k}}{Y}$.

Multiplying Equation (h) by $\dfrac{K}{K}$ derives:

(i) $\quad s = \dfrac{\dot{k}}{Y} \dfrac{K}{K} = \dfrac{\dot{k}}{K} \dfrac{K}{Y}$

Along the "golden age growth path" $\dfrac{\dot{k}}{K}$ = n and n = f'(k).
one obtains:

(j) $\quad s^* = f'(k) \dfrac{K}{Y} = \dfrac{rK}{Y}$.

Equation (j) states that the optimum saving ratio, s*, is
equal to capital's share of total output, rK/Y . It is at
this optimum saving rate that c* is at the maximum. Over-
saving such as depicted by the dotted $S_1 f(k)$ curve in Figure
3.1 would cause c* to fall.

The neoclassical view of saving and investment is rather
similar to the Malthusian saving-is-spending theorem. Both
theories assume perfect competition. But the broad
similarities stop here for Malthus had no notion of the
so-called "neoclassical parables."[13] Nor did he have any
clear conception of the price mechanism which eliminates the

_____

[13]See Charles E. Ferguson, THE NEOCLASSICAL THEORY OF PRO-
DUCTION AND DISTRIBUTION (London: Cambridge University
Press, 1969), pp. 252-254. The label "neoclassical
parables: is coined by G.C. Harcourt in his SOME CAMBRIDGE
CONTROVERSIES IN THE THEORY OF CAPITAL (London: Cambridge
University Press, 1972). For more discussions of the
"neoclassical parables," see PART II of this book.

"Harrodian knife-edge problem" in the neoclassical growth model. Malthus' general policy recommendation for avoiding under-consumption was to do everything possible to encourage "unproductive consumption" by the propertied class. His view was colored by his conservative ideology. As pointed out by Mark Blaug: "Since the landlord is the principal unproductive consumer, the prosperity of the community depends on the wealth and spending power of landlords. Indeed, Malthus' defense of the corn laws and his theory of gluts are cut out of the same cloth."[14]

---

[14]See Mark Blaug, op. cit., pp. 88-89.

CHAPTER 4

CAUSALITY IN CLASSICAL ECONOMICS

The Newtonian Heritage

The intellectual heritage or world view of classical economics is that of Newtonian mechanics. Sir Isaac Newton (1642-1727) taught the philosophers of the Enlightenment to think in terms of a force of gravity which reached out from the sun millions of miles away and kept the plants in their orbits. This concept gave rise to the view that nature was rational and orderly. Consequently, the universe could be conceived as a "world machine," which would be invariant for all time. Accurate prediction of the future was therefore considered possible. "It follows," observed Sir James Jeans, "that changes of the world at any instant depend only on the state of the world at that instant, the state being defined by the positions and velocities of the particles; changes in position are determined by the velocities, and changes in velocities by the forces, which in turn are determined by the positions."[1]

The Newtonian world view was epitomized by the following assertion of the French mathematician Pierre Simon, Marquis de Laplace (1749-1827) in his ESSAY ON PROBABILITY (1812):

> if the state of the world at its creation were specified in its minutest details to an infinitely capable and infinitely industrious mathematician, such a being would be able to deduce the whole of its subsequent history.[2]

---

[1] Sir James Jeans, PHYSICS AND PHILOSOPHY (Ann Arbor, Michigan: Michigan University Press, 3rd Printing, 1966, p. 109.

The aspiration of Laplace still dominates contemporary economic theory. The opening paragraph of Edwin Burmeister and A. Rodney Dobell's MATHEMATICAL THEORIES OF ECONOMIC GROWTH (1970) provides ample evidence to this point:

> The mathematician Laplace is reputed to have said, "Give me only the equations of motion, and I will show you the future of the Universe." Likewise, economists studying the evolution of a large general equilibrium system ask only for the equations of motion [3] in order to bring their work to completion.

John Hicks and Causality in Economics

The Newtonian world view brought with it a new interpretation of causality. According to John Hicks, the "Old Causality" in which "causes are always thought of as actions of either a human agent or a supernatural agent" was replaced in Newtonian physics by a system of thought which Hicks calls the "New Causality." The Aristotelian grip on intellectual thought was completely broken by this new concept.[4] Hicks writes:

---

[2] As quoted in Sir James Jeans, op. cit., p. 110.

[3] Edwin Burmeister and A. Rodney Dobell, MATHEMATICAL THEORIES OF ECONOMIC GROWTH (New York: The Macmillan Co., 1970), p.1.

[4] The Aristotelian "final cause" gave nature its teleology or purpose. The goal of medieval science was to explain the teleology of natural phenomena. "The secret of the success of modern science was the selection of a new goal for scientific activity. This new goal, set by Galileo and pursued by his successors, is that of obtaining quantitative descriptions of scientific phenomena independently of any physical explanations" (p. 184), Morris Kline, MATHEMATICS IN WESTERN CULTURE (New York: Oxford University Press, 1964).

96

Causation can only be asserted, in terms of the New Causality, if we have some theory, or generalization, into which observed events can be fitted; to suppose that we have theories into which all events can be fitted, is to make a large claim indeed. It was nevertheless a claim that thinkers of the eighteenth century, dazzled by the prestige of Newtonian mechanics, were tempted to make.[5]

We venture to add that economists today are still attempting to fit observed events into some theory (for example: the fitting of consumption functions, demand and supply curves, production functions and so forth).

"Causality is closely bound up with time's arrow; the cause must precede the effect. The relativity of time has not obliterated this order."[6] Hicks points out that there is one basic difference between economics and experimental sciences with respect to time. "Experimental science, in its nature, is out of historical time; it has to be irrelevant, for the significance of an experiment, at what date it is made, or repeated."[7] Economics, conversely, is always in historical time. Hicks writes:

> The economist is concerned with the future as well as with the past; but it is from the past that he has to begin. It is the past that provides him with his facts, the facts which he uses to make his generalizations; he then uses these generalizations as

[5] Sir John Hicks, CAUSALITY IN ECONOMICS (New York: Basic Books, Inc., Publishers, 1979), p. 8

[6] These are the words of Sir Arthur Eddington. See his THE NATURE OF THE PHYSICAL WORLD (Ann Arbor Paperback, 1958), p. 295.

[7] Sir John Hicks, op. cit., p. 3.

bases for predictions and for advice on planning.[8]

Hicks gives a timely warning to economists who try to ape the experimental sciences:

> It is just that economics is in time, in a way that the natural sciences are not. All economic data are dated; so the inductive evidence can never do more than establish a relation which appears to hold within the period to which the data refer. If a relation has held, with no more than intelligible exceptions, over (say) the last fifty years, we may reasonably guess that it will continue to hold this year, and perhaps next year, and perhaps for the year after that. But we cannot even reasonably guess that it will continue to hold for the next fifty years. In the sciences such guesses are reasonable; in economics they are not.[9]

Hicks distinguishes three kinds of causality in relation to time: (1) Sequential causality in which cause precedes effect; (2) contemporaneous causality in which both cause and effect relate to the same time period and (3) static causality in which both cause and effect are permanencies.

Static Causality in Classical Economics

Adam Smith was in the circle of eighteenth century intellectuals impressed and influenced by the Newtonian world view. His thinking was in terms of both "Newtonian mechanics" and the "New Causality." The textual evidence for his application of the Newtonian method is cited by Mark Blaug. He calls attention to the fact that Smith, in his post-humously

---

[8] Sir John Hicks, op. cit., p. 4.

[9] Sir John Hicks, op. cit., p. 38.

published essay, THE PRINCIPLES WHICH LEAD AND DIRECT PHILO-SOPHICAL ENQUIRIES; ILLUSTRATED BY THE HISTORY OF ASTRONOMY (written only 60 years after Newton's PRINCIPIA) described the Newtonian method as one in which we lay down "certain principles, primary or proved, in the beginning, from whence we account for the several phenomena, connecting all together by the same chain."[10]

Adam Smith's commitment to the "New Causality" is evidenced by his search for "laws," or generalizations on the basis of which he tried to fit various events. As stated in Chapter 1 of this book, the main theme and unifying principle of the WEALTH OF NATIONS is capital accumulation.

The causality in Smith's writings is "static" in the Hicksian sense. Smith regarded the causes and effects of capital accumulation as permanencies. To him they were the invariant and universally applicable principles governing the increase in the wealth of nations. As pointed out by Hicks, the theories of Adam Smith did have direct reference to facts during Smith's time. For instance, in Book I, Chapter 3 of the WEALTH OF NATIONS, Smith discussed his famous dictum that the division of labor is limited by the extent of the market. He wrote:

> As by means of water-carriage a more extensive market is opened to every sort of industry than what land-carriage alone can afford it, so it is upon the sea-coast, and along the banks of navigable rivers, that industry of every kind naturally begins to subdivide and improve itself, and it is frequently not till a long time after that those improvements extend themselves to the inland parts of the country.[11]

---

[10] Mark Blaug, THE METHODOLOGY OF ECONOMICS (London: Cambridge University Press, 1980), p. 57.

[11] Adam Smith, op. cit., p. 18.

The relation between the costs of water and land transport was a fact which appeared in Smith's time to be quite permanent. Another fact in the same category was that the techniques of production were not changing rapidly. Hence it seemed reasonable to Smith that the technical coefficient of production was fixed and that the natural prices of commodities were determined by technical conditions. It appeared plausible that relative prices would remain constant over time.

It should be noted that "static causality" is not limited to the Smithian writings. The theorems of neoclassical economics (which will be considered in Part II of this book) belong to the same category. The so-called "neoclassical parables" assert the following to be permanencies in the Hicksian sense: (a) that higher values of capital per man employed are associated with lower rates of profit; (b) that lower rates of profit are associated with higher capital-output ratios; and so forth. We may also include C.W.J. Granger's causality test and that of Christopher A. Sims[12] in the Hicksian "static causality." In both their tests, the time series are assumed to be "permanencies" or "stationary," i.e., the means and variances of the information sets are invariant with respect to time.

The institutional and factual elements which figured so prominently in the WEALTH OF NATIONS faded into the background in the writings of Ricardo. He and his followers consciously emulated Newtonian mechanics. Like Greek tragedies, the Ricardian theorems seemed to be inescapable. Mark Blaug observes: "On the one hand, Ricardo wrote to Malthus that his object was to elucidate principles and,

------

[12] See C.W.J. Granger, "Investigating Causal Relations by Econometric Models and Cross-Spectral Methods," ECONOMETRICA (July 1969), pp. 424-438 and Christopher A. Sims, "Money, Income and Causality," AMERICAN ECONOMIC REVIEW (September 1972), pp. 540-552.

therefore, he 'imagined strong cases...that might show the operation of these principles;' on the other hand, he was forever telling Parliament that some of the conclusions of economics were as certain as the principle of gravitation."[13] The Ricardian "stationary state" implies static causality, for once established, all the variables and their ratios in the model remain unchanged. Thus Hicks does not exclude Ricardo from the category of "static causality."

What about Malthus? In spite of the "glut controversy," Malthus' methodology was not substantially different from that of Ricardo. Malthus seemed to be groping for some sort of "correspondence principle" to supplement the Ricardian comparative static analysis. This point is made clear as one ponders the following passage from Samuelson's FOUNDATIONS OF ECONOMIC ANALYSIS:[14]

> The equations of comparative statics are...a special case of the general dynamic analysis. (Most likely that was Ricardo's methodology.) They can indeed be discussed by abstracting completely from dynamical analysis. In the history of mechanics, the theory of statics was developed before the dynamic problems were even formulated. (It will be recalled that both Smith and Ricardo emulated Newtonian mechanics.) But the problem of stability of equilibrium cannot be discussed except with reference to dynamical considerations, however implicit and rudimentary. (Malthus was aiming, though unsuccessfully, at the same thing.) We find ourselves confronted with the paradox: in order for the comparative-statics analysis to yield fruitful results, we must first develop a theory of dynamics.

---

[13]Mark Blaug, op. cit., p. 58.

[14]Paul Anthony Samuelson, FOUNDATIONS OF ECONOMIC ANALYSIS (Cambridge, Mass.: Harvard University Press, 1958). The words in the brackets are ours.

Malthus never questioned the possibility of the Ricardian "stationary state." What he wanted to point out was the possibility that, even before the arrival of the "stationary state," over-saving on the part of the propertied class would reduce effective demand which, in turn, would cause the rate of profit to fall.[15] Consequently, capital accumulation would be choked off.[15] Thus, it seems safe to say that Malthus never succeeded in escaping from the grips of "static causality."

---

[15] See Thomas Sowell, CLASSICAL ECONOMICS RECONSIDERED (Princeton, N.J.: Princeton University Press, 1974), p. 48.

PART II

Contemporary Re-Interpretations of the

Neoclassical Synthesis

CHAPTER 5

THE "GOLDEN AGE" OF THE "NEOCLASSICAL SYNTHESIS"

Early expositions of the Keynesian revolution conceived of the economy at the aggregate in terms of homogeneous flows of total expenditures; thereby paying little attention to the microfoundations of macro- economics. This trend in analysis has been referred to by Alan Coddington (1976) as "hydraulic Keynesianism." As Coddington states,

> It is the belief that there are indeed stable relations among the various overall flows in the economy that provides a basis for 'the government' to pursue its policy goals regarding the overall level of economic activity and hence, relatedly, of the level of employment.[1]

After the initial conquest of "hydraulic Keynesianism," the economics profession began to look inward to consider the issue of the microfoundations of Keynesian macroeconomics. Long before the popularization of the "Neoclassical Synthesis" John Hicks (1939) made what he considered to be a "breakthrough." This is reflected in the following remarks:

> I believe I have had the fortune to come upon a method of analysis which is applicable to a wide variety of economic problems.[2]

---

[1] See Alan Coddington, "Keynesian Economics: The Search for First Principles," in JOURNAL OF ECONOMIC LITERATURE, Vol. XIV, No. 4, December 1976, p. 1265.

[2] Sir John Hicks, VALUE AND CAPITAL (Oxford, England: Oxford University Press, 1939), p. 1.

It turns out, on investigation, that most of the problems of several variables, with which economic theory has to concern itself, are problems of the interrelation of markets. Thus, the more complex problems of wage-theory involve the interrelations of the market for labour, the market for consumption goods, and (perhaps) the capital market.... What we mainly need is a technique for studying the interrelations of markets.[3]

This technique developed by Hicks was essentially a Walrasian general equilibrium analysis without the auctioneer. "So viewed," noted E. Roy Weintraub, "general equilibrium theory is coextensive with the theory of the micro-foundations of macroeconomics."[4]

The perception of economic problems as involving the interrelationships of markets, and the need for a technique to study such interactions opened a floodgate of advance in economic analysis. During the period from 1939 to 1956, the economics profession witnessed rapid progress in the clearing of conceptual underbrush and the sharpening of analytical tools. Samuelson (1947) introduced "stability analysis" and clarified ambiguities in comparative statics with his "correspondence principle."[5] In the early 1950s, Kenneth J.

---

[3]Sir John Hicks, ibid., p. 2.

[4]See E. Roy Weintraub, "The Microfoundations of Macroeconomics: A Critical Survey," JOURNAL OF ECONOMIC LITERATURE, Vol. XV, No. 1, March 1977, pp. 1-2.

[5]Paul A. Samuelson, FOUNDATIONS OF ECONOMIC ANALYSIS; op.cit. Samuelson wrote: "...the problem of stability of equilibrium is intimately tied up with the problem of deriving fruitful theorems in comparative statics. This duality constitutes what I have called the correspondence principle" (p. 258). He added: "We find ourselves confronted with this paradox: in order for the comparative-static analysis to yield fruitful results, we must first develop a theory of dynamics" (pp. 262-263).

Arrow, Gerard Debreau and other distinguished mathematical economists completed rigorous proofs of the existence of competitive equilibria.[6] This was a productive and exciting period in the development of economic analysis. "Henceforth study of models could proceed mechanically from existence proofs through uniqueness of equilibrium arguments to stability analysis of equilibrium states."[7] The stability analysis of the standard IS-LM model as well as the causal determinancy and stability of dynamic equilibrium in the two-sector neoclassical growth model are two familiar illustrations of this procedure.[8]

In 1956 Don Patinkin integrated monetary and value theory within the neo-Walrasian general equilibrium

---

[6] See Kenneth J. Arrow and Gerard Debrau, "The Existence of An Equilibrium for a Competitive Economy," in ECONOMETRICA, July 1954, Vol. 22, No. 3, pp. 265-290.

[7] These are the words of E. Roy Weintraub. See Weintraub, op. cit., p. 3.

[8] Obviously the increasing sophistication of "hydraulic Keynesianism" and its eventual exposition as the "Neo-classical Synthesis" did not rest well with those who envisioned the Keynesian Revolution to imply a more radical departure from the existing state of economic analysis than simple cases of rigid prices and slow adjusting markets. The perceptions of these interpreters of Keynes, the so-called "fundamentalist Keynesians," will be explored in Part III of this volume. Indeed, it may be these differing views of what Keynes meant to say, and the resulting differences in models and implications that prompted Hicks, reflecting upon the development of the IS/LM model, to express the concern of doing a disservice to the profession by over-simplifying the important contributions of Keynes and giving fuel to his detractors.

framework.[9] E. Roy Weintraub states:

> In any event, by say 1960, the microfoundations
> problem appeared, on the surface, to be settled.
> There existed a detailed model of a competitive
> private ownership economy for which a stable
> equilibrium was known to exist. Patinkin had shown
> that money could be introduced into that system in
> a 'natural' way respecting the stability of that
> equilibrium.[10]

The joint efforts of these writers made the grand "Neoclassical Synthesis" the reigning paradigm in economics and
the "Keynes vs. Classics" debate was put to rest. The period
from the 1950s to the end of the 1960s was indeed the "golden
age" of the "Neoclassical Synthesis." In the following
section, we shall consider the nature of a "standard" macroeconomic model in the spirit of the "Neoclassical Synthesis."

A "Standard" Macroeconomic Model of the "Neoclassical Synthesis"

The "standard" macroeconomic model of the "Neoclassical
Synthesis" paradigm is illustrated by a simplified version of
a model presented by Don Patinkin.[11] This general equi-

---

[9] Don Patinkin, MONEY, INTEREST AND PRICES, Second Edition
(New York: Harper and Row, 1965).

[10] E. Roy Weintraub, op. cit., p. 4.

[11] See Don Patinkin, op. cit., Part II: Macroeconomics.
Patinkin writes: "Each of the foregoing aggregate functions
is assumed to reflect absence of money illusion. Each is
also assumed to remain unaffected by any change in the
distribution of real income or financial assets (bonds and
money)" (p. 200).

108

librium model consists of four markets: the market for labor services, the market for commodities, the market for bonds and the market for money. For each market there are three equations: a demand equation, a supply equation and an equilibrium condition. Walras' Law holds at each moment, in that if any three equilibrium equations are satisfied, the remaining one must also be satisfied. Money in this model is "outside" money. Perfect competition, absence of "money illusion," and absence of "distribution effects" are assumed for the supply and demand equations.

The Market for Labor Services

(1) $Y = \phi(N, K_o)$.

(2) $N^d = Q\left(\frac{W}{P}, K_o\right)$.

(3) $N^s = R\left(\frac{W}{P}\right)$.

(4) $N^d = N^s$.

Figure 5.1

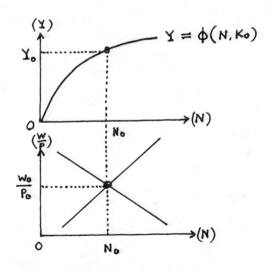

Equation (1) is a linearly homogeneous production function with fixed capital stock, K_o. Equation (2) is the demand function for labor which states that the demand for labor, N^d, is inversely related to the real wage rate, w/p. Equation (3) is the supply-of-labor function indicating that the supply of labor, N^s, is positively related to the real wage rate. Equation (4) is the equilibrium condition for the labor market. The determination of the full-employment output, Y_o, by the above-mentioned equations is depicted graphically in Figure 5.1.

The Market for Commodities

(5) $C = g(Y, r, \frac{M_o^H}{P})$.

(6) $I = h(Y, r, \frac{M_o^F}{P})$.

(7) $G = G_o$.

(8) $E = F(Y, r, \frac{M_o}{P})$.

(9) $F(Y, r, \frac{M_o}{P}) \equiv g(Y, r, \frac{M_o^H}{P}) + h(Y, r, \frac{M_o^F}{P}) + G_o$.

(10) $Y = S(\frac{w}{P}, K_o)$.

(11) $E = Y$.

Equation (5) is the aggregate consumption function, which states that aggregate consumption expenditure, C, is a function of real income, Y, the rate of interest, r, and real money balances held by households, $\frac{M_o^H}{P}$. Equation (6) is the aggregate investment function, which pinpoints the three major determinants of investment expenditures; namely, Y, r and the real money balances held by firms, $\frac{M_o^F}{P}$. Equation (7) states that government spending is determined exogeneous to the model. Equation (8) is the aggregate demand function. "Real balances" ($\frac{M_o}{P}$) is listed as one of the three major determinants. The inclusion of real balances makes aggregate demand sensitive to price changes. Equation (9) is an identity equation ($E = C + I + G$). Aggregate supply is

110

Figure 5.2

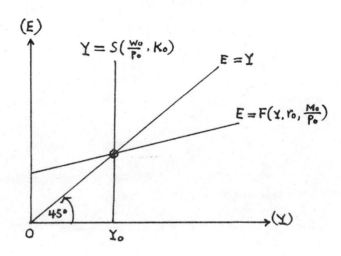

depicted by Equation (10), while Equation (11) is the equilibrium condition for the commodity market. The full-employment equilibrium situation is explained graphically in Figure 5.2.

<u>The Market for Bonds</u>

$$(12) \quad \frac{B^d}{rP} = H\left(Y, \frac{1}{r}, \frac{M_o^H}{P}\right).$$

$$(13) \quad \frac{B^s}{rP} = J\left(Y, \frac{1}{r}, \frac{M_o^F}{P}\right).$$

$$(14) \quad B^d = B^s.$$

Equation (12) is the demand function for bonds in real terms. It depicts the behavior of lenders. The symbol B^d represents the number of bonds demanded. The expression $1/r$ represents per-unit bond price in dollars. The real value of bond holdings demanded is given by the expression $\frac{B^d}{rP}$, where p is the absolute price level and depends on Y, r and $\frac{M^g}{P}$. Patinkin states that:

> The demand curve B^d also depicts Keynes' basic proposition that there is a minimum positive rate of interest on which individuals insist in order to compensate themselves for the loss of liquidity involved in holding bonds instead of money....For the given real income Y_H, the initial money balances M_0 and the price level P_0, the r at which the desired amount of bond holdings become zero is r_2. This is the economic meaning of the fact that above the price $1/r_2$, the demand curve for bonds is identical with the vertical axis.[12]

Equation (13) is the supply-of-bonds function which explains the behavior of borrowers. The expression $\frac{B^s}{rP}$ represents the real value of bond offerings. The "real balance effect" is again incorporated into this function in the form of $\frac{M_0^F}{P}$. Equation (14) is the equilibrium condition in the bond market. Figure 5.3 depicts the determination of the equilibrium bond price.

Figure 5.3

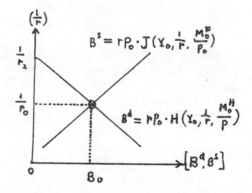

---

[12]Don Patinkin, op. cit., p. 215.

The Market for Money

(15) $\dfrac{M^d}{P} = L(Y, r, \dfrac{M_o}{P})$.

(16) $M^s = M_o$.

(17) $M^d = M_o$.

Equation (15) is the demand function for real money holdings M^d/P, where M^d represents the amount of nominal money holdings demanded by both households and firms. In nominal terms, the demand function for money may be written as: $M^d = P \cdot L(Y, r, \dfrac{M_o}{P})$. Equation (16) states that the nominal supply of money is determined exogenously and is treated as a datum, M_o. Equation (17) is the equilibrium condition for the money market. The determination of the equilibrium rate of interest is graphically depicted in Figure 5.4.

Figure 5.4

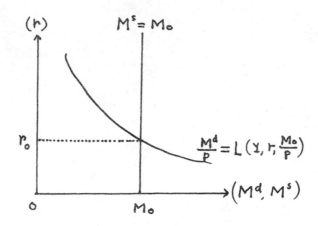

The initial full employment equilibrium situation is presented in Figure 5.5, which consists of four panels.

113

Figure 5.5

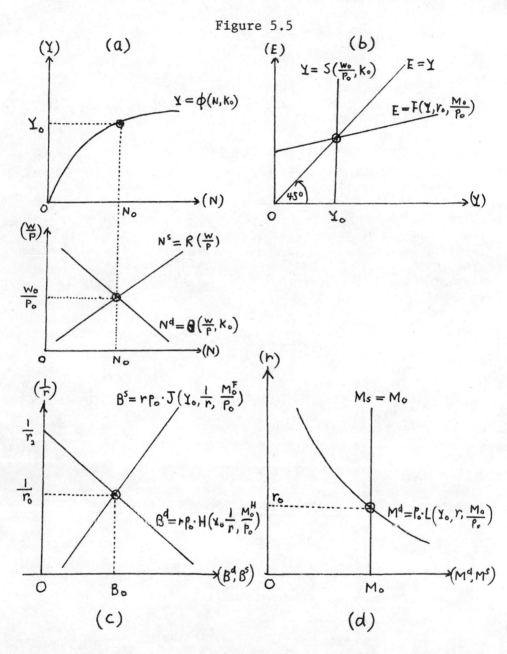

Panel (a) shows the full-employment magnitude of labor N_o; the corresponding real wage rate $^{w_o}/_{p_o}$; and the full-employment level of output Y_o. Panel (b) shows that at the equilibrium price level, p_o, with corresponding equilibrium rate of interest, r_o, and given money supply, M_o, aggregate effective demand, E_o is just sufficient to clear the market for output Y_o. Panel (c) of Figure 5.5 describes the determination of the equilibrium bond price, $1/r_o$, which is consistent with the full-employment values of p_o, w_o, Y_o and M_o. Panel (d) depicts the determination of the equilibrium rate of interest in the money market.

Following Patinkin's discussion, the workings of the model are graphically described in Figure 5.6. Starting with Panel (b): suppose, for some reason, aggregate effective demand falls from E_o to E_1. Consequently, producers reduce both prices and output in order to avoid unintended accumulation of inventories. Thus, the output level temporarily falls from Y_o to Y_1 and the price level declines from p_o to p_1. The disturbance in the commodity market will have immediate repercussions in the other three markets. First look at the labor market (Panel a). Suppose, as a first approximation, the nominal price level and wage rate fall proportionately and simultaneously. In this case, the real wage rate remains unchanged $\left(^{w_o}/_{p_o} = ^{w_1}/_{p_1}\right)$. However, there will be an involuntary departure of firms from their labor demand curve as revealed by point A, "which is the simple counterpart of their involuntary departure from their commodity supply curve as revealed by point G" in Panel (b).[13] "Not being able to sell all they want, they cannot employ all they want. This is the neglected obverse side of involuntary unemployment."[14] As long as the demand conditions in the commodity market continue to be described by the curve E_1, the corresponding demand conditions in the labor market are described by the kinked curve $RTAN_1$ in Panel (a). Thus invol-

---

[13] Don Patinkin, op. cit., p. 322.

[14] Don Patinkin, op. cit., p. 322.

untary unemployment is measured by the distance $N_o - N_1$; and (given the aggregate production function) output falls correspondingly from Y_o to Y_1.

Turning to Panel (d) of Figure 5.6, we see that the demand for money curve shifts downward from the original M^d to M^d due to the "real-balance effect." The determinants of the demand for money as described by Equation 15 are Y, r and M/p. With money supply remaining unchanged at M_o, the decline in the price level from p_o to p_1 increases the real value of the given money balances held by wealth holders in the economy. Hence, they wish to hold less money balances; liquidity preference, therefore, declines and consequently the rate of interest falls from r_o to r_1.

The fall in the rate of interest in the money market causes the price of bonds to rise from the original $1/r_o$ to $1/r_1$. The "real-balance effect" is the equilibrating force behind the new and higher bond price. It should be noted that the price level, p, appears in the demand for bonds equation $B^d = rP \cdot H(Y, 1/r, M_w/p)$ twice. The p outside of the parentheses indicates that an increase (decrease) in the price level will result in a proportional increase (decrease) in B^d. The second p appears inside the parentheses in the denominator of real balances, M_o/p. Therefore, when the price level increases (decreases), real balances fall (rise). In the present case, the fall in the price level causes M_o/p_1 to rise. Since the demand for bonds is equivalent to lending, the "real-balance effect" in this case will increase B^d, attennuating the force exerted by the p outside the parentheses to cause a proportionate decrease in B^d. The combined effect is that the demand for bonds falls, but less than proportionately.

On the supply side of the bond market, Equation 13 states that the supply of bonds, B^s, in nominal terms may be stated as: $B^s = rP \cdot J(Y, 1/r, M_o/p)$. The price level again appears twice in this equation. The first p, outside the parentheses, indicates that a fall in the price level will lead to a proportionate fall in B^s. The second p inside the

Figure 5.6

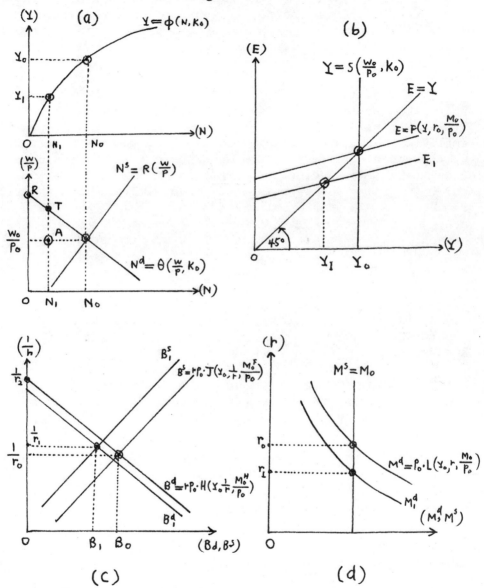

parentheses will cause B^S to decline further since B^S is the same as the firms' borrowing, and a rise in their real balances will certainly decrease their need for borrowing. Thus, the combined effect implies that B^S declines with p, but more than proportionately.

The combined effects of the lower p and r cause the aggregate demand curve in Panel (b) to be restored to its original full-employment position. Simultaneously, full employment is also restored in the labor market as revealed by the disappearance of the kinked demand for labor curve in Panel (a). The involuntary departures from the firms' demand curve for labor and supply curve for commodities are entirely removed, as price flexibility finally restores full employment equilibrium. This is the "tatonnement" process which not only "states that the free market itself acts like a vast computer,"[15] but that it also assures the stability of the system.[16]

Walrasian general equilibrium analysis forms the microfoundation of this "standard" static model. The following important features of the model have been pointed out by E. Roy Weintraub:

1. The system is firmly choice-theoretic, all agents being supposed to make simultaneous (but non- binding) decisions to optimize, taking prices as given;

2. an equilibrium is characterized by agents not modifying their decisions, so that the prices taken as parameters for each agent, who optimizes subject to them are, in equilibrium,

---

[15] Don Patinkin, op. cit., p. 38

[16] Don Patinkin pointed out: "...a stable system is one in which the process of tatonnement will succeed in establishing equilibrium prices; an unstable system is one in which it will not." Op. cit., p. 39.

precisely those prices that result (in the market) from such optimizing behavior;

3. all transactions are, in consequence, co-terminal and subsequent to the decision process. Put briefly, the salient feature of the system is that it is timeless, and since stable, always in equilibrium.[17]

In such a static world with a constant money stock, price flexibility assures full employment. But the question then arises as to how this model can be reconciled with Keynesian macroeconomics which permits an extended period of underemployment equilibrium. "The [neoclassical] assumption that the agents all face the same price system," observes Jean Michel Grandmont, "...means that they have a common and perfect foresight of future prices and interest rates. While this theory is a very useful framework of reference, its extreme assumptions make it an inadequate tool for representing the world we live in."[18] Patinkin was probably the first to call attention to the important point that "the attempt to interpret Keynes' analysis of unemployment within a static equilibrium framework makes it mandatory, by definition, to assume the existence of wage rigidities."[19] This is the negative conclusion of the "Neoclassical Synthesis" on

---

[17] E. Roy Weintraub, op. cit., p. 4

[18] Jean Michel Grandmont, "Temporary General Equilibrium Theory: in ECONOMETRICA, Vol. 45, No. 3, April 1977, p. 535.

[19] Don Patinkin, "Price Flexibility and Full Employment," originally appeared in AMERICAN ECONOMIC REVIEW, XXXVIII (1948). This article is reprinted in Don Patinkin STUDIES IN MONETARY ECONOMICS (New York: Harper & Row, Publishers, 1972), pp. 8-30. The quotation is taken from page 30 of STUDIES IN MONETARY ECONOMICS.

Keynes' contribution to economic theory. The conclusion is that the GENERAL THEORY, in the realm of static general equilibrium analysis, is but a special case of classical theory, obtained by imposing a restrictive assumption on the latter. "This broad proposition gives a thumbnail description of the so-called 'Neoclassical Synthesis.' It embodies a concept of the state of art which is perhaps better described in Professor Clower's term, as 'the Keynesian Counterrevolution' for it represents the final rejection of Keynes' every claim to being a major theoretical innovator."[20] "But," Patinkin wrote in 1965, "this narrowing of the analytical distance between Keynesian and Classical economics does not generate a corresponding narrowing of the policy distance. It still leaves Keynes insisting that the inefficacy of the automatic adjusting process is so great as to be remediable only by a direct government investment in public works."[21]

The Theoretical Heritage of the "Neoclassical Synthesis"

Subjective utility theory, stemming from the so-called "marginal revolution" in the 1870s, forms the theoretical heritage of the "Neoclassical Synthesis." The "revolution" was a revolt against the Ricardian theory of value and distribution that was considered in Chapter 2 of this book. Ricardo's preoccupation with the growth process prompted him to make a sharp distinction between those commodities that could not be reproduced by the application of labor and raw materials, such as old masters' paintings, and those that were reproducible. Clearly the first category of goods has

---

[20] These were the words of Axel Leijonhufvud. See his ON KEYNESIAN ECONOMICS AND THE ECONOMICS OF KEYNES (New York: Oxford University Press, 1968), p. 8.

[21] Don Patinkin, MONEY, INTEREST AND PRICES, Second Edition, p. 340.

nothing to do with economic growth while the second does. Since he had no interest in the first category of goods, Ricardo focused his full attention on the exchange value of the second category of commodities.

The marginalists recognized the dichotomy of the Ricardian analysis and attempted to achieve a more unifying theory of value and distribution. In doing so they replaced the classical objective real cost theory of value with the more elegant subjective value theory which culminated in a unified general theory of economic choice. As Hicks pointed out in 1939:

> What begins as an analysis of the consumer's choice among consumption goods ends as a theory of economic choice in general. We are in sight of a unifying principle for the whole economy.[22]

The foundation for this unifying principle was first laid by Carl Menger (1840-1921) who applied the theory of subjective value directly to the evaluation of productive services. Menger pointed out that factors of production exhibit the character of goods because they derive their want-satisfying power from the consumer goods which they help to create. In the parlance of the Austrian school, consumer goods are "first order" ("lower order") goods, while resources are second, or higher order goods, depending on the number of processes they are removed from the final products. George J. Stigler observed: "This is the germ of the theory of distribution through 'imputation'--i.e., the derivation of the value of productive agents from the value of their

---

[22]Sir John Hicks, op. cit., p. 24.

products."[23] Stigler added: "Menger does make one specific
contribution to production theory, a contribution the
importance of which literally cannot be exaggerated. That
contribution consists in the realization that the proportions
in which productive agents may be combined to secure the same
product are variable--later known as the law of 'proportion-
ality' or 'substitution.'"[24] This law leads directly to the
marginal productivity theory of distribution.

The precise link between the factor and good markets was
finally provided by Philip Wicksteed (1844-1927) and A.W.
Flux (1867-1942) who introduced the linearly homogeneous
production function into the neoclassical theory of
production. Once the Euler Theorem was invoked, the marginal
productivity theory of distribution was born. The aesthetic
sense of symmetry of this new approach is best described by
C.E. Ferguson:

> There is basically one neoclassical theory
> embracing production, distribution, capital, and
> growth....(it) is a beautiful edifice erected upon
> the foundations of microeconomic production
> functions (and input-output pricing processes). If
> these production functions, and the aggregate
> production function derived from them, possess
> certain characteristics (linearly homogeneous), the
> central results of neoclassical theory are obtained

[23] George J. Stigler, PRODUCTION AND DISTRIBUTION THEORIES:
THE FORMATIVE PERIOD (New York: The Macmillan Co., 1946),
p. 139. Stigler wrote: "The greatest contribution of the
theory of subjective value to theoretical economic analysis
lies in the development of a sound theory of distribution.
This means the view of distribution as the allocation of
the total product among the resources which combine to
produce it, through valuation by imputation." op. cit., pp.
151-152.

[24] George J. Stigler, op. cit., p. 149.

and the theory of production and distribution is validated. That is, if certain production relations hold, one may prove that the permanently sustainable consumption stream varies inversely with the rate of interest and that the maximum sustainable consumption per capita is attained when the rate of growth equals the rate of interest (or capital rent).[25]

Based on the work of Ferguson, the central theorems of the neoclassical system may be stated as follows:

(a) $y = f(k)$ $f'(k) > 0$, $f''(k) < 0$.

Equation (a) is the aggregate linearly homogeneous production function in per capita terms. The symbol y stands for per capita output, Y/L; and k represents capital per man, K/L. This neoclassical production function is the foundation of production theory. It stands or falls with the validity of the homogeneous k inserted in the bracket. There are basically two strands of neoclassical thought in neoclassical capital theory, (i) the Austrian theory of capital and

---

[25] C.E. Ferguson, THE NEOCLASSICAL THEORY OF PRODUCTION AND DISTRIBUTION (England: Cambridge University, 1969), pp. 11-12. The words in the first and third bracket are ours. It is interesting to note that Professor Ferguson in replying to the "Cambridge Criticism" of neoclassical theory said: "Until the econometricians have answers for us, placing reliance upon neoclassical economic theory is a matter of faith. I personally have the faith; but at present the best I can do to convince others is to invoke the weight of Samuelson's authority as represented, for example, by the flyleaf quotation." In the flyleaf of the book, Samuelson wrote: "Until the laws of thermodynamics are repealed, I shall continue to relate outputs to inputs--i.e., to believe in production functions...."

interest expounded by Eugene von Bohm-Bawerk (1851-1914), who adopted the concept of the "average period of production" to avoid the thorny problem of capital measurement; and (ii) the real homogeneous capital model of the American economist, John Bates Clark (1847-1938).[26] The homogeneous k in equation (a) follows the Clarkian concept.

(b) $f'(k) = r$

where $f'(k)$ stands for the marginal product of capital and r denotes the rate of profit.

(c) $w = f(k) - f'(k)k$.

where w represents the real wage rate per man. Equation (c) may be used to illustrate the marginal productivity theory of distribution. We can rewrite Equation (c) as:

(d) $f(k) = w + f'(k)k$, or $y = w + rk$.

If we multiply both sides of the preceding Equation by L, we obtain:

(e) $Y = wL + rK$.

Equation (e) is the familiar "production exhaustion" theorem stating that under perfect competition, if each factor is paid according to its marginal product, then total output will be exhausted by factor payments, no more or less. Figure 5.7 is a graphical representation of the marginal productivity theory of distribution in per capita terms.

(f) $dr/dk = f''(k)$ $f''(k) < 0$

---

[26] For excellent discussions of Bohm-Bawerk and J.B. Clark, see George J. Stigler, op. cit., Chapters 8 and 9.

Figure 5.7

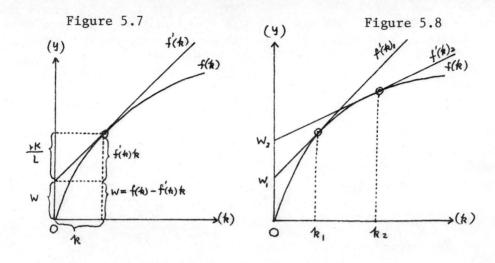

Figure 5.8

Figure 5.9

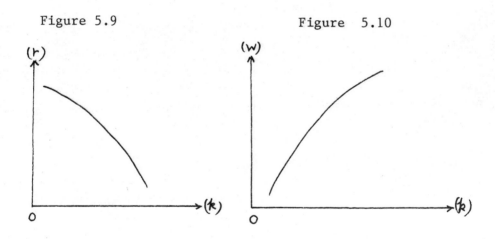

Figure 5.10

125

Equation (f) is one of G.C. Harcourt's "Neoclassical Parables"[27] and states that there is an association between a lower rate of profit and higher values of capital per man. This particular relation is depicted by Figures 5.8 and 5.9.

$$\text{(g)} \quad dw/dk = \frac{d}{dk} f(k) - f'(k)k = f'(k) - f'(k) - kf''(k) =$$

$$-kf''(k).$$

Equation (g) describes still another "Neoclassical Parable," which links a rising real wage per man to an increasing value of capital per man. It is another way of stating the traditional belief that capital accumulation is the best way to raise the standard of living. This positive correlation is described graphically in Figure 5.10.

$$\text{(h)} \quad \eta = \frac{-\frac{dw}{w}}{\frac{dr}{r}} = -\left(\frac{dw}{dr}\right)\frac{r}{w} = -(-k)\frac{r}{w} = \left(\frac{K}{L}\right)\frac{r}{w} = \frac{rK}{wL}.$$

The Marshallian elasticity of the factor-price frontier is the ratio of aggregate factor shares, which is the meaning of Equation (h). We thus arrive back to the marginal productivity theory of distribution once again.

Since the neoclassical theorems are derived from the per capita production function, all relevant variables are dependent functions of k. The preceding eight equations are forceful testimonies of this essential feature. In addition, savings per man, capital widening and capital-deepening can also be stated as functions of k. These relations are described by the following equations:

$$\text{(i)} \quad S/L = I/L = sf(k),$$

where s denotes the constant saving ratio.

---

[27]See G.C. Harcourt, SOME CAMBRIDGE CONTROVERSIES IN THE THEORY OF CAPITAL (England: Cambridge University Press, 1972), p. 122.

$$\text{(j)} \quad \dot{K}/K = \dot{L}/L = n, \quad \text{or } \dot{K} = nK, \quad \text{or } I/L = nk = sf(k),$$

where n represents the exogenously determined constant growth rate of the labor force. Equation (j) depicts the "golden age" rate of capital accumulation, or capital widening. In other words, the "golden age" rate means $\dot{k} = 0$.

$$\text{(k)} \quad \dot{k} = sf(k) - nk, \quad \text{or } \dot{k} = \psi(k).$$

Equation (k) describes capital-deepening, or the increasing value of the capital-labor ratio, k. It will be recalled that this equation is the fundamental equation of Solow's one-sector growth model, which has been referred to in Chapter 3, of this book.[28]

The general equilibrium analysis of the "standard" macro model, considered in the preceding section, stems from the pioneering work of Leon Walras (1834-1910).[29] It is interesting to note that both Walras and Marx were great post-Ricardians. Michio Morishima observes:

---

[28] See Robert M. Solow, "A Contribution to the Theory of Economic Growth," 1956, op. cit.

[29] Recent studies of Walrasian general equilibrium theory have been mainly devoted to his pure economics which was expounded in ELEMENTS OF PURE ECONOMICS OR THEORY OF SOCIAL WEALTH (1874). It should be noted that Walras also made intensive studies of practical issues. His contributions in this area were incorporated in two collections of essays: Etudes d'economic social (1896) and Etudes d'economie politique appliquee (1898). Ben B. Seligman in his MAIN CURRENTS IN MODERN ECONOMICS (New York: The Free Press of Glencoe, 1962) wrote: "In the main, the general outlook expressed in his less technical writings was a reflection of the spirit of 1848. Society, he knew, was an association of all men, not merely a device to facilitate the exploitation of some by others. He also knew of the intense disparities that had accompanied economic

Both Walras and Marx founded their respective scientific socialisms on their economics--in the case of Walras, on his pure economics and, in the case of Marx, on his scientific economics. We may say, therefore, that Marx would have held Walras in as much respect as he did Ricardo. It is not right to assume that Marx and Walras would have been completely antagonistic towards each other, as many contemporary economists believe. They were the two greatest disciplies--or critics--of Ricardo.[30]

Post-Keynesian developments in general equilibrium analysis have focused on the problem of proving, re-proving or generalizing the theorems of Walras. The following statement made by Kenneth J. Arrow and Gerard Debreu (1954)[31] provides ample evidence of this development:

29,cont.

  development. Wages then were as depressed in France
  as they had been in Britain during the industrial
  revolution; the distress of the working class was plain for
  all to see;...the socialists had ample reason to grumble.
  The outcome of this exacerbating situation had been the
  inevitable explosion of 1848. Although the irrepressible
  faith in progress which overthew Louis Philippe appeared
  perfectly sound to Walras, he abhorred revolution. Change,
  he thought, should be slow and scientific. Men ought to
  search carefully for the correct social ideal and, when
  this was discovered, should advance toward it steadily and
  without fear. Science at all times, said Walras, would
  have to be the guide to practice" (pp. 369-370).

[30] Michio Morishima, WALRAS' ECONOMICS: A PURE THEORY OF CAPITAL AND MONEY (England: Cambridge University Press, 1977), p. 6.

[31] Kenneth J. Arrow and Gerard Debreu, "Existence of an Equilibriun for A Competitive Economy," ECONOMETRICA, Vol. 22, No. 3, July 1954, pp. 265-290.

L. Walras first formulated the state of the economic system at any point of time as the solution of a system of simultaneous equations representing the demand for goods by consumers, the supply of goods by producers and the equilibrium condition that supply equal demand in every market. It was assumed that each consumer acts so as to maximize his utility, each producer acts so as to maximize his profit, and perfect competition prevails, in the sense that each producer and consumer regards the price paid and received as independent of his own choices. Walras did not, however, give any conclusive arguments to show that the equations, as given, have a solution. The investigation of the existence of solutions is of interest both for descriptive and normative economics.[32]

The Arrow-Debreu general equilibrium theory is undoubtedly a major intellectual achievement. Unfortunately, it evidenced a significant gap between itself and the macroeconomics of Keynes. Frank Hahn voiced this concern as follows:

General Equilibrium Theory is an abstract answer to an abstract and important question: Can a decentralized economy relying only on price signals for market information be orderly? The answer of General Equilibrium Theory is clear and definitive: One can describe such an economy with these properties. But this does not mean that any actual economy has been described. An important and interesting theoretical question has been answered and in the first instance that is all that has been done. This is a considerable intellectual achieve-

---

[32] Kenneth J. Arrow and Gerard Debreu, op. cit., p. 265.

ment, but it is clear that for praxis a great deal
more argument is required.[33]

Some of the additional arguments required are to be
considered in the following chapter.

---

[33]Frank Hahn, "General Equilibrium Theory" in Daniel Bell and
Irving Kristol, eds., THE CRISIS IN ECONOMIC THEORY, op.
cit., p. 126.

CHAPTER 6

THE REVISIONISTS OF THE "NEOCLASSICAL SYNTHESIS"

The "standard" macro model described in the preceding chapter reflects the attempts of writers within the camp of the "Neoclassical Synthesis" to force the economics of Keynes into a market equilibrium framework. "The result has been to leave conventional macroeconomics with an embarrasingly weak choice-theoretic basis, and to associate with it important implications which are difficult to reconcile with observed phenomena."[1] Critics of the "Neoclassical Synthesis" usually attribute these attempts to the writings of Hicks (1937), Reddaway (1936), Meade (1937) and Patinkin (1956).[2]

DON PATINKIN'S DISEQUILIBRIUM MACROECONOMICS

Ironically, Patinkin is one of the early revisionists of the "Neoclassical Synthesis." In Chapter 13 of MONEY, INTEREST AND PRICES (1956), Patinkin reinterprets Keynesian macroeconomics in the context of "temporary equilibrium with quantity rationing."[3] By denying that Keynesian involuntary

---

[1] These are the words of Robert J. Barro and Herschel I. Grossman. See their "A General Disequilibrium Model of Income and Employment," THE AMERICAN ECONOMIC REVIEW, Vol. LXI, No. 1, March 1971, p. 82.

[2] J.R. Hicks, "Mr. Keynes and the 'Classics:' A Suggested Interpretation," ECONOMETRICA, April 1937; W.B. Reddaway, "The General Theory of Employment, Interest and Money," ECONOMIC REVIEW, June 1936; J.E. Meade, "A Simplified Model of Mr. Keynes' System," REVIEW OF ECONOMIC STUDIES, Feb. 1937; Don Patinkin, op. cit.

[3] Jean Michel Grandmont observes: "Systematic efforts have been made recently by general equilibrium theorists...to

unemployment has its origin in wage rigidities, Patinkin claims that his analysis is "more Keynesian that Keynes."[4] Involuntary unemployment of labor is considered by Patinkin to be a direct consequence of disequilibrium in the commodity market. This analysis that supposedly "out Keynes" Keynes may be summarized as follows.

The labor market and the commodity market are depicted by Figures 6.1 and 6.2. The initial equilibrium in the commodity market is indicated by point B and in the labor market by point M. The equilibrium values of the variables are: Y_o, N_o, K_o, r_o, P_o, w_o and M_o.

Suppose aggregate demand for some reason decreases from E_o to E_1. A "glut" is created in the commodity market measured by the distance BC. The pressure of this excess output causes firms to bid down the prices of commodities, and also decreases the demand for labor. At the real wage rate $(w/p)_o$, less of the labor input is now demanded. According to Patinkin, "at an unchanged real wage rate their

---

3,cont.

move closer to economic reality. The idea underlying these works is not new and can be found in the writings of J. Hicks, under the label temporary equilibrium. The method was also adopted by Patinkin....According to this viewpoint, at each date every agent has to make decisions in the light of his expectations about his future environment, which depends upon his information on the state of the economy in the current and past periods. One can then study the state of the market in the current period either by postulating that adjustments are made only by price movements (temporary competitive equilibrium), or by assuming that prices are temporarily fixed during the period and that adjustments are made by quantity rationing (temporary equilibrium with quantity rationing)." op. cit., p. 536.

[4] Don Patinkin, op. cit., p. 340.

Figure 6.1 Figure 6.2

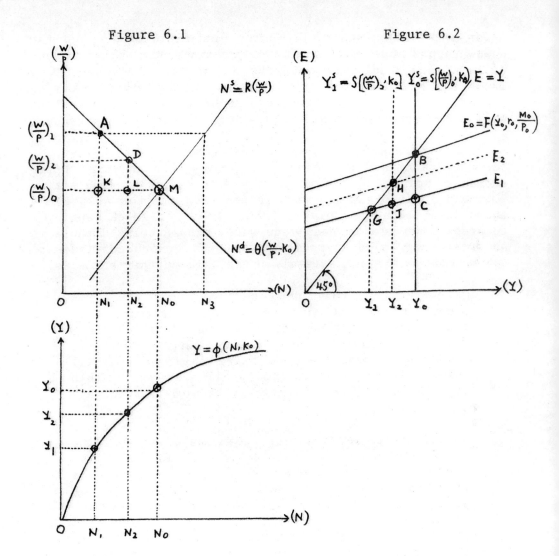

labor input consists of N_2 units instead of N_o." But the downward pressure will continue, for at Y_2 the firms' output will still exceed their sales by HJ units. "Only when this input has been reduced to N_1 with a corresponding reduction in output to Y_1 will these pressures cease; for only then will firms finally succeed in selling all that they produce."

Through this process the economy is brought to a position described by point K in Figure 6.1 and its corresponding point, G, in Figure 6.2. Patinkin emphasizes: "...this position is not one of equilibrium; for at point K there is an excess supply of labor, $N_o - N_1$, which continues to press down on the money wage rate, and at point G there is an excess supply of commodities, $Y_o - Y_1$, which continues to press down on the price level.[5] Patinkin further stresses:

> In particular, the involuntary departure of firms from their demand curve as revealed by point K is the simple counterpart of their involuntary departure from their commodity supply curve as revealed by point G. Not being able to sell all they want, they cannot employ all they want. This is the neglected obverse side of involuntary unemployment.[6]

> (Involuntary unemployment) can have no meaning within the confines of static equilibrium analysis. Conversely, the essence of dynamic analysis is involuntariness: its domain consists only of positions off the demand or supply curves. Indeed, it is this very departure from these curves, and the resulting striving of individuals to return to the optimum behavior which they represent, which provides the motive power of the dynamic process itself. Thus our first task in studying

---

[5] Don Patinkin, op. cit., pp. 320-321.

[6] Don Patinkin, op. cit., p. 323.

involuntary unemployment is to <u>free ourselves of the mental habit--long ingrained by the method of static analysis--of seeing only the points on the demand or supply curve</u>.[7]

The Patinkin arguments have been further clarified by Robert J. Barro and Herschel I. Grossman.[8] They point out that if the real wage rate should decline to $(w/p)_3$ in Figure 6.1, the supply and effective demand for labor will be equilibrated at point C. "At point C, involuntary unemployment has vanished, but clearly this situation is not optimal. The reduced real wage has induced MK man-hours of labor to leave the labor force. Employment remains MK man-hours below the level associated with general equilibrium. Involuntary, i.e. excess supply, unemployment has been replaced by voluntary unemployment."[9] Barro and Grossman further emphasize:

The conclusion is that too high a real wage was not the cause of the lower employment, and a reduction in the real wage is only a superficial cure. The real cause of the problem was the fall in commodity demand, and only a reflation of commodity demand can restore employment to the proper level....Thus disequilibrium analysis of the labor market suggests that real wages may move procyclically. This result differs from the conventional view that employment and real wages must be inversely related.[10]

---

[7] Don Patinkin, op. cit., p. 323. The underlines are ours.

[8] Robert J. Barro and Herschel I. Grossman, "A General Disequilibrium Model of Income and Employment," <u>American Economic Review</u>, Vol. 61, #1, March 1971, p. 82.

[9] R.J. Barro and H.I. Grossman, op. cit., pp. 86-87.

[10] R.J. Barro and H.I. Grossman, op. cit., pp. 86-87.

In as much as point K in the labor market and point G in the commodity market are not optimal positions, excess supply in the two markets reinforce each other, exerting downward pressure on both wages and prices. Assume for the moment that these decline in the same proportion. What will be the equilibrating mechanism? Again, it is the old reliable "real-balance effect." The "real-balance effect" gradually pushes the aggregate demand curve upward and eventually restores it to its original position. Full-employment general equilibrium is again attained.

Patinkin points out that the essential nature of this equilibrating process is not changed if wages and prices do not initially fall in the same proportion. We shall not describe the equilibrating process since the main thrust of the Patinkin arguments has already been stated. To conclude, we quote the following perceptive statements of Patinkin:

First we see that involuntary unemployment can exist even in a system of perfect competition and wage and price flexibility.[11]

(Although involuntary unemployment need not have its origin in wage rigidities,) our theory does depend on rigidities. For, by definition, any system which fails to respond quickly and smoothly to equilibrating market forces is suffering from rigidities. But the offending rigidities are not those of extraneous monopolistic elements....They are the rigidities of sovereign consumers and investors unwilling to modify their expenditure habits on short notice.[12]

---

[11] Don Patinkin, op. cit., pp. 323-324.

[12] Don Patinkin, op. cit., p. 343. The words in the brackets are ours.

Disequilibrium Macroeconomics and Robert W. Clower

Robert Clower's revision of the "Neoclassical Synthesis" and Don Patinkin's disequilibrium analysis should be considered as complements. As Barro and Grossman point out, "Patinkin's model involves utility maximization subject to an employment constraint."[13] The former concentrates on the distinction between effective and notional demand for labor; the latter emphasizes the difference between effective and notional demand for output.

Clower (1965) demonstrates that the Keynesian consumption function and the associated "income-constrained" multiplier process can be explained in a general equilibrium framework without removing relative prices.[14] In Clower's words, "Keynesian economics is price theory without Walras' law, and price theory with Walras' law is just a special case of Keynesian economics."[15] To understand Clower's statement, first consider the derivation of Walras' law within conventional general equilibrium theory.

Assume that there are 100 goods being exchanged in a closed economy under conditions of perfect competition. If the 10th good is selected as the numeraire, then the price of the 10th good is determined, $P_{10}=1$. This means that there will be 99 equilibrium prices yet to be determined. To determine the equilibrium prices of each of the 99 goods, three notional equations are required:

---

[13] R.J. Barro and H.I. Grossman, op. cit., p. 88.

[14] Robert W. Clower, "The Keynesian Counter-Revolution: A Theoretical Appraisal" in F.H. Hahn and F.P.R. Brechling, eds., THE THEORY OF INTEREST (London: Macmillan, 1965), Chapter 5, reprinted in Robert W. Clower. ed. MONETARY THEORY (England: Penguin Modern Economics Readings, 1969), pp. 270-297.

[15] Robert W. Clower, op. cit., p. 295.

A demand equation: $Q_{12} = D_{12}(P_{12}, P_2, \ldots, P_{99})$

A supply equation: $Q_{12} = S_{12}(P_{12}, P_2, \ldots, P_{99})$

An equilibrium condition: $D_{12} = S_{12}$, or, $D_{12} - S_{12} = 0$.

The three equations are notional in that they are based on the implicit assumption that all transactors can buy and sell all they want at market clearing prices. In the demand equation, one of the prices, say P_{14}, is the market clearing wage rate, which provides the desired labor income for the household. Thus, the actual (current) variable is not included in the demand function.

General equilibrium requires that all 100 excess demand equations be equal to zero. If money is only a unit of account, then the following identities hold:

Demand for goods $\equiv$ Supply of money.
Symbolically,

$$\sum_{i=1}^{99} P_i D_i \equiv S_{10}.$$

Supply of goods = Demand for money. $\sum_{i=1}^{99} P_i S_i \equiv D_{10}.$

The total demand as measured in money value for the 100 goods is:

$$\sum_{i=1}^{100} P_i D_i \equiv \sum_{i=1}^{99} P_i D_i + D_{10} \equiv S_{10} + D_{10}, \quad i = (1, 2, \ldots, 100).$$

The total supply as measured in money value for the 100 goods is:

$$\sum_{i=1}^{100} P_i S_i \equiv \sum_{i=1}^{99} P_i S_i + S_{10} \equiv D_{10} + S_{10}, \quad i - (1, 2, \ldots, 100).$$

It follows that the total money value of all items demanded must equal the total money value of all items supplied. In algebraic notation, this means that:

$$\sum_{i=1}^{100} P_i D_i \equiv \sum_{i=1}^{100} P_i S_i.$$

This identity is called "Walras' law." However, it is relevant only under full employment conditions. As pointed out by Clower:

> Clearly, orthodox analysis does not provide a general theory of disequilibrium states: firstly, because it yields no direct information about the magnitude of realized as distinct from planned transactions; secondly, because it tacitly assumes that the forces at any instant to change prevailing market prices are independent of realized transactions at the same moment (this includes as a special case the assumption, made explicitly in all 'tatonnement,' 'recontract' and 'auction' models, that no disequilibrium transactions occur.[16]

As shown by Barro and Grossman, Clower's price theory without Walras' law may be succinctly stated as follows:

(a) Maximize $U = U(N^s, y^d, \frac{M}{P} + m^d)$.

Equation (a) is the household's utility function. The choice variables are all notional in nature. N^s represents the notional supply of labor time; y^d denotes notional demand for output; M/P represents real money balances; and m^d is the notional demand for additional money balances. Utility maximization implies that N^s, y^d and m^d are all functions of the real wage rate, w, real money balances, M/P and non-labor income, π .

(b) Subject to the budget constraint:

$$wN^s + \pi = y^d + m^d.$$

"The important point is that the notional demand functions for commodities and additional money balances do not have the forms of the usual consumption and saving functions

---

[16] Robert W. Clower, op. cit., pp. 275-276.

with income as an argument, because the household simultaneously chooses the quantity of labor to sell."[17] In other words, effective demands for commodities and money balances arising from realized income are indistinguishable from notional demands assuming a state of full employment. All household decisions are accomplished simultaneously and instantaneously. This is what Clower termed the "unified decision hypothesis."[18]

In contrasting the above notional process to a situation in which labor services are in excess supply, Clower points out that the utility function in the latter case would be written as follows:

$$(c) \quad U = U(N, y^{d'}, \frac{M}{p} + m^{d'}),$$

where N represents the realized employment which is smaller than the notional labor supply, N^s. The representative household is unable to sell its notional labor supply and obtain its notional labor income. Thus, actual income differs from full-employment income and the disappointed household is forced to revise its consumption and savings plans. This is what Clower calls the "dual decision hypothesis."[19] The consumption function (savings function) effective in the market is the one which is obtained after this re-examination, and is the foundation of the Keynesian consumption function. In this situation, "labor income," as observed by Barro and Grossman, "is no longer a choice variable which is maximized out, but is instead exogenously given."[20] As a result, the utility maximization problem

---

[17] These are the words of Barro and Grossman, op. cit., p. 87.

[18] Robert W. Clower, op. cit., p. 286.

[19] Robert W. Clower, op. cit., p. 287.

[20] R.J. Barro and H.I. Grossman, op. cit., p. 87.

140

amounts to the optimal disposition of the realized income, $wN_s + \pi$, which is smaller than the notional income $wN^s + \pi$. The effective budget constraint is:

(d) $wN + \pi = y^{d'} + m^{d'}$,

where $y^{d'}$ and $m^{d'}$ denote the effective demand for commodities and the effective demand for money. Utility maximization now implies

(e) $y^{d'} = y^{d'}(wN + \pi, \frac{M}{p})$,

and

(f) $m^{d'} = m^{d'}(wN + \pi, \frac{M}{p})$.

This type of analysis leads Clower to the following conclusions:

> Firstly, orthodox price theory may be regarded as a special case of Keynesian economics, valid only in conditions of full employment.

> Secondly, an essential difference between Keynesian and orthodox economics is that market excess demands are in general assumed to depend on current market transactions in the former, and to be independent of current market transactions in the latter. This difference depends, in turn, on Keynes' tacit use of a dual-decision theory of household behavior and his consequent rejection of Walras' law as a relevant principle of economic analysis.

> Thirdly, chronic factor unemployment at substantially unchanging levels of real income and output may be consistent with Keynesian economics even if all prices are flexible; this problem has yet to be

141

investigated within the context of a Keynesian model of market price formation.[21]

The Disequilibrium Macroeconomics
of Axel Leijonhufvud

Building upon the analysis of Robert Clower, Axel Leijonhufvud suggested "that the 'Keynes and the Classics' issues are better approached from a dynamic rather than comparative static perspective."[22] Although the model of Keynes was static, his theory is dynamic. Leijonhufvud emphasizes this, stating that "the subject of his (Keynes') work is not 'unemployment equilibrium' but the nature of the macroeconomic process of adjustment to a disequilibrating disturbance."[23] In contrast, the macroeconomic process of adjustment in the Walrasian general equilibrium model relies on the "tatonnement" process.[24] In Walrasian general equilibrium theory, all transactors are regarded as price

---

[21] Robert W. Clower, op. cit., p. 294.

[22] Axel Leijonhufvud, ON KEYNESIAN ECONOMICS AND THE ECONOMICS OF KEYNES (New York: Oxford University Press, 1968), p. 389.

[23] Axel Leijonhufvud, op. cit., p. 50.

[24] Axel Leijonhufvud writes: "Tatonnement (literally 'groping') was Walras' term for the hypothetical trial and error auction process which he sketched as a simulation suggesting how an actual economic system might arrive at the equilibrium vector of prices. His sketch assumed that actual economic activities were suspended during the 'groping' process and only resumed when the right solution was found." See his TWO LECTURES ON KEYNES' CONTRIBUTION TO ECONOMIC THEORY (England: The Institute of Economic Affairs, 1969), p. 30 note one.

takers. As noted by Kenneth J. Arrow (1959):[25]

> The standard development of the theory of behavior
> under competitive conditions has made both sides of
> any market take price as given by some outside
> agency. Thus, for a single market,
>
> $$D = f(p), \quad S = g(p) \qquad (1)$$
>
> where D is the demand for the commodity, S its
> supply, and p its price. The functions $f(p)$ and
> $g(p)$ represent the behavior of consumers and
> producers respectively. But relation (1) con-
> stitutes only two equations with the three unknowns
> D, S and p.
>
> The theoretical structure is usually completed by
> adding the condition of equality of supply and
> demand,
>
> $$S = D \qquad (2)$$
>
> What is the rationale of relation (2) ?...it is
> regarded as the limit of a trial-and-error process
> (tâtonnement) describable by an equation of the
> general type:
>
> $$dp/dt = h(S - D) \qquad (3)$$
>
> where
>
> $$h' < 0, \quad h(0) = 0.$$
>
> ...It is not explained whose decision it is to
> change prices in accordance with equation (3).

---

[25] Kenneth J. Arrow, "Toward A Theory of Price Adjustment" in
THE ALLOCATION OF ECONOMIC RESOURCES (Stanford, California:
Stanford University Press, 1959, pp. 41-51.

Each individual participant is supposed to take prices as given...there is no one left over whose job is to make a decision on price.[26]

Arrow's question was no doubt recognized by Walras. That is probably why Walras entrusted the "job of making a decision on price" to a deus ex machina--the "auctioneer," who was supposed to supply price-takers with the "true" market-clearing prices at zero cost. Just like Maxwell's demon in the theory of thermodynamics, the Walrasian "demon" was to perform the sorting process during the tatonnement process and ensure that the system could hop blithely from one equilibrium vector of prices to another. "False trading" at "false prices" was eliminated and the stability of the system was assured.[27]

To make the transition from Walras' world to that of Keynes, the Walrasian "demon" has to be exorcised. Leijonhufvud views Keynes, the exorcist, as reversing the Marshallian ranking of price and quantity-adjustment speeds.[28] As observed by Leijonhufvud, "Keynes' long struggle to escape seems primarily to have been a struggle with the dynamics of the Marshallian period-analysis."[29] If prices do not adjust instantly, transactions will be concluded at disequilibrium prices. Hicks (1939) called this

---

[26] Kenneth J. Arrow, op. cit., pp. 42-43. The word in brackets is ours.

[27] See Don Patinkin, op. cit., p. 39.

[28] In the Marshallian analysis, price can be altered more easily than the rate of output, which in turn can be altered faster than the size of the plant. "In the Marshallian short run...the speed of price adjustment is regarded as infinite, that of capital stock as zero." A. Leijonhufvud, op. cit., p. 52.

[29] Axel Leijonhufvud, op. cit., p. 53.

144

type of transaction "false trading."[30] Leijonhufvud points out:

> Clower's contribution forces a drastic revision of this view (Hicksian) of false trading. Here the attention is focused not on the distribution effects caused by transactions that do in fact take place at false prices, but on the aggregative income effects caused by the transactions which do not take place because of the false prices. Clower considers the specific instance of a disequilibrium price pertaining to the market for factor services supplied by households, thus staying close to the theoretical structure of the GENERAL THEORY ("Wages are rigid"). Current household receipts ("income") are determined not by the quantity of services a household would want to supply at the price at which such services are currently bought, but by how much it will actually succeed in selling. Its effective demand in other markets will be constrained by the income actually achieved. This is the crucial point. Realized transaction quantities enter as arguments of the excess demand functions in addition to prices.[31]

The Keynesian multiplier analysis is characteristic of Keynesian quantity-adjustment models. In the opinion of Leijonhufvud, the quantity-adjustment model "implies an information process which, like the Walrasian tâtonnement, functions apart from the trading process itself, but relates to quantities, not to prices. Households are informed of their real income 'before any trade takes place'...The two 'pure' models differ in terms of the kind of information which they assume will be available to transactors in the

---

[30] J.R. Hicks, VALUE AND CAPITAL, op. cit., p. 128.

[31] Axel Leijonhufvud, op. cit., pp. 55-56. The words in brackets are ours.

short run when a previous equilibrium has been disturbed. Both types of models confine attention to information that is available at zero cost."[32]

To complete the exorcism, information cost must be taken into consideration. In the nontâtonnement world of Keynes, ignorance and uncertainty abound. Here Leijonhufvud invokes the analysis of Armen A. Alchian with respect to information costs.[33] Alchian observed:

> A large and costly portion of so-called marketing activity is information-dissemination activity. Advertisement, window displays, sales clerks, specialist agents, brokers, catalogs, correspondence, phone calls, market research agencies, employment agencies, licensing...facilitate the spread and acquisition of knowledge about potential demanders and suppliers and their goods and about prices they can expect to see prevail.[34]

Building upon Alchian's analysis, Leijonhufvud (1969) emphasizes: "When 'in the real world' the market situation is changing, it is not possible to have all transactors making decisions just on quantities but never on prices. They must decide what prices to charge or to accept."[35] Thus, when excess supply develops in the output market, sellers must decide on their "reservation-price;" when excess supply develops in the labor market, the worker in the process of

---

[32] Axel Leijonhufvud, op. cit., pp. 74-75.

[33] Armen A. Alchian, "Information Costs, Pricing and Resource Unemployment" in Edmund S. Phelps, ed., MICROECONOMIC FOUNDATIONS OF EMPLOYMENT AND INFLATION THEORY (New York: W.W. Norton & Co., Inc., 1970), pp. 27-52.

[34] Armen A. Alchian, op. cit., p. 28.

[35] Axel Leijonhufvud, Two Lectures, op. cit., p. 31.

searching for a new job must set himself a "reservation-wage." Leijonhufvud writes:

> As the sampling of job openings progresses, his knowledge of the current state of the market improves and his reservation-wage will be adjusted accordingly--downwards or upwards, depending upon whether the market is found worse or better than initially anticipated. At some point, the rate at which the best offer known improves will appear to no longer warrant the costs of further research and he will accept a job.[36]

A similar situation will confront sellers. At some point of the transitional process, sellers will realize that their reservation prices have to be lowered owing to increasing search costs. Hence, the final outcome will be consistent with the predictions of the "standard" model of the "Neoclassical Synthesis." However, the nature of the macroeconomic process of adjustment is entirely different. Leijonhufvud's reinterpretation of Keynes' GENERAL THEORY makes the "standard" model a special case of Keynes' more general theory, for it relies on the tatonnement process to restore full employment equilibrium. In Leijonhufvud's own words:

> The only thing which Keynes removed from the foundations of classical theory was the deus ex machina--the auctioneer which is assumed to furnish, without charge, all the information needed to obtain the perfect coordination of the activities of all traders in the present and through the future. Which, then, is the more general theory and which the special case? Must

---

[36] Axel Leijonhufvud, op. cit., p. 31.

one not grant Keynes his claim to having tackled the more general problem?[37]

The Revisionism of the Monetarists

The Monetarists' criticisms of the "Neoclassical Synthesis" focus on three areas: (a) macroeconomic theory, (b) economic stabilization policy and (c) economic research methodology. Our emphasis here is on macroeconomic theory with some implications for stabilization policy.

The Monetarists criticize the Keynesians of the "Neoclassical Synthesis" persuasion for failure to (i) make a clear distinction between nominal and real quantities of money and (ii) differentiate between the phenomenon of high interest rates and that of rising interest rates. The Monetarists emphasize that the nominal quantity of money is an exogenous policy variable. The real quantity of money is an endogenous variable, the equilibrium solution of which is determined by the general equilibrium of the real and monetary sectors of the economy. Hence, real money balances are not under the direct control of the monetary authority. This important distinction is made more clear with the aid of the Patinkin diagram[38] reproduced in Figure 6.3.

The vertical axis of Figure 6.3 measures the value of money, which is the reciprocal of the price level $(1/p)$; and the horizontal axis measures the quantity of nominal money demanded and supplied. The initial equilibrium situation is

---

[37] Axel Leijonhufvud, "Keynes and the Keynesians: A Suggested Interpretation" (1967), AMERICAN ECONOMIC REVIEW, Vol. 57, No. 2, pp. 401-410, reprinted in Robert W. Clower, ed., Penguin Modern Economics Readings in Monetary Theory, op. cit., pp. 307-308.

[38] See Don Patinkin, op. cit., p. 47.

Figure 6.3

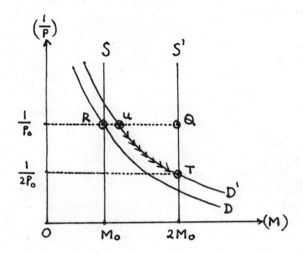

point R where the supply of nominal money M_o intersects the demand for money D. The equilibrium value of the real quantity of money is depicted by the rectangle $0\ 1/p_o\ R\ M_o$. The equilibrium price level associated with M_o, the exogenously given money supply, is p_o.

Suppose the monetary authority increases the supply of nominal money from M_o to $2M_o$. This will cause a rightward shift of the supply curve to S'. The increased quantity of nominal money disturbs the original optimal portfolio balance of wealth holders. The original optimal money holding is M_o/p_o. If the price level remains at p_o, the increased nominal quantity of money would be in excess supply. As pointed out by Patinkin, "not all of the increased endowment is expended in the commodity markets. That is, there is also a real-balance effect in the money market. This is reflected diagrammatically as a rightward shift from D to D': at the same level of absolute prices, individuals--because of their increased wealth--feel themselves able to indulge in a higher level of liquidity."[39]

The dynamic process by which the money market moves from R to T is described as follows. At the price level p_o, the amount of excess supply of nominal money is measured by the distance UQ. Wealth holders will dispose of the excess money directly (Cantillon-Hume mechanism), or indirectly via the bond market (Thornton-Wicksell mechanism), raising aggregate demand in the commodities market. Thus, pressures exist in the commodity markets to drive p up and 1/p down. Both the money market and the commodity market will be simultaneously in equilibrium again when the price level is bid up to $2p_o$. Equilibrium in the money market is depicted by point T, at which the excess supply of nominal money is eliminated and the equilibrium solution of the real quantity of money is represented by the rectangle, $0 \ 1/2p_o \ T \ 2M_o$.

Several important points follow from the above-mentioned dynamic process:

> (1) The demand-for-money function is the logical link between the real and monetary sectors. This is the reason Milton Friedman calls attention to the fact that
>
>> The quantity theory is in the first instance a theory of demand for money...and the theory of the demand for money is a special topic in the theory of capital.[40]

---

[39] Don Patinkin, op. cit., p. 47.

[40] Milton Friedman, ed., STUDIES IN THE QUANTITY THEORY OF MONEY (Chicago: University of Chicago Press, 1956), p. 4.

150

(2) The real quantity of money is an endogenous variable beyond the control of the monetary authority.

(3) Monetarists have a monetary theory of the price level.

(4) The monetary dynamics illustrate the renowned theorems of the quantity theory of money: short-run nonneutrality and long-run neutrality of money.

(5) The Monetarists's emphasis on the close relation between nominal money and the price level is the basis for their rejection of the liquidity preference theory as a general theory of money and interest rates. As observed by David I. Fand:

> Monetarists, following the Quantity Theory, do not accept...the liquidity preference theory of interest rates for several reasons: First, they suggest that an increase in money may directly affect expenditures, prices and a wide variety of implicit yields on physical assets, and need not be restricted to a small set of conventional yields on assets. Second, they view the demand for money as determining the desired quantity of real balances, and not the level of interest rates. Third, and most fundamentally, they reject the notion that the authorities can change the stock of real balances--an endogenous variable--and thereby bring about a permanent change in interest rates, except for very special circumstances.[41]

---

[41]David I. Fand, "A Monetarist Model of the Monetary Process," in William E. Gibson and George G. Kaufman, eds.,

With regard to the distinction between high and rising interest rates, the Monetarists, following Irving Fisher, relate monetary growth to market interest rates via changes in the price level.[42] They argue that in a fully anticipated inflation, market interest rates will be high, reflecting the rate of inflation, even though real rates (the interest rates implied by the rate of exchange between present and future goods) remain unchanged. Rising market interest rates (the rate represents an exchange between money now and money in the future) is a phenomenon reflecting "adaptive expectations of the rate of inflation." The market rates will continue to rise until the rate of inflation is fully anticipated.

The Monetarists' emphasis on the role of price expectations has important policy implications since it provides the rationale[43] for two paradoxical statements made by Milton Friedman:

(1) Monetary policy "cannot peg interest rates for more than very limited periods" and

---

41,cont.

MONETARY ECONOMICS: READINGS ON CURRENT ISSUES (New York: McGraw-Hill Book Co., 1971), p. 75.

[42] Irving Fisher's analysis of "Gibson Paradox" (the well documented empirical association between high market nominal interest rates and high prices) is stated in his APPRECIATION AND INTEREST (Macmillan, 1930) and THE THEORY OF INTEREST (Macmillan, 1930). Also see J.M. Keynes, A TREATISE ON MONEY (Macmillan, 1930).

[43] Milton Friedman, "The Role of Monetary Policy" in his ed., THE OPTIMUM QUANTITY OF MONEY AND OTHER ESSAYS (Chicago: Aldine Publishing Company, 1969), Chapter 5.

(2) Monetary policy "cannot peg the rate of unemployment for more than very limited periods."[44]

It has been generally recognized that the first paradoxical statement is designed to show "why interest rates are
such misleading indicators of whether monetary policy is
'tight' or 'easy.' For that, it is far better to look at the
rate of change of the quantity of money.[45] Figure 6.4
depicts the arguments made by Friedman against using the
level of market interest rates as an indicator of monetary
policy.

Figure 6.4

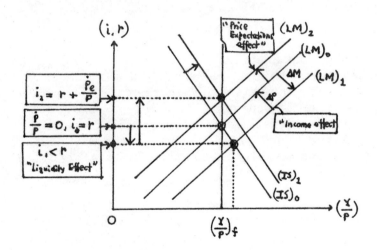

[44] Milton Friedman, op. cit., p. 99.

[45] Milton Friedman, op. cit., p. 101.

The diagram is the familiar IS-LM model. The nominal rate of interest is represented by i and r represents the real rate. The initial full-employment equilibrium is indicated by the intersection of the $(IS)_0$ and $(LM)_0$ curves. With $\dot{p}/p = 0$, $i = r$. Suppose the monetary authority increases the nominal quantity of money. Consequently, $(LM)_0$ shifts downward to $(LM)_1$; the "liquidity effect" drives i down to i_1 which is below the real rate. The lower nominal rate of interest not only induces an increase of aggregate demand but also causes the demand for assets or speculative money balances to increase. The "income effect" generated by the increase in aggregate demand forces the transactions demand for nominal money balances to increase. Since the economy is already at full employment, the increase in aggregate demand will lead to an increase in prices. The joint force of increases in both the demand for money and rising prices push the $(LM)_1$ curve back to $(LM)_0$. Simultaneously, the nominal rate of interest rises. However, this is not the end of the dynamic movements. As the price level continues to rise, a "price expectations effect" is invoked. The LM curve is pushed further back to $(LM)_2$. Simultaneously, the high money cost of investment projects (at the same real rate) will push the IS curve to the right--from $(IS)_0$ to $(IS)_1$. The dynamic adjustment process comes to an end when $(IS)_1$ intersects $(LM)_2$ and the new equilibrium market rate is $i_2 = r + \dot{p}_e/p$, which is higher than the initial equilibrium rate. Thus Friedman observes:

These subsequent effects explain why every attempt to keep interest rates at a low level has forced the monetary authority to engage in successively larger and larger open market purchases. They explain why, historically, high and rising nominal interest rates have been associated with rapid growth in the quantity of money, as in Brazil or Chile or in the United States in recent years, and why low and falling interest rates have been associated with slow growth in the quantity of money,

154

as in Switzerland now (1969) or in the United
States from 1929 to 1933.[46]

Turning to the second paradoxical statement made by
Milton Friedman, it has been generally recognized that
monetary policy cannot peg the rate of unemployment for more
than very limited periods, representing another way of
stating the hypothesis of the natural rate of unemployment.
Friedman and Edmund Phelps argue that Phillips curve trade-
offs will disappear as soon as expectations of workers adapt
to actual inflation experience. To them, the long-run
Phillips curve is vertical at the natural rate of unemployment, the rate at which the expected rate of inflation equals
the actual rate of inflation and the real wage rate is at its
equilibrium level. The adaptive expectations hypothesis and
the vertical Phillips curve are graphically explained by
Figure 6.5.

Suppose the economy is initially at point U_o where both
the actual and expected rates of inflation are equal to zero
and the rate of unemployment is at its natural level. Assume
that the monetary authority implements an expansionary
monetary policy with the objective of moving the unemployment
rate to a lower level, say U_1. In the diagram, the trade-off
for this lower unemployment rate is represented as 4 percent
inflation. This is shown by the movement from U_o to point A
on the short-run Phillips curve S_1. The trade-off is made
possible by the fact that workers at first do not fully
anticipate the 4 percent inflation. Sooner or later, however, their expectations will adapt to the actual rate of
inflation and workers will incorporate the fully anticipated
inflation rate into their wage bargains. The real wage rate
will rise which, in turn, will cause the employers to cut
back on employment. Consequently, the economy will move from
A to B on the long-run Phillips curve. In the next round,
the short-run Phillips curve will be S_2. If the monetary
authority still wishes to maintain the target rate U_1, it can

---

[46]Milton Friedman, op. cit., p. 100.

155

Figure 6.5

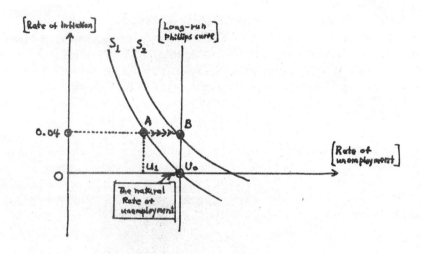

only do so by accelerating the increase in the rate of inflation. Thus, Friedman asserts:

> There is always a temporary trade-off between
> inflation and unemployment; there is no permanent
> trade-off. The temporary trade-off comes not from
> inflation per se, but from unanticipated inflation,
> which generally means, from a rising rate of
> inflation...The monetary authority controls nominal
> quantities--directly, the quantity of its own
> liabilities...It cannot use its control over
> nominal quantities to peg real quantity--the real
> rate of interest, the rate of unemployment, the

level of real national income, the real quantity of money, the rate of growth of real national income, or the rate of growth of the real quantity of money.[47]

Turning to fiscal policy, it is well known that Monetarists generally assert that government spending, financed either by taxing or borrowing from the public, "crowds out" private spending. This view had long been popularized by macroeconomics textbooks before 1972.[48] The Monetarist position was usually depicted by a vertical LM curve reflecting the assumption that the interest elasticities of the demand for and supply of money are zero. Milton Friedman (1972) argued, however, that the slope of the LM curve was irrelevant to the "crowding out" phenomenon. Instead, Friedman based the monetarist position on the "wealth effect." He wrote:

> One way to characterize the Keynesian approach is that it gives almost exclusive importance to the first-round effect. This leads it to attach importance primarily to flows of spending rather than to stocks of assets. Similarly, one way to characterize the quantity-theory approach is to say that it gives almost no importance to first-round effects...The empirical question is how important the first-round effects are compared to the ultimate effects. Theory cannot answer the question.[49]

Friedman's "first-round" and "ultimate" effects may be explained graphically by Figure 6.6.

---

[47] Milton Friedman, op. cit., pp. 104-105.

[48] See William H. Branson, MACROECONOMIC THEORY AND POLICY (New York: Harper & Row Publishers, 1972), p. 281.

[49] Milton Friedman, "Comments on the Critics," JOURNAL OF POLITICAL ECONOMY, Vol. 80, September-October 1972, pp.

Figure 6.6

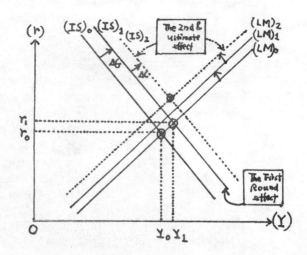

49, cont.

906-950. See p. 922 for the quotation. Similar
views were advanced by Karl Brunner and Allan H. Meltzer in
their essay, "Money, Debt and Economic Activity," JOURNAL
OF POLITICAL ECONOMY, Vol. 80, September-October 1972, pp.
951-977. As observed by Roger W. Spencer and William P.
Yohe, the "crowding out" hypothesis is not a new one. They
write: "It was, in fact, the dominant view before the
Keynesian Revolution of the 1930s. Classical economists
including Adam Smith and David Ricardo, and neo-classicists
including F.A. Hayck and R.C. Hawtrey found little use for
fiscal stabilization efforts." See Federal Reserve Bank of
St. Louis REVIEW (October 1970), p. 14. The more recent
renewal of the "crowding out" controversy, as observed by
Keith M. Carlson and Roger W. Spencer (Federal Reserve Bank
of St. Louis REVIEW, December 1975), is traceable primarily
to the empirical results published by Anderson and Jordan
in 1968 and supporting studies by Keran in 1969 and 1970,"
p. 3.

Figure 6.6 presents the familiar IS-LM diagram in which the initial equilibrium levels, r_o and Y_o, are given by the intersection of $(IS)_o$ and $(LM)_o$. An increase in government spending is indicated by the outward shift of the IS curve to $(IS)_1$. Consequently, income rises from Y_o to Y_1. If the increased spending is financed by borrowing, the "wealth effect" of the increased bond holdings by the public, together with the income increase, will lead to higher consumption and lower saving. Hence, the IS curve will shift further outward to $(IS)_2$. This is what Friedman refers to as the "first-round" effects. The "second round" effects refer to the leftward shifts of the (LM) curve, since the "wealth effect" will affect the financial markets also. As household wealth increases, the demand for both money and bonds will also increase. As a result, $(LM)_o$ will shift leftward to $(LM)_1$. But the shift will not stop at $(LM)_1$, for as long as government's deficits persist, the LM curve will continue to shift leftward. Such shifts have a deflationary impact on the level of national income. They may potentially swamp the "first round" stimulative effects of deficit spending. This is why Friedman said: "Theory cannot answer that question."

An answer to Friedman was provided by Alan S. Blinder and Robert M. Solow in 1973.[50] They demonstrated that "certain theoretical arguments can be adduced in support of the conventional view that fiscal policy works."[51]

The main purpose of the Blinder-Solow analysis was to determine whether the effect of financing a government deficit by issuing bonds differs from that produced when the deficit is financed by money creation. The Blinder-Solow

---

[50] Alan S. Blinder and Robert M. Solow, "Does Fiscal Policy Matter?" JOURNAL OF PUBLIC ECONOMICS, Vol. 2, 1973, pp. 319-337.

[51] Alan S. Blinder and Robert M. Solow, ibid, p. 323.

model consists of the following nine equation:[52]

(1) (goods market equilibrium) $\quad Y = C + I + G$

(2) (consumption function) $\quad C = C(Y + i_B - T, W)$

(3) (net investment function) $\quad I = I(r)$

(4) (tax function) $\quad T = T(Y + i_B)$

(5) (demand for real balances) $\quad \dfrac{M^d}{P} = L(r, Y, W)$

(6) (exogenous money supply) $\quad M^S = \bar{M}$

(7) money market equilibrium $\quad M^S = M^d$

(8) definition of wealth) $\quad W = K + \dfrac{M}{P} + \dfrac{B}{rp}$

(9) (government budget constraint) $\quad G + i_B + Tr = T_x + \dfrac{\dot{B}}{rp} + \dfrac{\dot{M}}{P}$

In the wealth equation, $\dfrac{B}{rp}$ is the real value of the stock of government bonds. The symbol i_B represents interest payments by the government on bonds. While interest payments represent an expenditure to the government, they are also income to the recipients, income on which taxes are paid. Hence, such interest payments are included in both the consumption function and the tax function. The government budget constraint requires that, in each period, total government expenditure ($G + i_B + T_r$) must equal the total flow of financing from all sources, including the printing of money ($T_x + \dot{B}/rP + \dot{M}/P$). The symbol T represents net taxes ($T \equiv T_x - T_r$).

Blinder and Solow point out that "the IS-LM model usually treats the price level as exogenously fixed, and we

---

[52] The notation follows that of Blinder and Solow with some minor alterations. A dot over a variable denotes a time derivative.

shall adhere to this convention. However, it should be noted that we do this strictly for simplicity. There are no real difficulties in adding a production function and a labor market and allowing the price level to be endogenously determined."[53] If P is set equal to 1, the symbol P will drop out in equations (5), (8) and (9). The equation for the government budget constraint will then be:

$$(10) \qquad G + i_B = T + \frac{\dot{B}}{r} + \dot{M}$$

Blinder and Solow further point out: "Suppose that we ignore the dynamics of the model and look only at the long-run steady-state solution (in addition, interest payments are abstracted). This means $\dot{M} = \dot{B}/_r = 0$, so that (9) implies $G = T(Y)$, that is the government budget must be balanced in the long run."[54] It follows that

$$(11) \qquad dG = T'dY \qquad or \qquad dY/dG = 1/T'$$

"Observe that this long-run multiplier expression holds regardless of how the deficit is financed, and is independent of all functional relations in the model except the tax function. In a word, if the model is stable under each mode of financing (so that it actually approaches its steady state), the long-run multipliers for bond and money-financed deficit spending are identical."[55]

A different result is obtained, however, when interest payments are not abstracted from the long-run steady state solution. In this case the "steady state" equation for the government budget constraint is

---

[53] Alan S. Blinder and Robert M. Solow, op. cit., p. 324 note.

[54] Alan S. Blinder and Robert M. Solow, op. cit., p. 326. The words in brackets are ours.

[55] Alan S. Blinder and Robert M. Solow, op. cit., p. 326.

(12) $\qquad G + i_B - T(Y + i_B) = 0$

so that

(13) $\qquad dY/dG = \dfrac{1 + (1 - T') \; dB/dG}{T'}$.

If the deficits are financed by money creation, then $dB/dG = 0$ and, as before, $dY/dG = 1/T'$. On the other hand, if the deficits are bond financed, the long-run "steady-state" multiplier is greater under bond financing than under money creation, since

$$\frac{1 + (1 - T') \; dB/dG}{T'} > \frac{1}{T'} ,$$

assuming $(1 - T') > 0$ and $dB/dG > 0$.

According to James Barth, "The interpretation of the difference between the two multipliers given by Blinder and Solow is based upon 'second round' effects. Starting from equilibrium with a balanced government budget, an increase in government spending financed by money creation will cause a shift in the IS curve which produces an increase in the equilibrium level of income. This is the explanation offered in 'traditional' IS-LM analysis; that is, the 'first round' effect. If the deficit is financed by bonds, however, 'second round' effects will also occur due to wealth effects and the fact that interest payments on bonds must be made. There are two reasons that a deficit financed by bond sales will be larger than that financed by money creation: (1) income rises less so that the induced tax receipts are smaller and (2) the increased debt will require increased interest payments. The increase in the number of bonds outstanding requires a greater rise in income to induce an increase in tax receipts sufficient to cover the additional interest payments and to cover the deficit in order to achieve long-run steady-state equilibrium."[56]

Although Blinder and Solow have provided "certain theoretical arguments" in support of the conventional view that fiscal policy works, the "crowding out" controversy has yet to be put to rest. As observed by Keith M. Carlson and Roger W. Spencer,

> Apparently these issues will not approach solution until additional structural models are developed and tested. The Keynesians (of the "Neoclassical Synthesis" persuasion) have developed many models, but these models have not been tested as inter-dependent units. Monetarists, on the other hand, have not offered structural models to go along with their reduced form results.[57]

The Counter-Revolution of the Rational Expectations School

The advocates of rational expectations are purists. In their view, the "Keynesian counter-revolution" accomplished by the architects of the "Neoclassical Synthesis" is not thorough enough. To them, too many irrational elements and inconsistencies of Keynesian economics are retained in the

---

[56] James Barth, "Introduction to Crowding Out: Theory and Evidence" in MACROECONOMICS: SELECTED READINGS (Revised Edition), edited by Ching-Yao Hsieh, James Barth and Salih Neftci (Lexington, Mass.: Xerox Individualized Publishing, 1977), pp. 7-8.

[57] Keith M. Carlson and Roger W. Spencer, op. cit., pp. 15-16.

analysis.[58]   Thus, the main objective of the rational expectations school is to apply neoclassical utility optimization principles to all economic problems, specifically to the problems of expectations formation and macroeconomic policy. Neil Wallace raises the pertinent question:

> Perhaps the main problem confronting macroeconomics is the explanation of observed positive correlations between aggregate demand variables, on one hand, and output and employment, on the other hand. More directly, why do not shifts in aggregate demand impact only on prices as is implied by what

----

[58]Mark H. Willes succinctly summarizes the shortcomings of Keynesian models as follows: (1) Irrational expectations: "Macro-model builders have generally given their agents 'adaptive expectations.' Agents who have adaptive expectations expect the future to be essentially a continuation of the past...The model consequently has no way of formulating expectations for a future that is substantially different from the past." (2) Inconsistencies: "Conventional modeling is inconsistent because its premises about aggregate behavior are based on conflicting assumptions about individual behavior...Conventional models often treat consumption and labor as unrelated variables, which implies that agents are inconsistent or even schizoid....the things Keynes has thrown away have made macro models impotent for evaluating policies." (3) Arbitrary measures of success: "In Keynesian models the success of a policy cannot be clearly determined. Because these models replace individual decisions with aggregate actions, they say nothing about individual welfare....Policies designed to reduce employment fluctuations, even if they succeed, can reduce people's economic welfare over the course of the business cycle." See his essay, "Rational Expectations as a Counterrevolution," in Daniel Bell and Irving Kristol, eds., THE CRISIS IN ECONOMIC THEORY, op. cit., pp. 85-90.

might be called the 'classical' full employment flexible wage and price macroeconomic model?[59]

The "classical" model referred to by Wallace has nothing to do with the Smithian or Ricardian models. The term "classical," in essence, is neoclassical theory and refers to a series of composite models constructed by contemporary writers with the sole purpose of sharpening understanding of the differences between Keynesian economics and the pre-Keynesian views. Only in the money market equations can one detect the heritage of Richard Cantillon, David Hume, Henry Thornton and other monetary theorists of the classical period.

To highlight the relationship between the "classical" macroeconomic model and the macroeconomics of the rational expectations school, we attempt to trace the roots of rational expectations modeling by presenting Branson's "classical model" as background (Figure 6.7).[60]

Demand-side equilibrium:

(1) Output market equilibrium:

$$y - c[y-t(y)] = i(r) + g \quad ; \quad \text{(the IS curve)}$$

(2) Money market equilibrium:

$$\frac{\bar{M}}{\bar{P}} = l(r) + k(y) \quad ; \quad \text{(the LM curve)}$$

---

[59] Neil Wallace, "Microeconomic Theories of Macroeconomic Phenomena and Their Implications for Monetary Policy" in RATIONAL EXPECTATIONS AND THE THEORY OF ECONOMIC POLICY, PART II: ARGUMENTS AND EVIDENCE, Thomas J. Sargent and Neil Wallace (Minneapolis: Research Department, Federal Reserve Bank of Minneapolis, 1976), p. 24.

[60] See William H. Branson, MACROECONOMIC THEORY AND POLICY (New York: Harper & Row, Publishers, 1979) 2nd edition, pp. 129-131; also Chapters 4 and 6.

Supply-side equilibrium:

(3) Aggregate production function:

$$y = y(N, \bar{K})$$

(4) Labor market equilibrium:

$$Pf'(N) = P^e g(N)$$

Equation (1) is the output (goods) market equilibrium condition. The symbol y stands for real income; the expression $y - c[y - t(y)]$ represents real consumption; the symbol t denotes net tax revenue in real terms: $t = t(y)$; $t' > 0$. The symbol i is investment expenditure in real tems, and g is government spending in real terms.

In Equation (2) the two components of the demand for real money balances are $l(r)$ and $k(y)$. The former stands for transactions demand and the latter for speculative and asset demand. The supply of money is represented by the symbol M, which is assumed to be determined exogenously.

The intersection of the IS and LM curves determines the equilibrium levels of r and y simultaneously.

The aggregate demand curve is derived by asking "what happens to equilibrium output demanded as the price level, p, changes, allowing other variables, such as the interest rate, also to adjust to their equilibrium levels."[61]

The aggregate supply curve is derived from Equations (3) and (4). The left-hand side of Equation (4) symbolizes the demand for labor and the right-hand side, the supply of labor. The demand-for-labor function is:

---

[61] William H. Branson, op. cit., p. 69.

166

Figure 6.7

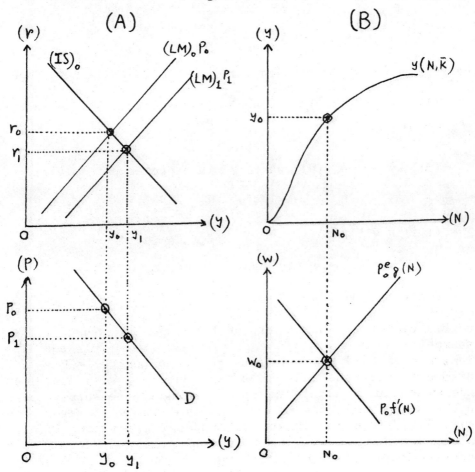

$$w = \frac{W}{P} = f'(N) = \frac{\partial y}{\partial N},$$

or $W = P.f'(N)$.

The supply-of-labor function is:

   (i) $N^S = N^S(w^e)$, where w^e is expected real wage rate.

   or

   (ii) $w^e \equiv \frac{W}{P^e} = g(N)$, where P^e is expected price level.

   or

   (iii) $W = P^e g(N)$.

   (iv) $W = \frac{W}{P^e} \cdot \frac{P^e}{P}$. By substitution, we obtain:

   (v) $W = P^e g(N)$.

In the "classical" case, perfect foresight is assumed. This assumption implies that $P^e = P$. We begin with full equilibrium where P^e and P are indexed to 1, so that $P^e = P = 1$.[62] This means that the full-employment output y_o is determined independent of aggregate demand. The aggregate supply curve in the "Classical" case is vertical as depicted in Figure 6.8 (A). Figure 6.8 (B) shows that under these assumptions an autonomous shift of aggregate demand will only lead to an increase in prices without any impact on y_o.

It should be noted that the vertical aggregate supply curve is associated with the concept of the "natural rate of unemployment," for full employment does not means 100 percent employment of the existing labor force. It always includes a certain percentage of "frictional unemployment."

---

[62] William H. Branson, op. cit., p. 125.

Figure 6.8 (A)   Figure 6.8 (B)

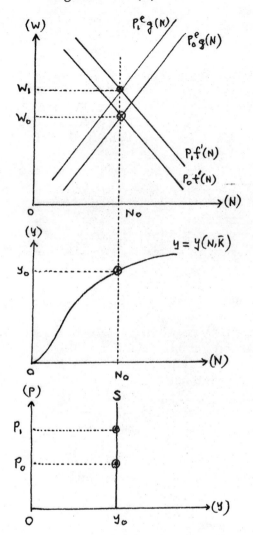

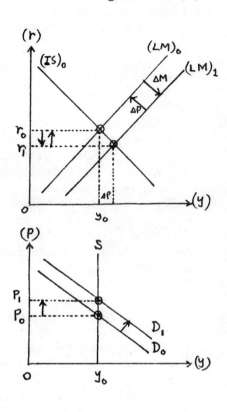

169

With the "classical" macroeconomic model as background, consider the following simple macroeconomic model illustrative of the rational expectations school.

(1) The Aggregate Supply Function: $y_t - \bar{y} = a(P_t - P_t^e) + U_t$
where y_t is the current supply of output; and $\bar{y}$ stands for the full-employment output (same as y_o in the "classical" model) corresponding to the "natural rate of unemployment." The symbols P_t, P_t^e, and U_t represent the price level of the current period, the expected price level of the current period and deviations of output from the full-employment level, $\bar{y}$. The equation states that expectational errors will cause y_t to deviate from $\bar{y}$, and that the deviations will disappear when expectational errors vanish. Expectations in this simple model refer mainly to price expectations. The microfoundation of this assertion, in the words of James Barth, is based on the assumption:

> ...that a firm will supply output based on relative prices. The market price is not known to the firm. This requires that the firm form an expectation about this price. With less than perfect knowledge, the firm's expectations will be correct only on average. Sometimes it will err on the high side, while other times it will err on the low side. It is assumed, however, that these errors cancel. This is what is meant by rational expectations: an individual or firm will on average be correct, so that any errors tend to cancel and these errors are the 'smallest' given available information (that is, not only unbiased[63] but also 'best' forecasts are formed).

[63] This quotation is taken from an unpublished paper by James Barth entitled, "Notes on Classical, Keynesian and Rational Expectations Models" (November 1978), p. 5.

Thus, it should be stressed that rational expectations do not imply "perfect foresight." In this respect, the rational expectations school parts company with the "classical" model. It also diverges from the "adaptive expectations" hypothesis, for economic agents who have "adaptive expectations" always base their expectations entirely on the past. Nothing is said about formulating expectations for a future that is not a continuation of the past. Thus, the rational expectations school considers "adaptive expectations" to be irrational expectations.

(2) <u>The Demand-side Price Formation Process</u>: $P_t = \alpha M_t + V_t$
where M_t is the stock of money in existence at period t; and V_t is a proxy for all other variables that may affect the price level. This equation describes the inflation-generating process of the simple model and is essentially the quantity theory of money. It states that the price level is determined basically by the stock of money and by some transitory disturbances other than the growth of money stock. The monetary authority attempts to adjust money growth according to some sort of feedback control, viz. the current rate of money growth is treated as a function of last period's excess demand for money and some other random disturbances. Rational expectations of the movements of the price level should be the same as the price formation processes represented by Equation (2) of this simple model.

(3) <u>Rational Price Expectations</u>: $P^e = \alpha M_t^e + V_t^e$
The information available to each agent frequently includes some unwanted "noise." Rational expectations imply that each agent will, through the process of trial and error, eventually purge these unwanted "noises." (This procedure is often referred to as the "signal extraction problem.") Consequently, V_t^e will be reduced to zero and $P_t^e = \alpha M_t^e$. This is the essence of the notion that expectations are "rational" in the Muthian

171

sense, and hence equal the predictions of the theory.[64]

(4)   The Reduced Form of the Simple Model:

$$Y_t - \bar{y} = \alpha\, b(M_t - M_t^e) + bV_t + U_t$$

Equation (4) is derived from substituting equations (2) and (3) into (1) and indicates that any deviation from the full-employment output is attributable to two causes: (a) the unwanted "noises" represented by V_t and U_t, and (b) unanticipated changes in the money supply indicated by $(M_t - M_t^e)$. Rational expectations will render V_t^e and U_t equal to zero. Hence, only unanticipated changes in money supply matter. However, if rational people can correctly anticipate the systematic or predictable component of monetary policy, then $(M_t - M_t^e)$ will also equal zero. Under these conditions,

---

[64] See John F. Muth, "Rational Expectations and the Theory of Price Movements," ECONOMETRICA, Vol. 29 (July 1961), pp. 315-335. Muth defines rational expectations as "that expectations of firms (or more generally, the subjective probability distribution of outcomes) tend to be distributed, for the same information set, about the predictions of the theory (or the 'objective' probability distribution of the outcomes)," op. cit., p. 316. More recently, P.A.V.B. Swamy, James R. Barth and P.A. Tinsley in their paper, "The Rational Expectations Approach to Economic Modeling" (JOURNAL OF ECONOMIC DYNAMICS AND CONTROL, Vol. 4, 1982, pp. 125-147, North Holland), pointed out "that conventional formulations of the rational expectations postulate violate the axiomatic basis of modern statistical theory by confounding 'objective' and 'subjective' notions of probability. It is logically impossible to test the rationality of subjective expectations by comparison with observable frequencies. If a rational expectations conjecture is simply imposed on a model, conditions for identification of the model are more stringent than indicated in earlier literature", p. 125.

$y_t - \bar{y}$ will equal zero ($y_t = \bar{y}$), the "classical" perpendicular aggregate supply curve emerges and the economy
is always on the vertical long-run Phillips curve. Consequently, in this view systematic monetary policy cannot affect real economic activity, not even short-run
trade-offs between the rate of inflation and the rate of
unemployment.

The general conclusions of the rational expectations
hypothesis seem to present a dilemma. Thomas J. Sargent and
Neil Wallace make the following observations:

> The conundrum facing the economist can be put as
> follows. In order for a model to have normative
> implications, it must contain some parameters whose
> values can be chosen by the policymaker. But if
> these can be chosen, rational agents will not view
> them as fixed and will make use of schemes for
> predicting their values. If the economist models
> the economy taking these schemes into account, then
> those parameters become endogenous variables and no
> longer appear in the reduced-form equations for the
> other endogenous variables. If he models the
> economy without taking the schemes into account, he
> is not imposing rationality.[65]

In spite of the criticisms leveled at this school, we
should not obscure one of its major accomplishments. We
agree with the following observation made by Rodney Maddock
and Michael Carter:

> The development of rational expectations theory
> will make a more significant contribution to
> economics in the impetus it gives to research on

---

[65]Thomas J. Sargent and Neil Wallace, "Rational Expectations
and the Theory of Economic Policy," JOURNAL OF MONETARY
ECONOMICS, Vol. 2, 1976, pp. 169-183, North-Holland
Publishing Company.

the vital areas of learning and expectations
formation. It brings to the fore questions about
the availability and use of information. Instead
of being the finale of the monetarist's case
against policy intervention, it should be seen as
th prologue for a revitalized theory of expectations, information and policy.[66]

Criticisms from the Austrian School

Austrian economists are subjectivists. They are the
true descendants of the theory of Carl Menger. As pointed
out by Israel M. Kirzner, the two distinct insights of the
Austrian school are:

First, there is the insight that human action is
purposeful, and Second, there is the insight that
there is an indeterminancy and unpredictability
inherent in human preferences, human expectations
and human knowledge.[67]

The distinctive methodology of the Austrians is praxeology, which is defined as the general theory of purposeful
human action. The term was first applied by Ludwig von Mises
(1949).[68] Praxeology asserts that individual agents adopt

---

[66] Rodney Maddock and Michael Carter, "A Child's Guide to
Rational Expectations," JOURNAL OF ECONOMIC LITERATURE,
Vol. XX, No. 1, March 1982, pp. 39-51. The quotation
appears on page 49.

[67] Israel M. Kirzner, "On the Method of Austrian Economics"
in Edwin G. Dolan, ed., THE FOUNDATIONS OF MODERN AUSTRIAN
ECONOMICS (Kansas City: Sheed & Ward, Inc., 1976), p. 42.

[68] See Ludwig von Mises, HUMAN ACTION: A TREATISE ON ECONOMICS
(New Haven: Yale University Press, 1949).

goals and believe, whether erroneously or correctly, that they can achieve these by the employment of certain means.

The common thread that ties the various specific Austrian doctrines together is the notion of historical (calendar) time. Time is also the central thrust of the Austrian critique of the "Neoclassical Synthesis." Murray N. Rothbard observes:

> All action in the real world, furthermore, must take place through _time_; all action takes place in some _present_ and is directed toward the _future_ (immediate or remote) attainment of an end. If all of a person's desires could be instantaneously realized, there would be no reason for him to act at all. Furthermore, that a man acts implies that he believes action will make a difference....Action therefore implies that man does not have omniscient knowledge of the future; for if he had such knowledge, no action of his would make any difference. Hence, action implies that we live in a world of an _uncertain_, or not fully certain, future.[69]

As did Mises, the Austrian economists consider purposeful human action an unchanging phenomenon to be regarded as the "absolutism" in economics. Mises wrote:

> The philosophy of historical relativism—historicism—fails to see the fact that is something unchanging that, on the one hand, constitutes the sphere of history or historical events...and, on the other hand, enables man to deal with these events....This alone distinguishes human history from the history of changes going on outside the field of human action....In human history we are

[69] Murray N. Rothbard, "Praexology: The Methodology of Austrian Economics" in Edwin G. Dolan, ed., THE FOUNDATIONS OF MODERN AUSTRIAN ECONOMICS, op. cit., p. 20. The underlines are ours.

dealing with the ends aimed at by the actors, that is, with final causes. In natural history, as in the other branches of the natural sciences, we do not know anything about final causes.[70]

The axioms of praxeology are valid a priori. "They are not subject to verification or falsification on the ground of experiences and facts." Its statements and propositions are, like those of logic and mathematics, a priori. Friedrich A. Hayek stresses:

In fact most of the objects of social or human action are not 'objective facts' in the special narrow sense in which this term is used by the (natural) sciences....They cannot be defined in physical terms.[71]

The praxeology of the Austrian school emphasizes a much broader notion of purposeful human action than the Robbinsian concept (Figure 6.9 presents a comparison of Robbinsian and Austrian school concepts). Recall that Lionel Robbins (1932) defined the subject-matter of economics as follows:

Economics is concerned with that aspect of behaviour which arises from the scarcity of means to achieve given ends. The economist is not concerned with ends as such. He is concerned with the way in which the attainment of ends is limited. The ends may be noble or they may be base. They may be 'material' or 'immaterial'--if ends can be so described. But if the attainment of one set of

---

[70] Ludwig von Mises, "Epistemological Relativism in the Science of Human Action" in Helmut Schoeck and James W. Wiggins, eds., RELATIVISM AND THE STUDY OF MAN (Princeton, New Jersey: D. Van Vostrand Co., Inc., 1961), p. 129.

[71] Friedrich A. Hayek, THE COUNTER-REVOLUTION OF SCIENCE (London: The Free Press of Glencoe, 1955), pp. 26-27.

Figure 6.9

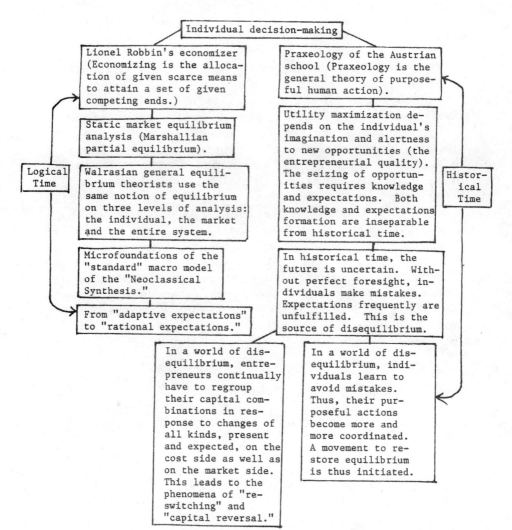

Individual decision-making

Lionel Robbin's economizer (Economizing is the allocation of given scarce means to attain a set of given competing ends.)

Static market equilibrium analysis (Marshallian partial equilibrium).

Walrasian general equilibrium theorists use the same notion of equilibrium on three levels of analysis: the individual, the market and the entire system.

Microfoundations of the "standard" macro model of the "Neoclassical Synthesis."

From "adaptive expectations" to "rational expectations."

Praxeology of the Austrian school (Praxeology is the general theory of purposeful human action).

Utility maximization depends on the individual's imagination and alertness to new opportunities (the entrepreneurial quality). The seizing of opportunities requires knowledge and expectations. Both knowledge and expectations formation are inseparable from historical time.

In historical time, the future is uncertain. Without perfect foresight, individuals make mistakes. Expectations frequently are unfulfilled. This is the source of disequilibrium.

In a world of disequilibrium, entrepreneurs continually have to regroup their capital combinations in response to changes of all kinds, present and expected, on the cost side as well as on the market side. This leads to the phenomena of "reswitching" and "capital reversal."

In a world of disequilibrium, individuals learn to avoid mistakes. Thus, their purposeful actions become more and more coordinated. A movement to restore equilibrium is thus initiated.

Logical Time

Historical Time

ends involves the sacrifice of others, then it has
an economic aspect.[72]

The Mises's concept of human action embodies an insight
about man that is absent in the Robbinsian view. As observed
by Kirzner,

> This insight recognizes that men are not only
> calculating agents but are also alert to
> opportunities. Robbinsian theory only applies
> after a person is confronted with opportunities;
> for it does not explain how that person learns
> about opportunities in the first place. Misesian
> theory of human action conceives of the individual
> as having his eyes and ears open to opportunities
> that are 'just around the corner.' He is alert,
> waiting, continually receptive to something that
> may turn up....This alertness is the entrepre-
> neurial element in human action, a concept lacking
> in analysis carried out in exclusively Robbinsian
> terms. At the same time that it transforms alloca-
> tive decision making into a realistic view of human
> action, entrepreneurship converts the theory of
> market equilibrium into a theory of market
> process.[73]

It is interesting to note that the Austrian view of
entrepreneurship is compatible with G.L.S. Shackle's emphasis
on the role of imagination in the general theory of choice.
According to Shackle, the very act of choice involves the
imagination of the chooser. For "choice must concern itself

---

[72]Lionel Robbins, AN ESSAY ON THE NATURE AND SIGNIFICANCE OF
ECONOMIC SCIENCE (London: Macmillan & Co., Ltd., 1952), p.
24-25.

[73]Israel M. Kirzner, "Equilibrium versus Market Process," in
Edwin G. Dolan, ed., THE FOUNDATIONS OF MODERN AUSTRIAN
ECONOMICS, op. cit., pp. 119-120.

with time to come" and "the future is imagined by each man
for himself, and this process of the imagination is a vital
part of the process of decision."[74] Expressing Shackle's
ideas in the more familiar jargon of economics, one may say
that utility maximization depends not only on the decision-
maker's preferences, budget constraint and the objectively
specified alternatives facing him, but also on the imagined
future outcomes of his choice. Shackle says:

> Reports from the field [of choosable entities] are
> labeled with the name of the present in which they
> are received. In that identified present, 'what
> is' is not open to choice. It has already chosen
> itself. Choice must concern itself with time-to-
> come. The entities that are rivals for election by
> the chooser and are mutually exclusive for his
> choice, must, before his choice is made, be co-
> existent in his thought. They are not reports of
> 'what is' but imaginations of what might be.[75]

A subset of man's imagination is what Shackle calls
expectations. Imagination could be unconstrained, but
expectations about the future outcomes of an individual's
choices must be consistent with the individual and constraints. However, both imagination and expectations are
essentially subjective in nature. S.C. Littlechild observes:

> The concept of entrepreneurial alertness
> shares many of the properties of imagination: both
> provide a vehicle for moving outside the static
> neoclassical economizing problem, and thereby

---

[74] See G.L.S. Shackle, EPISMETICS AND ECONOMICS (Cambridge:
Cambridge University Press, 1972), p. 3.

[75] G.L.S. Shackle, "Imagination, Formalism, and Choice" in
Mario J. Rizzo, ed., TIME, UNCERTAINTY, AND DISEQUILIBRIUM
(Lexington, Massachusetts: D.C. Heath & Co., 1979), p. 22.
The words in the brackets and the underline are ours.

provide the basis for a dynamic market process taking place over <u>time</u>.[76]

The Austrian emphasis of dynamic market process taking place in historical time leads to a second major point: The Austrian writers criticize "Neoclassical Synthesis" for obscuring the element of unpredictability in human expectations and knowledge in the real world of uncertainty. They attribute these shortcomings to the microfoundations of the "Neoclassical Synthesis." Ludwig M. Lachmann argues that the Walrasian general equilibrium analysis should be abandoned, pointing out that:

> Walrasians, in using the same notion of equilibrium on three levels of analysis--the individual, the market, and the entire system--succumbed to the fallacy of unwarranted generalizations: They erroneously believed that the key that unlocks one door will also unlock a number of others. Action controlled by one mind is, as Mises showed, necessarily consistent. The actions of a number of minds in the same market lack such consistency, as the simultaneous presence of bulls and bears shows. Consistency of action in a number of markets within a system constitutes an even greater presumption.[77]

The Austrians' disenchantment with general equilibrium analysis is reiterated by Edwin G. Dolan:

---

[76] S.C. Littlechild, Comment: Radical Subjectivism or Radical Subversion," in Mario J. Rizzo, ed., TIME, UNCERTAINTY, AND DISEQUILIBRIUM, op. cit., p. 46. The underline is ours.

[77] Ludwig M. Lachmann, "On the Central Concept of Austrian Economics: Market Process," in Edwin G. Dolan, ed., op. cit., p. 131.

The theory of general equilibrium poses a number of attractive puzzles for neoclassical economists, particularly those wishing to display their virtuosity in mathematical analysis....But from the point of view of an Austrian theorist bent on making the world intelligible in terms of human action the puzzles of general equilibrium are simply not the whole story. Far from being deterred by the fact that the decision-making process of the entrepreneur is not easily expressed in mathematical notation , a writer like Kirzner is able to exercise his own virtuosity at verbal-deductive analysis and produce a variety of useful insights.[78]

The dynamic market process, according to Hayek, is also an equilibrating mechanism. As observed by Mario J. Rizzo, the concept of equilibrium is not timeless, "for it involves the consistency of individual plans in the context of a near or remote future. The activity of planning necessarily implies a temporal framework or horizon."[79] Disequilibrium in the Hayekian sense implies lack of coordination of plans. In other words, in disequilibrium, man's knowledge is imperfect. A movement from disequilibrium to equilibrium must be one in which men gradually learn to avoid mistakes, so that their actions become more and more coordinated. The Austrian theorists do not reject the concept of equilibrium. As succinctly put by Kirzner, "If we reject this hypothesis, then we reject the basis for viewing the market process as an equilibrating mechanism--that is, rejecting the claim that economics can tell us anything definite about the unintended market consequences of human actions."[80]

------

[78] Edwin G. Dolan, "Austrian Economics as Extraordinary Science," in Edwin G. Dolan, ed., op. cit., p. 9.

[79] These are the words of Mario J. Rizzo. See his TIME, UNCERTAINTY, AND DISEQUILIBRIUM, op. cit., p. 3.

[80] Israel M. Kirzner, "On the Method of Austrian Economics," in Edwin G. Dolan, ed., op. cit., p. 49.

The central concept of a dynamic market process taking place over time is further reflected in the Austrian theory of capital. They reject the fundist-materialist dichotomy Hicks made in 1974. Hicks wrote:

> There are some for whom Real Capital is a Fund--I shall call them Fundists; and there are some for whom it consists of physical goods--I shall venture in this paper to call them Materialists....Not only Adam Smith, but all (or nearly all) of the British Classical Economists were Fundists; so was Marx (how else should he have invented 'Capitalism?'); so was Jevons. It was after 1870 that there was a Materialist Revolution. It is not the same as the Marginalist Revolution; for some of the Marginalists, such as Jevons and Bohm-Bawerk, kept the Fundist flag flying. But most economists, in England and America, went Materialist. Materialism, indeed, is characteristic of what nowadays reckoned to be the 'neoclassical' position. Not only Cannan, but Marshall and Pigou, and J.B. Clark, were clearly materialists. Anyone, indeed, who uses a Production Function, in which Product is shown as a function of labor, capital, and technology, supposed separable, confesses himself to be (at least while using it) a Materialist....But the rethinking of capital theory and of growth theory, which followed from Keynes, and from Harrod on Keynes, led to a revival of Fundism. If the Production Function is a hallmark of Materialism, the capital-output ratio is a hallmark of modern Fundism.[81]

The Austrian economists occupy a position that is neither fundist nor materialist. As pointed out by Kirzner:

---

[81] John Hicks, "Capital Controversies: Ancient and Modern," AMERICAN ECONOMIC REVIEW, May 1974, p. 315.

Austrians reject the fundist-materialist dichotomy because of the special understanding of the role individual plans play in the market process. A capital good is not merely a produced factor of production. Rather it is a good produced as part of a multiperiod plan in which it has been assigned a specific function in a projected process of production. A capital good is thus a physical good with an assigned productive purpose.[82]

According to Kirzner, the Austrians vigorously reject the attempt to collapse the multidimensional collection of capital goods into a homogeneous quantity. "They defy aggregation not only because of physical heterogeneity but also, more importantly, because of the diversity of the purposes to which these goods have been assigned."[83] Based on their fundamental tenets, the Austrian theorists provide an additional cause for the "reswitching" and "capital reversal" phenomena expounded by the post-Keynesian economists during the stage of "Cambridge controversies in the theory of capital." Lachmann observes:

> In a world of disequilibrium, entrepreneurs continually have to regroup their capital combinations in response to changes of all kinds, present and expected, on the cost side as well as on the market side. A change in the mode of income distribution (the essential argument of the post-Keynesians) is merely one special case of a very large class of cases to which the entrepreneur has to give constant attention. No matter whether switching or reswitching is to be under-taken, or

---

[82] Israel M. Kirzner, "The Theory of Capital," in Edwin G. Dolan, ed., op. cit., p. 137. The underlines are ours.

[83] These are the words of Kirzner, op. cit., p. 138.

any other response to market change, <u>expectations</u> play a part, and the individuality of each firm finds its expression in its own way.[84]

It should be noted that the only argument in the post-Keynesian economics (to be discussed in Part III of this book) acceptable to the Austrians is that of capital re-switching. They reject post-Keynesian macro-economics (or what Austrians refer to as "neo-Ricardians") just as intensely as Carl Menger attacked Ricardian value theory. For the same reason, they even disown Bohm-Bawerk as a legitimate Austrian capital theorist. Lachmann stresses:

> Bohm-Bawerk never meant to be a capital theorist. He was essentially a Ricardian who asked a Ricardian question: "Why are the owners of imper-manent resources able to enjoy a permanent income and what determines its magnitude?" The notion of temporal capital structure consisting of a sequence of stages of production was a mere by-product of an inquiry into the causes and the magnitude of the rate of return on capital and not the main subject. In pursuit of this Ricardian inquiry Bohm-Bawerk battled on and failed like a Ricardian.[85]

---

[84] Ludwig M. Lachmann, "On Austrian Capital Theory," in Edwin G. Dolan, ed., op. cit., p. 150.

[85] Ludwig M. Lachmann, op. cit., p. 145.

CHAPTER 7

CAUSALITY IN THE "NEOCLASSICAL SYNTHESIS"

The workings of the "standard" macroeconomic model described in Chapter 5 of this book show both cause and effect taking place in the same time period. For instance, an exogenous decrease in aggregate demand (the cause) leads to changes in the price level, bond prices and wage rate (the effects), leaving the real variables unchanged. The causality in the "standard" model is "contemporaneous" in the Hicksian sense.

In handling "contemporaneous causality," the modern economist has learned to think in terms of accounting periods. As pointed out by Hicks,

An accounting period is not like the 'period' of statics [static causality] which goes on indefinitely; it is a historical period, with a beginning and an end. A whole economy, like a firm, will begin its accounting period with inheritance from the past of a given stock of equipment. Though new equipment may be added during the period, the beginning-stock sets limits upon production possibilities; whatever is possible during the period must be consistent with it. The end-stock is not the same way a limiting factor. It can be changed by current performance; it is nevertheless of great importance just how it is changed.[1]

Thus, "contemporary causality" has its advantages, but it also creates many thorny methodological problems for the modern economists, such as the length of the time period, the

---

[1] Sir John Hicks, CAUSALITY IN ECONOMICS, op. cit., p. 65. The words in the brackets are ours.

fitting together of stocks and flows, expectations, un-
certainties and so forth. This is the reason why students of
economics have to face a bewildering variety of methodol-
ogies: the Marshallian "short period", the temporary equilibrium method of the Swedish school,[2] the Hicksian temporary
equilibrium method of VALUE AND CAPITAL and Keynes' fixed-
price static equilibrium method. They also have to grope
their way out of the jungle of expectations elasticities;
adaptive expectations, regressive expectations, rational
expectations and whatever other ways exist for dealing with
those unquantifiables.

In dealing with "contemporaneous causality," one has to
resort to the temporary equilibrium method. Hicks observes:

> (Suppose that) we are seeking to explain the level
> of income (which, at a given level of money wages,
> carries with it the level of employment) that was
> obtained in some particular past year, say 1975.
> We know the facts of that year, what investment (I)
> and income (Y) were in that year. We have to
> compare them with what they would have been if some
> cause, which in the present inquiry we are prepared

---

[2] The architect of the temporary equilibrium method, as
observed by Hicks, was Eric Lindahl (1891-1960), who was a
student of Knut Wicksell. The methodological problem was
discussed by Lindahl in his STUDIES IN THE THEORY OF MONEY
AND CAPITAL (1939). Hicks, in his CAPITAL AND GROWTH,
observes: Lindahl "reduced the [Wicksellian cumulative
process] of change to a sequence of single periods, such
that, in the interior of each, change could be neglected.
Within the single period, quantities and prices could thus
be determined in what resembles a 'static' kind of analysis
(which we have attributed to Smith and Marshall) save for
one thing; the expectations are explicitly introduced as
independent variables in the determination of the single-
period equilibrium," op. cit., p. 60. The words in the
first brackets are ours.

to treat as exogenous, had been different. This is
not on record; it can only be deduced with the aid
of a theory. We have to construct a model, in
which the exogenous element is allowed to vary,
while other things, so far as possible, are to be
kept unchanged.[3]

The deduced results of the "standard" model are by means
of the tatonnement process. Implicit in the tatonnement
process is the assumption of unitary elasticity of expectations. Both prices and price expectations are thus recipro-
cally determined in the adjustment process. Perfect competition in this case is a necessary condition. Hick's VALUE AND
CAPITAL is a book of perfect competition throughout; so is
Keynes's GENERAL THEORY. As observed by Hicks, "Keynes was
undoubtedly right in insisting that the model must be constructed consistently; so that the equality of saving and
investment which is a pure accounting identity (at the beginning of the period), must hold in the model, as it does in
fact."[4] In Keynes's formal model, the consistency problem is
solved by Keynes' use of the consumption function to establish the comparative-static multiplier. In this way, the
temporary equilibrium method is validated. In the same vein,
Keynes treated the difficult problem of expectations by
making investment flows depend on long-run expectations,
which would be so far in the future that any change in them
would not matter much in the present. "So to this extent one
could talk, and think, of unchanged expectations over the
period."[5]

Although causality in Keynes' formal model is "contemporaneous," there is one essential part of Keynes' theory that

----

[3]Sir John Hicks, op. cit., pp. 74-75. The words in the first
brackets are ours.

[4]These are the words of John Hicks. Op cit., p. 75.

[5]These are the words of John Hicks. Op cit., p. 82.

187

is not at home under this methodological umbrella. This is his liquidity preference theory. It does not fit well with the other relations of the model. In the quantity theory of money, the bridge is provided by the velocity of circulation. Thus, Milton Friedman (1971) relied on the stable demand-for-money function to construct "A Monetary Theory of Nominal Income."[6] The "velocity bridge" is missing in Keynes' theory. To Keynes, money is not only the link between the past and the present; it is also the link between the present and the future. Thus the proper place for liquidity preference is in the realm of "sequential causality" (in which cause precedes effect) which will be considered in Part III of this book. This point has been recognized by Arrow and Hahn, as evidenced by their statement: "If a serious monetary theory comes to be written, the fact that contracts are indeed made in terms of money will be of considerable importance."[7] It is also the rationale for Paul Davidson's MONEY AND THE REAL WORLD.[8]

The disequilibrium analysis of Patinkin, Clower and Leijonhufvud fall into the same category of "contemporaneous causality." All of them developed their analyses in the framework of Walrasian general equilibrium. Furthermore, the concept of equilibrium can make room for disequilibrium. For instance, in his VALUE AND CAPITAL, Hicks did not suppose that equilibrium prices are established immediately; rather there may be a good deal of "false" trading before they are established. While the prices adjust, expectations are adapting themselves to the information that becomes evident in the course of trading. In the cases of the disequilibrium

---

[6] See Milton Friedman, "A Monetary Theory of Nominal Income," JOURNAL OF POLITICAL ECONOMY, March/April, 1971.

[7] K.J. Arrow and F.H. Hahn, GENERAL COMPETIVE ANALYSIS (San Francisco: Holden-Day Inc., 1971), p. 356-357.

[8] Paul Davidson, MONEY IN THE REAL WORLD (New York: John Wiley and Sons, 1972, 1978), 2nd edition, p. 147.

analyses of Patinkin and Leijonhufvud, the final outcomes of their respective theories are consistent with those of the "standard" model of the "Neoclassical Synthesis." Only during the transitional period does disequilibrium come in to its own. Clower's analysis is more Keynesian than Keynes, for his "dual decision hypothesis" supplied the missing chapter in the GENERAL THEORY. However, the causality in his model is not different from that of Keynes.

Monetarism is very much at home with "contemporaneous causality." Their perpendicular aggregate supply curve (corresponding to their natural rate of unemployment) and the associated neutrality of money thesis fit the equilibrium method much better than Keynes' theory. Their adaptive expectations hypothesis is also consistent with the framework. In essence, it may be viewed as a temporary equilibrium model "in which the exogenous element is allowed to vary, while other things, as far as possible, are to be unchanged."

Monetarism breaks away from the confines of "contemporaneous causality," when Milton Friedman delves into the question of optimal quantity of money.[9] In this connection, monetarism joins the company of the "Golden Rule of Accumulation" and sails into the realm of "static causality" in which both cause and effect are permanencies in the Hicksian sense.

In the strong rational expectations hypothesis, economic agents are assumed to have perfect information about the behavior of the economy at the present and in the future. If one could penetrate its impressive stochastic mask, one could say that the strong rational expectations hypothesis (like the "classical" model) is very much at home with "contemporaneous causality."

---

[9] See Milton Friedman, THE OPTMUM QUANTITY OF MONEY AND OTHER ESSAYS (Chicago: Aldine Publishing Company, 1969), Chapter 1.

With regard to the Austrian school, their economics do
not fit into the pigeon-hole of "contemporaneous causality."
Practically all modern Austrian economists reject the
equilibrium analysis of the "Neoclassical Synthesis." They
stress that the central concept of Austrian economics is a
market process taking place over historical time. The un-
predictable nature of knowledge and unfulfilled expectations
in a world of uncertainty are also emphasized. Thus, one may
say that their verbal economics (for they abhor mathematical
formulations and econometrics) seem to be at home with
"sequential causality."

PART III

CONTEMPORARY RE-INTREPRETATIONS OF

POST KEYNESIANISM

CHAPTER 8

THE POST-KEYNESIAN ALTERNATIVE PARADIGM

The Post-Keynesians are more revolutionary than the revisionists of the "Neoclassical Synthesis."[1] Instead of simply altering the Walrasian general equilibrium framework, they attempt to overthrow the entire microfoundations of the "Neoclassical Synthesis." The Post-Keynesians argue that Walras and the Neoclassical Synthesis omit the very factor that Keynes contributed--historical time.[2] The views of the Post-Keynesians on this point are aptly summarized by Joan Robinson:

---

[1]The advocates of Post-Keynesian economics have been called by various names, such as "Neo-Keynesians," "Neo-Ricardians" and the "Anglo-Italian School." The writers of this school prefer to be called "Post-Keynesians." Some of the leading figures are: Joan Robinson, N. Kaldor, L. Pasinetti, D.M. Nuti, P. Sraffa and J.A. Kregel in England; P. Garegnani, L. Spaventa, A. Roncaglia in Italy; A. Asima-Kopulos, G.C. Harcourt in Australia; A. Bhaduri and K.R. Bharadwaj in India; T.K. Rymes in Canada; and S. Weintraub, Paul Davidson, E.J. Nell, A.S. Eichner, J. Cornwell, P. Kenyon, B. Moore and many others in the U.S.A. Axel Leijonhufvud is not included in this group. As pointed out by Joan Robinson, "Leijonhufvud has made an heroic effort to show how a theory of unemployment could be derived from a Walrasian model--Walras without the auctioneer. But this in fact was not the basis of the argument." See her Richard T. Ely Lecture, "The Second Crisis of Economic Theory." THE AMERICAN ECONOMIC REVIEW, Dec. 27-29, 1971, op. cit., reprinted in Joan Robinson, CONTRIBUTIONS TO MODERN ECONOMICS (New York: Academic Press, 1978), p. 4.

[2]Joan Robinson in 1962 wrote: "Keynes brought back time into economic theory. He woke the Sleeping Princess from the long oblivion to which 'equilibrium' and 'perfect foresight'

A system of simultaneous equations need not specify any date nor does its solution involve history. But if any proposition drawn from it is applied to an economy inhabited by human beings, it immediately becomes self-contractory. Human life does not exist outside history and no one has correct foresight of his own future behavior, let alone of the behavior of all other individuals which will impinge upon his.[3]

Thus, the Post-Keynesians couch their analysis in historical time and emphasize the all-pervading influence of uncertainty on economic behavior and economic institutions. This orientation leads to two basic tenets of Post-Keynesian economics, namely (1) the critical role of investment at both macroeconomic and microeconomic levels and (2) sequential causality.

In historical time, the influence of past history and current expectations about the uncertain future are linked together through the act of investment. Keynes confined his investment theory to the short run (the Keynesian investment multiplier or the "demand-generating effect" of investment). By combining Keynes' insight with Ricardo's vision, the Post-Keynesians treat investment as the leading determinant

---

[2]Cont. had condemned her and led her out into the world here and now." See her ECONOMIC PHILOSOPHY (Chicago: Aldine Publishing Company, 1963), copyright 1962 by Joan Robinson, p. 76.

[3]Joan Robinson, CONTRIBUTION TO MODERN ECONOMICS, op. cit., p. 127. A.S. Eichner and J.A. Kregel in their paper, "An Essay on Post-Keynesian Theory: A New Paradigm in Economics," JOURNAL OF ECONOMIC LITERATURE, Vol. XIII, No. 4, Dec. 1975 point out: "Post-Keynesian theory, in contrast to other types of economic analysis, is concerned primarily with the depiction of an economic system expanding over time in the context of history," p. 1294.

of both income distribution and economic growth.[4] Furthermore, the Post-Keynesians, like the Institutionalists, carefully monitor institutional changes in the capitalist
economy.[5] Wallace Peterson observes:

> I like to view Keynesianism and institutional
> economics as two trains which started out on
> parallel tracks toward a common destination. That
> destination is an understanding of the workings of
> our complex, but essentially capitalist system.
> One train--the Keynesian train--spurted ahead, but
> was almost imperceptibly shunted onto another
> track, one which took it further and further away
> from its original destination. This was the
> neoclassical synthesis. What is now needed is to

---

[4]Alfred S. Eichner points out: "This follows from an underlying belief that in a dynamic, expanding economy (para-
phrasing neoclassical terminology), the income effects
produced by investment and other sources of growth far
outweigh the substitution effects, resulting from price
movement." See his A GUIDE TO POST-KEYNESIAN ECONOMICS
(White Plains, New York: M.E. Sharp, Inc., 1978, 1979), p.
12.

[5]John Cornwall observes: "Post-Keynesian macrodynamics can be
seen as an attempt to incorporate both the institutional
framework of an advanced market economy and the manner in
which this institutional framework changes over time into
the explanation of growth and cyclical process. Unlike
neoclassical macrodynamics, it strives to encompass the real
world of uncertainty, oligopolies, new products and tech-
nologies, a world in which the 'human element' is reflected
in the quality of the entrepreneurial class." See John
Cornwall, "Macrodynamics" in Alfred S. Eichner, ed., A GUIDE
TO POST-KEYNESIAN ECONOMICS, op. cit., pp. 29-30.

get the trains back on parallel tracks.[6]

The Post-Keynesian emphasis on the critical role of investment together with the impact of institutional change on economic activities is clearly reflected in their specific doctrines. A schematic representation of the Post-Keynesian alternative paradigm is depicted in Figure 8.1. In the following sections of this chapter we shall address these specific doctrines.

The Post-Keynesian Theory of Distribution

It will be recalled that the so-called "neoclassical parables" described in Chapter 5 of this book, laid the foundations of the orthodox marginal productivity theory of distribution. "For marginal productivity to be a determinate quantity," observed K.R. Ranadive, "the factors need to be capable of variation by small increments and also substitutable at the margin, so that the same output could be obtained by a number of alternative combinations of factors. For the validity of both the assumptions, viz. divisibility of factors and variability of coefficients, the factors need to

---

[6] Wallace C. Peterson, "Institutionalism, Keynes and the Real World" in CHALLENGE, Vol. 20, No. 2, May/June 1977, p. 23. Peterson writes: "Although institutionalism cannot boast of a precise structure of theory, there is one viewpoint common to institutionalists of nearly every persuasion. This is the rejection of the idea that the economic system can be adequately organized through markets and the free play of individual self-interest...economic activity is part of an ongoing process, not part of a mechanistic system tending toward a state of balance or equilibrium....We cannot ignore history and time. When we bring history and time into our analysis it means that the economic system never returns to the same condition, as much as we might wish otherwise" (p. cit., pp. 23-25.

Figure 8.1

The Post-Keynesian Alternative Paradigm

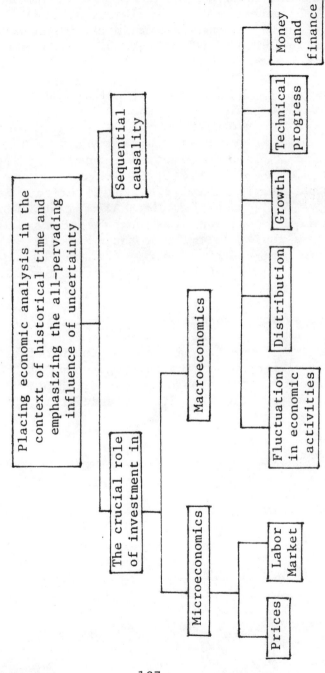

be defined in their ultimate rather than their intermediate form."[7] In other words, the classical concept of capital as a collection of commodities must be rejected; the Sraffian analysis in "PRODUCTION OF COMMODITIES BY MEANS OF COMMOD-ITIES" has to be ignored.

The neoclassical parable of capital-deepening (the assertion that there is an association between lower rates of profit and higher capital per man) requires the applicability of the marginal productivity theory to be confined to the long period. As pointed out by Ranadive, "Not only is it necessary to confine the applicability of the Cobb-Douglas production function to the long period, but a unique aggregate production function also cannot be postulated except under conditions of long period equilibrium of the system as a whole, which, ipso facto, entails equilibrium for every decision-making unit."[8] This means that the rationalization of the unique aggregate production function which is the foundation of the beautiful edifice of neoclassical theory (borrowing a phrase from Ferguson) requires the long-run general equilibrium of the system.

The Post-Keynesians argue that the neoclassical parables have many limitations. The opening rounds of the debate were concerned with the question of reswitching of techniques.[9] However, as emphasized by Eichner and Kregel, the Post-

---

[7]K.R. Ranadive, INCOME DISTRIBUTION: THE UNSOLVED PUZZLE (Bombay, India: Oxford University Press, 1978), p. 211.

[8]K.R. Ranadive, op. cit., pp. 212-213.

[9]See G.C. Harcourt, SOME CAMBRIDGE CONTROVERSIES IN THE THEORY OF CAPITAL, op. cit., Chapter 4. For a survey of this question, see Ching-yao Hsieh, Ahmad A. Abushaikha and Anne Richards, A SHORT INTRODUCTION TO MODERN GROWTH THEORY, op. cit., Chapter 11.

Keynesian arguments are not necessarily tied to the question of capital reswitching.[10] In addition to the theoretical problems noted by Ranadive, there is a deeper logical weakness in the marginal productivity theory of distribution, namely the treatment of capital as a mere instrument of production (in the aggregate production function) in developing a theory of distribution. Borrowing from Marx's treatment of capital, A. Bhaduri writes:

> The central consequence of treating 'capital' as a mere physical instrument of production results in the prevalent neo-classical methodology of treating 'production' and 'distribution' as two separable branches of inquiry. The conventional 'production function' is supposed to depict the pure production aspect of an economy, and the profit-maximizing behavior leading to marginal calculations gives a corresponding 'marginal productivity theory' of distribution. The single most important consequence of accepting the Marxian definition of 'capital,' on the other hand, is to recognize the logical untenability of the separation between 'production' and 'distribution' in a general conceptual scheme.[11]

---

[10] Eichner and Kregel write: "Trying to grasp the potential (of the alternative paradigm) from the arguments about capital reversal and double-switching, however, is likely to be just as treacherous as trying to understand the marginalist revolution...from the debate over the 'wages fund' doctrine,"op. cit., p. 1249.

[11] A. Bhaduri, "On the Significance of Recent Controversies on Capital Theory: A Marxian View," ECONOMIC JOURNAL, Vol. 79, 1969, pp. 532-539, reprinted in G.C. Harcourt and N.F. Laing, eds., CAPITAL AND GROWTH, op. cit., p. 254. Marx claimed that capital as an aid to labor in the production process should be viewed in the context of a social organization. Each type of economic organization develops

A. Bhaduri then proceeds to demonstrate the artificiality of the marginal productivity theory of distribution as follows:[12]

(1) y = rk + w. This is a definitional equation depicting the distribution of the net national income, y, between profits, rk, and wage income, w. The equation is stated in per capita terms.

(2) dy = rdk + kdr + dw. This equation is obtained by totally differentiating equation (1) and shows that the marginal product of capital, dy/dk, does not in general equal the rate of profit, r.

Bhaduri points out that, "it is clear that the 'marginal productivity' relation will hold provided, by fluke or by assumption,"

(3) kdr + dw = 0, which in turn implies -dw/dr = k. This expression is equivalent to Samuelson's condition that the elasticity of the "factor-price frontier" equal the distributive

_____

11, cont. its own "relations of production" or "rules of the game," often sanctioned by law or religion. Economic theory which ignores such "rules of the game" is ahistorical in spirit. Distribution is also related to the "relations of production," for it is a social ownership relation giving rise to capitalists' income. In the Marxian view, means of production are not 'capital' unless owned by the capitalists. This is the reason why Marx criticized Ricardo for ignoring the concept of "mode of production."

12 A. Bhaduri, op. cit., pp. 255-256.

200

shares, when the factors are paid
according to their marginal products
in an economy with a homogeneous
production function of degree one in
labor and capital.[13]

Bhaduri further points out that the Samuelson condition is
based on very restrictive assumptions and employs P.
Garegnani's diagram (1970) to illustrate this point.[14]

Figure 8.2

. The Garegnani Diagram Showing the
Restrictive Assumptions of the Samuelson Condition

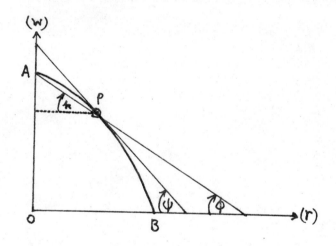

[13] See Paul A. Samuelson, "Parable and Realism in Capital
Theory: The Surrogate Production Function," REVIEW OF
ECONOMIC STUDIES, Vol. 29, 1962, pp. 193-206.

[14] See P. Garegnani, "Heterogeneous Capital, The Production
Function and the Theory of Distribution," REVIEW OF
ECONOMIC STUDIES, Vol. 37 (3), pp. 407-436.

In Figure 8.2, the wage-profit frontier for a technique is represented by the curve AB. Samuelson needs a linear relation between profit and wage in order to rationalize the marginal productivity theory of distribution. The explanation is as follows:

(4) The value of capital per man is: $k = \dfrac{y - w}{r}$. This equation is derived from Equation (1). In the diagram, the value of capital is given by tan ϕ , which is the slope joining the points A and P.

(5) From Equation (1), by setting $r = 0$, the maximum wage is depicted by OA in the diagram. Similarly, setting the wage to 0 , one obtains the maximum profit OB.

(6) The slope of the AB wage-profit frontier at point P is given by tan ψ which does not coincide with tan ϕ .

(7) Therefore, only a linear relation between wage and profit will make

$$- dw/dr = k = \frac{y - w}{r}$$

or tan ψ = tan ϕ .

Bhaduri further points out: "The assumption which Professor Samuelson makes to produce a straight-line frontier is the uniform 'capital-labour ratio' in all lines of production. In Marx's terminology this is equivalent to the assumption of uniform 'organic composition of capital' in all lines of production--exactly the assumption which Marx himself made in the first two volumes of his CAPITAL to avoid the famous 'transformation problem' that appears only in the third volume. Professor Samuelson rediscovered the importance of this assumption about a hundred years later!"[15]

[15] A. Bhaduri, op. cit., pp. 256-257.

The Post-Keynesian rejection of the marginal productivity theory of distribution is, in effect, an indirect challenge to the entire microfoundations of the "Neoclassical Synthesis." In order to offer an alternative explanation of income distribution, the Post-Keynesians seek the determinants outside the sphere of market exchange. They have found them in investment and oligopolistic market structure. As observed by J.A. Kregel, the following relations make up the central core of the Post-Keynesian approach to the distribution of income:

(1) The control of investment and thus growth, by profit recipients (either entrepreneurs or large corporations) and the control of prices by producers (oligopolistic corporations).

(2) The dependence of the rate of change of output per worker on the rate of gross investment and technical progress.

(3) An interdependence between the growth of output on the one hand and the distribution of income between wages and profits on the other hand (with that interdependence affecting the willingness and ability of entrepreneurial organizations to carry out investment).[16]

Nicholas Kaldor's "widow's cruse" theory of distribution can be considered as the basic model of the Post-Keynesian approach to distribution. The Kaldoran model can be outlined as follows:

Writing S_w and S_c for aggregate savings out of wages and profits respectively, Kaldor formulates the following income identity:

---

[16] J.A. Kregel, "Income Distribution" in A GUIDE TO POST-KEYNESIAN ECONOMCIS, op. cit., p. 53.

(1) $Y = W + P$, where W stands for wage-earners' income and P represents capitalist's income.

(2) $S = S_w + S_c$, the definitional equation for aggregate savings.

(3) $S_w = s_w W$.

(4) $S_c = s_c P$.

(5) $I = \bar{I}$, stating investment to be a exogenous variable.

As pointed out by Kaldor, "The interpretative value of the model depends on the 'Keynesian' hypothesis that investment, or rather, the ratio of investment to output, can be treated as an independent variable, invariant with respect to changes in the two savings propensities."[17]

(6) $\bar{I} = S$, the condition for dynamic equilibrium.

It should be noted that this equilibrium condition is that of the "steady state" or "golden age" growth path. The Post-Keynesians recognize the "steady state" to be an artificial setting and try to avoid it to the extent possible. The objective in employing this device in the present case is to provide a theoretical framework for highlighting the determinants of the rate of profit other than those given by the marginal productivity theory. Only in the "steady state" setting are the rate of profit on capital (which is ex-ante and forward-looking, expressing expectations of returns to be obtained from the finance invested) and the ex-post rate of

---

[17] Nicholas Kaldor, "Alternative Theories of Distribution," originally published in REVIEW OF ECONOMIC STUDIES, Vol. 23, No. 2, 1955-1956, reprinted in Kaldor's ESSAYS ON VALUE AND DISTRIBUTION (Illinois: The Free Press of Glencoe, 1969), p. 229.

profit (which is a calculation of the returns actually realized) the same. Only in such an artificial setting could the determinants of the equilibrium rate of profit be more precisely identified. By substitution, Kaldor obtains:

$$(7) \quad \bar{I} = s_c P + s_w W = s_c P + s_w (Y - P) = (s_c - s_w) P + s_w Y.$$

Dividing Equation (7) by Y, the equation for the profit share in income is derived by:

$$(8) \quad \frac{P}{Y} = - \frac{s_w}{s_c - s_w} + \frac{1}{s_c - s_w} \frac{\bar{I}}{Y}.$$

The equation for the rate of profit is obtained by dividing Equation (7) by K:

$$(9) \quad r = \frac{P}{K} = \frac{s_w}{s_c - s_w} \frac{Y}{K} + \frac{1}{s_c - s_w} \frac{I}{K}.$$

Equation (8) states that, given the wage-earners' and capitalists' propensities to save, the share of profit in income depends on the ratio of investment to output. [18] This is the so-called "widow's cruse" theory of distribution for the equation indicates that the more capitalists invest, the

_____

[18] The expression "widow's cruse" is derived from Keynes' TREATISE OF MONEY, Vol. 1, p. 139, wherein Keynes considered profits as a "widow's cruse." Keynes wrote: "If entrepreneurs choose to spend a portion of their profits on consumption...the effect is to increase the profits on the sale of liquid consumption goods....Thus, however much of their profits entrepreneurs spend on consumption, the increment of wealth belonging to entrepreneurs remain the same as before. Thus profits, as a source of capital increment for entrepreneurs, are a widow's cruse which remains undepleted however much of them may be devoted to riotous living. When on the other hand, entrepreneurs are making losses, and seek to recoup these losses by curtailing their normal expenditure on consumption, i.e. by saving more, the cruse becomes a Danaid jar which will never be filled up; for the effect of this

higher will be the profit share in income. This proposition is described graphically in Figure 8.3.[19]

Kaldor points out that in the limiting case where $s_w = 0$ and $s_c = 1$, Equation (8) can be rewritten as:

$$(10) \quad \frac{P}{Y} = \frac{1}{s_c} \frac{I}{Y} \; .$$

The "widow's cruse" idea is brought out in sharp relief by this equation. Furthermore, this is what Pasinetti considers the "new answer to the old Ricardian problem." "For Ricardo the wage rate is fixed exogenously and all that remains (after paying rent) goes to profits. For Kaldor the rate of profit is determined exogenously by the natural rate of growth of output and the capitalists' propensity to save; and all that remains goes to wages. For the former it is profits that take up the feature of residual category; for the latter it is wages."[20]

Kaldor's "new answer" is most explicit in the limiting case where $s_w = 0$:

$$(11) \quad r = \frac{P}{K} = \frac{1}{s_c} \frac{I}{K} \; , \; \text{or} \; \frac{P}{K} = \frac{1}{s_c} \frac{\dot{K}}{K}.$$

----

18 cont. reduced expenditure is to inflict on the producers of consumption-goods a loss of an equal amount." Kaldor observes in the footnote of p. 227, ibid., "This passage, I think, contains the true seed of the ideas developed in the GENERAL THEORY--as well as showing the length of the road that had to be traversed before arriving at the conceptual framework presented in the latter work."

19 This is Ferguson's diagram. See C.E. Ferguson, op. cit., p. 315.

20 Luigi L. Pasinetti, op. cit., pp. 101-102.

Figure 8.3

The "Widow's Cruse" Distribution

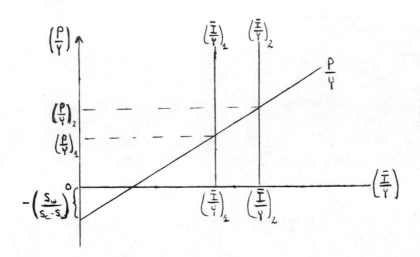

In "golden age" growth (Harrod's "natural rate of growth"), $\dot{K}/K = \dot{L}/L = n$. Substituting this equation into Equation (11), one obtains:

$$(12) \quad r = \frac{P}{K} = \frac{n}{s_c},$$

which pinpoints the determinants of the rate of profit beyond those given by the marginal productivity theory.

This basic model can also be employed to demonstrate the linkage between distribution and growth through the common critical determinant of investment. Recall that Harrod's growth model depicts the inherent instability of the capitalist system. This instability is the result of a divergence between the warranted growth rate of output and the natural growth rate. This has been termed the "knife-edge" problem. The "widow's cruse" theory of distributiuon is one resolution to the Harrodian problem.

Expressing the savings function $[S = s_w Y + (s_c - s_w)P]$ in a different form:

$$(13) \quad S = \frac{S}{Y} = s_w + (s_c - s_w) \frac{P}{Y}.$$

Incorporating the growth rate of output into this equation:

$$(14) \quad \frac{s}{\beta} = \frac{s_w + (s_c - s_w) \frac{P}{Y}}{\beta} \gtreqless n$$

where s/β is Harrod's "warranted growth rate" and n represent the "natural rate."

Kaldor emphasizes that: "The 'warranted' and the 'natural' rates of growth are not independent of one another; if profit margins are flexible, the former will adjust itself to the latter through a consequential change in P/Y."[21] What causes P/Y to change? The answer is given by Equation (8), or its simplified version, Equation (10). In the case where $s/\beta < n$, an increase in investment exceeding ex ante saving implies excess aggregate demand. Consequently, prices will rise and profit margins (P/Y) will also increase. If $s_c > s_w$, this redistribution of income in favor of profits will increase aggregate real saving and the "warranted" and "natural" rates will be brought into equality again. The

---

[21] N. Kaldor, op. cit., p. 232.

redistribution effect is applicable to the converse case as well. However, it is evident that $s_c > s_w$ is the stability condition. Furthermore, Kaldor pays more attention to institutional developments in the real world than most of the writers of the "Neoclassical Synthesis." He imposes the following constraints on his model:

(15) $w > w_{min}$, reflecting the influence of labor unions.

(16) $P/Y > m$, where m represents minimum profits.

Kaldor thereby stresses that there are limits to this equilibrating mechanism. The first limit is that the real wage cannot fall below a certain minimum and "the second is that the indicated share of profits cannot be below the level which yields the minimum rate of profit necessary to induce capitalists to invest their capital."[22] These constraints are illustrated by Figure 8.4.[23]

Post-Keynesian Growth Theory

Post-Keynesian growth theory is still in the formative stage. However, there are certain discernable features of its central core that can be outlined. The framework of this central core has been laid out by Joan Robinson. We will attempt to restate some of the important contributions of this pioneering Post-Keynesian theorist.

Joan Robinson emphatically rejects what she calls the "pseudo-causal models" of economic growth constructed by

---

[22]N. Kaldor, op. cit., p. 233.

[23]This is Kaldor's diagram adopted by G.C. Harcourt with slight modifications. See Harcourt, op. cit., p. 209.

Figure 8.4

The Kaldorian Constraints

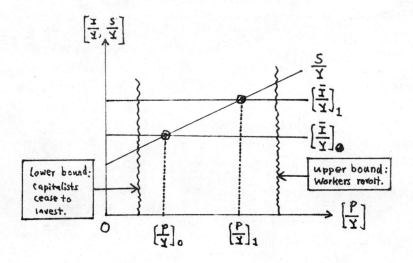

theorists of the "Neoclassical Synthesis." She writes:

> In a model depicting equilibrium positions there is
> no causation. It consists of a closed circle of
> simultaneous equations. The value of each element
> is entailed by the values of the rest. At any
> moment in logical time, the past is determined just
> as much as the future. In a historical model,
> causal relations have to be specified. Today is a
> break in time between an unknown future and an
> irrevocable past. What happens next will result
> from the interactions of human beings within the
> economy. Movement can only be forward.[24]

[24] Joan Robinson, ESSAYS IN THE THEORY OF ECONOMIC GROWTH (New
York: St. Martin's Press, Inc., 1962), p. 26.

Joan Robinson urges that "to build a causal model, we must start not from equilibrium relations but from rules and motives governing human behavior. We therefore have to specify to what kind of economy the model applies, for various kinds of economies have different sets of rules."[25]

The causal model that Joan Robinson outlines represents her initial attempt to analyze the growth process of the modern capitalist world. She groups the determinants of the growth process under seven headings: (1) technical conditions, (2) investment policy, (3) thriftiness conditions, (4) competitive conditions, (5) the wage bargain, (6) financial conditions and (7) the initial stock of capital goods and the state of expectations formed by past experience. The purpose of highlighting these determinants is twofold: (a) to distinguish the factors responsible for long-run growth of output from those responsible for short-run fluctuations around a trend line and (b) to show the possibility of various alternative growth paths to that of the "Golden Age" path, such as the "Limping Golden Age"--representing growth at less than full employment, "Leaden Age"--describing growth with rising rates of unemployment, "Bastard Golden Age," and so on.[26]

The causal links of Joan Robinson's model may be described as follows: "The dynamic force of a capitalist economy is capital accumulation and growth. The accumulation going on in a particular situation determines the level of profits obtainable in it, and thus determines the rate of profit expected on investment. The rate of profit in turn influences the rate of accumulation."[27] This is the double-sided relationship between the rate of profit (r = P/K) and the rate of accumulation (I/K) which Robinson depicts in the following diagram, Figure 8.5.

---

[25] Joan Robinson, op. cit., p. 34.

[26] Joan Robinson, op. cit., pp. 51-59.

[27] Joan Robinson, op. cit., p. 47.

Figure 8.5

The Double-Sided Relationship Between r and K̇/K

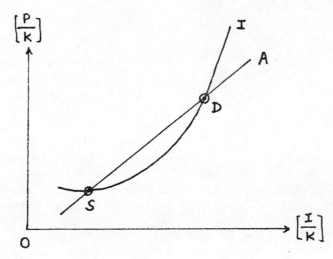

The diagram is designed to show the "short-period situations which chances and changes of history throw up."[28] This is the central mechanism of Joan Robinson's causal model. Why did she use a short-period model to analyze long-run growth? The answer is that Joan Robinson's view is similar to that of Michal Kalecki who stated: "The long-run trend is but a slowly changing component of a chain of short-period situations; it has no independent entity."[29] The short-period she employs is the Marshallian theory of the firm in the short run. Th double-sided relationship between

---

[28] Joan Robinson, op. cit., p. 48.

[29] Michal Kalecki, SELECTED ESSAYS ON THE DYNAMICS OF CAPITALIST ECONOMY (Cambridge: Cambridge University Press, 1971), p. 165.

the rate of profit and the rate of accumulation can be derived from the short-period production and pricing decisions of the firm. The Robinsonian short-period model is depicted in Figure 8.6.[30]

In Figure 8.6 the vertical axis measures aggregate supply (Z) and aggregate demand (D). The horizontal axis measures quantities of workers employed (N). The aggregate supply curve (Z_e) indicates alternative aggregate supply prices (expected sales-proceeds) which would leave producers satisfied for the alternative levels of employment that they could maintain. The market wage rate is assumed to be historically determined $(\bar{w})$, and $O\bar{w}N$ is the wage bill line. The vertical distance OA indicates the normal profits expected on the committed finance in the current period. The expected supply price of output is equal to the sum of the total wage bill and normal profits ($p = \bar{w}N + P$, where p represents supply price and P denotes normal profits).

Suppose that expected aggregate demand is ED_e. The point of intersection of aggregate supply and demand is Y. N workers will be hired to produce the total output YN. The expectations of the producers are fulfilled; the realized supply price consists of YG normal profits and GN in total wages. Under the conditions of "tranquility" where expectations are not disappointed, the double-sided relationship between the rate of profit and the rate of accumulation can be derived. This can be seen through equation and word. First, the aggregate supply price can be defined symbolically as:

(1) $Z = \bar{w}N + P.$

Let $\bar{w}N$ be some constant proportion (α) of Z, i.e.

(2) $\bar{w}N = \alpha Z.$

---

[30] Paul Davidson, op. cit., pp. 120-129.

Figure 8.6

Joan Robinson's Short-Period Model

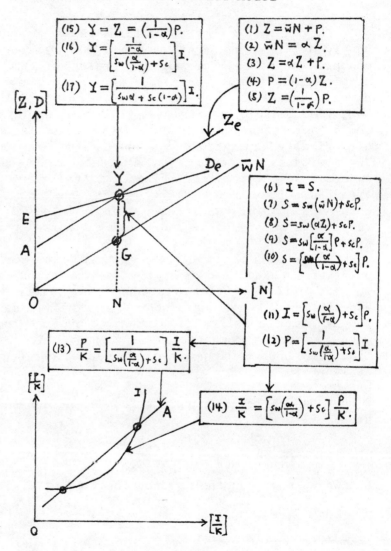

$(15) \quad Y = Z = \left(\frac{1}{1-\alpha}\right) P.$

$(16) \quad Y = \left[\frac{\frac{1}{1-\alpha}}{s_w\left(\frac{\alpha}{1-\alpha}\right)+s_c}\right] I.$

$(17) \quad Y = \left[\frac{1}{s_w\alpha + s_c(1-\alpha)}\right] I.$

$(1) \quad Z = \bar{w}N + P.$

$(2) \quad \bar{w}N = \alpha Z.$

$(3) \quad Z = \alpha Z + P.$

$(4) \quad P = (1-\alpha) Z.$

$(5) \quad Z = \left(\frac{1}{1-\alpha}\right) P.$

$[Z, D]$

Z_e

$D_e \quad \bar{w}N$

Y

E

A

G

$(6) \quad I = S.$

$(7) \quad S = s_w(\bar{w}N) + s_c P.$

$(8) \quad S = s_w(\alpha Z) + s_c P.$

$(9) \quad S = s_w\left[\frac{\alpha}{1-\alpha}\right] P + s_c P.$

$(10) \quad S = \left[s_w\left(\frac{\alpha}{1-\alpha}\right)+s_c\right] P.$

$O \quad N \qquad [N]$

$(11) \quad I = \left[s_w\left(\frac{\alpha}{1-\alpha}\right)+s_c\right] P.$

$(12) \quad P = \left[\frac{1}{s_w\left(\frac{\alpha}{1-\alpha}\right)+s_c}\right] I.$

$(13) \quad \frac{P}{K} = \left[\frac{1}{s_w\left(\frac{\alpha}{1-\alpha}\right)+s_c}\right] \frac{I}{K}.$

$\left[\frac{P}{K}\right]$

I

A

$(14) \quad \frac{I}{K} = \left[s_w\left(\frac{\alpha}{1-\alpha}\right)+s_c\right] \frac{P}{K}.$

$O \qquad \left[\frac{I}{K}\right]$

Substituting (2) into (1), one obtains:

(3) $Z = \alpha Z + P$.

Rearranging terms, we have:

(4) $P = (1 - \alpha) Z$, or

(5) $Z = (\frac{1}{1-\alpha}) P$.

Under conditions of "tranquility," ex ante saving equal ex ante investment, or

(6) $I = S$.

Total savings (S) is defined as:

(7) $S = s_w (\bar{w}N) + s_c P$.

Substituting (2) into (7), we have:

(8) $S = s_w (\alpha Z) + s_c P$.

Substituting (5) into (8), the following is derived:

(9) $S = s_w (\frac{\alpha}{1-\alpha})P + s_c P$.

Rearranging terms, we obtain the following three equations:

(10) $S = \left[s_w \left(\frac{\alpha}{1-\alpha}\right) + s_c \right] P$.

(11) $I = \left[s_w \left(\frac{\alpha}{1-\alpha}\right) + s_c \right] P$.

(12) $P = \left[\dfrac{1}{s_w \left(\frac{\alpha}{1-\alpha}\right) + s_c} \right] I$.

Dividing (11) by K, we obtain an equation stating that the rate of profit depends on the rate of capital accumulation:

(13) $\dfrac{P}{K} = \left[\dfrac{1}{s_w\left(\frac{\alpha}{1-\alpha}\right) + s_c} \right] \dfrac{I}{K}$.

215

Obtained by dividing (12) through by K, equation (14) states that the rate of accumulation is influenced by the rate of profit:

$$(14) \quad \frac{I}{K} = \left[S_w\left(\frac{\alpha}{1-\alpha}\right) + S_c \right] \frac{P}{K}.$$

The equilibrium level of output is given by

$$(17) \quad Y = \left[\frac{1}{S_w \alpha + S_c(1-\alpha)} \right] I.$$

which can be transformed into the Keynesian investment multiplier:

$$(18) \quad \Delta Y = \left[\frac{1}{S_w \alpha + S_c(1-\alpha)} \right] \Delta I.$$

Having derived the symbolic representation of the double-sided relationship between the rate of profit and the rate of capital accumulation, let us return to consider Figure 8.5. Curve A is the locus of all possible expected rates of profit that justify the investment plans drawn up by firms, oligopolistic or otherwise. Curve I is the locus of all possible investment plans of firms that are fulfilled by the realized rate of profit. Consequently, the "Golden Age" growth rate is indicated by point D in Figure 8.5. However, Joan Robinson warns: "The fact that the desired and actual rates of accumulation coincide in a particular short-period situation does not by itself guarantee that they will continue to do so."[31] "Uncertainty, through the volatility of expectations to which it gives rise, is continually leading the firms into self-contradictory policies. Now it needs no chance shocks to set an upswing going. The model is inherently unstable and fluctuates even in otherwise tranquil conditions."[32]

---

[31] Joan Robinson, op. cit., p. 49

[32] Joan Robinson, op. cit., p. 67.

Joan Robinson's ultimate concern is with the analysis of the economy in disequilibrim which is a salient attribute of historical time. Paul Davidson observes:

> Mrs. Robinson has cautioned that these neo-Keynesian models (such as those of Kaldor and Pasinetti) are only applicable to economies growing at constant rates through time and that in the current state of the economic arts these formal models could not readily explain how economies traverse from one growth rate to another, or how adjustments to disequilibrium are made when tranquility conditions are disturbed. Accordingly, the Cambridge (England) philosophy is to use these models to make comparisons between economies each growing at a uniform but different rate in conditions of tranquility as preliminary to attempting disequilibrium path analysis.[33]

Preliminary to her ultimate disequilibrium analysis, Joan Robinson employs the "Golden Age" model to make comparisons between economies, each growing at an uniform but different rate. One of her objectives in this is to provide a theoretical framework for investigating the determinants of the rate of profit beyond those given by marginal productivity theory. In this sense, her methodology is similar to those of Kaldor and Pasinetti. The comparative dynamics can be simply stated as follows: If firms in two "Golden Age" systems have the same "animal spirit" as

---

[33]Paul Davidson, op. cit., p. 132. The words in the brackets are ours. Davidson's observation may also provide an explanation as to why Joan Robinson did not employ any mathematical formulation in her two books: THE ACCUMULATION OF CAPITAL (1956) and ESSAYS IN THE THEORY OF ECONOMIC GROWTH (1962). In fact, Robinson does not employ any mathematical formulation in any of her writings on capital and growth.

reflected by the identical I-curves in Figures 8.7(a) and 8.7(b), and if the average propensity to save is higher in Economy B than that in A, then the rate of profit and the rate of accumulation will be lower in Economy B than in Economy A. The higher average propensity to save in Economy B is depicted by an A-curve in Figure 8.7(b) that lies lower than the A-curve in Figure 8.7(a). Consequently, r_B is lower than r_A. If one adopts the Ricardo-von Nuemann-Kalecki

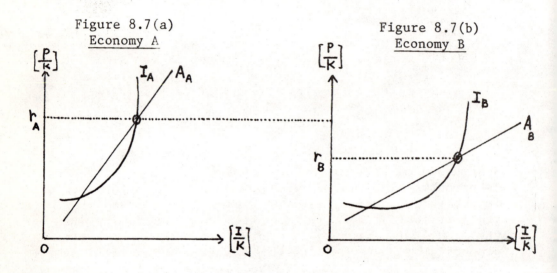

Figure 8.7(a)
Economy A

Figure 8.7(b)
Economy B

assumption that $s_w = 0$, the determinants of the rates profit of the two economies would be (a) the "natural growth rate" (n) and the average propensity to save out of gross profit (s_c). It should be noted that these determinants are the same as those in Kaldor's special case. In conclusion, we would like to summarize Joan Robinson's views on economic growth by the following schematic representation (Figure 8.8) of the key causal relationships in her theory.

The Post-Keynesian Approach to Technical Progress

The Post-Keynesian approach to technical progress varies significantly from those approaches adopted by writers of the "Neoclassical Synthesis" persuasion. A representative model of the latter is Robert Solow's embodied technical progress. In an important theoretical paper, Solow has shown that the neoclassical aggregate production function and its aggregate homogeneous capital can be modified to accommodate machines of different vintages.[34] The necessary and sufficient conditions for the aggregation of heterogeneous capital have been subsequently given by F.M. Fisher as follows:[35]

(a) linearly homogeneous production for every industry;

(b) capital-augmenting technical progress everywhere; and

---

[34] R.M. Solow, "Investment and Technical Progress," in MATHEMATICAL METHODS IN SOCIAL SCIENCES, edited by K.J. Arrow, S. Karlin and P. Suppes (Stanford, California: Stanford University Press, 1960), Chapter 7. For a simplified version of Solow's model, see Ching-Yao Hsieh, A.A. Abushaikha and A. Richards, op. cit., Chapter 6.

[35] F.M. Fisher, "Embodied Technical Change and the Existence of an Aggregate Capital Stock," THE REVIEW OF ECONOMIC STUDIES, Vol. 32, October 1965, pp. 263-287.

Figure 8.8

A Schematic Representation of Joan Robinson's
Causal Model

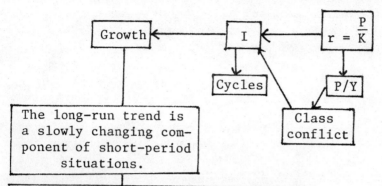

The long-run trend is
a slowly changing com-
ponent of short-period
situations.

The central mechanism is the desire
of firms to accumulate. The higher
the rate of investment, the greater
the rate of profit on investment.
Valuing the existing capital stock
on the basis of the same rate of
profit, one can then express firms'
investment plans in terms of a rate
of accumulation.

The double-sided relationship between
P/K and I/K.

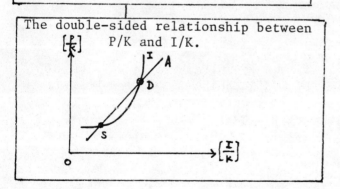

(c)   optimal allocation of the labor force so that the marginal product of labor is the same for all vintages of capital equipment in existence.

The vintage model that satisfies these conditions has been called the "putty-putty" case. The name reflects the fact that the model requires substitutability between machines and labor at all times before and after installation, according to the same Cobb-Douglas production function. Furthermore, labor is allocated to different vintages of machines under conditions of perfect competition. Less labor is allocated to older machines than to new machines. Thus the question of scrapping old machines does not rise. "In this case," quipped R.G.D. Allen, "machines (like old soldiers) never die but simply fade away."[36] It should be noted that, even though Solow treats investment as the transmission mechanism of technical progress, the source of technical progress remains exogenous to his model.

A model representative of the Post-Keynesian approach to technical progress is the technical progress function of N. Kaldor and J.A. Mirrlees (1962).[37] In their important paper, "A New Model of Economic Growth," Kaldor and Mirrlees present a "putty-clay" vintage model incorporating the concept of endogenous technical progress. Some important differences between the Kaldor-Mirrlees model and that of Solow are listed below:

----

[36]R.D.G. Allen, MACROECONOMIC THEORY (New York: St. Martin's Press, 1967), p. 283.

[37]Nicholas Kaldor and James A. Mirrlees, "A New Model of Economic Growth," reprinted from the REVIEW OF ECONOMIC STUDIES, Vol. 29 (June 1962), pp. 174-192 in Harold R. Williams and John D. Huffnagle, eds., MACROECONOMIC THEORY: SELECTED READINGS (New York: Appleton-Century-Crofts, 1969), pp. 504-527.

(a)   Whereas the question of obsolescence does not arise
      in the Solow model, this question is taken into
      consideration in the Kaldor-Mirrlees model. In the
      Kaldor-Mirrlees model factor substitution is
      impossible ex poste (after installation). Labor
      will not be released from older machines to man the
      machines of the latest vintage. The solution is,
      therefore, to scrap some old machines. Thus, the
      economic life of a machine of given vintage becomes
      an additional endogenous variable to be determined.
      The criterion for scrapping the machine as
      obsolescent is its quasi-rent. Along the "Golden
      Age" growth path, the real-wage rate rises and the
      quasi-rents of old machines continue to decline and
      eventually become zero. Hence, the additional
      equilibrium condition emerges, i.e., the
      obsolescence condition of zero quasi-rent.

(b)   Kaldor and Mirrlees give more emphasis on un-
      certainty and expectations about the future than
      Solow does in his 1960 model. This point is
      highlighted by their investment function. Under
      conditions of continuous technical progress,
      expectations concerning the future are uncertain
      and hazardous. "Hence, investment projects which
      qualify for adoption," pointed out by Kaldor-
      Mirrlees, "must pass a further test--apart from the
      test of earning a satisfactory rate of profit--and
      that is that the cost of the fixed assets must be
      'recovered' within a certain period--i.e., that the
      gross profit earned in the first h years of the
      operation must be sufficient to repay the cost of
      investment."[38] In other words, the two authors
      invoke fixed pay-off period criterion as a simple
      "rule of thumb" for investment decisions.

---

[38] N. Kaldor and J.A. Mirrlees, op. cit., p. 510.

(c) The concept of the aggregate production function and the marginal productivity theorems derived therefrom are absent in the Kaldor-Mirrlees model. The authors write: "A 'production function' in the sense of a single-valued relationship between some measure of capital, K_t, the labour force N_t and of output Y_t (all at time t) clearly does not exist. Everything depends on past history, on how the collection of equipment goods which comprises K_t has been built up. Thus Y_t will be greater for a given K_t (as measured by historical cost) if a greater part of the existing capital stock is of more recent creation; this would be the case, for example, if the rate of growth of population has been accelerating.[39]

The main thrust of the Kaldor-Mirrlees model is to show that the "Golden Age" solution is possible only if appropriate assumptions are made about its functional relationships. The following is a simplified version of their model.

(1) $S_t = s_c P_t$.

Equation (1) is the classical saving function assumed by the architects of the model. This savings assumption naturally leads to the "widow's cruse" theory of distribution. Hence, we have the following equation:

(2) $P_t / Y_t = \dfrac{1}{s} \dfrac{I_t}{Y_t}$.

As in any vintage model, two time variables are needed: one for time in the usual sense denoted by t and the other, τ, for the dating of vintage machines in use at time t.

(3) $L_t = L_0 e^{nt}$ and

_____

[39] N. Kaldor and J.S. Mirrlees, op. cit., p. 522.

$$(3') \quad L_t = \int_{t-T}^{t} L_\tau \, d\tau.$$

Equation (3) incorporates the Harrodian assumption about the growth of the labor force while (3') defines the total labor force.

$$(4) \quad \frac{1}{q_t} \frac{dq_t}{dt} = F\left(\frac{1}{i_t} \frac{di_t}{dt}\right).$$

Equation (4) is the technical progress function. $\frac{1}{q_t} \frac{dq_t}{dt}$ stands for the annual rate of growth in gross investment per worker operating on new machines; and $\frac{1}{i_t} \frac{di_t}{dt}$ denotes the rate of growth in gross investment per worker.

The microfoundations of the Kaldor-Mirrlees model consist of two equations: one behavioral equation depicting the firm's decision to invest and a second expressing the condition for obsolescence.

$$(5) \quad i_t = h q_t - \int_{t}^{t+h} w_x \, dx.$$

Equation (5) is the investment function. The fixed payoff period set in advance is indicated by the symbol h. The symbol x is a running time variable for integration from t to t + h; q_t stands for output per worker produced by the new machine; and w represents the real-wage rate. Defining p_t to be profit per worker, the initial level of profit per worker from the new machine can be expressed as: $p_t = q_t - w$. This is the identity equation behind Equation (5). Note that Equation (5) is stated in per capita terms. The total function is:

$$(6) \quad I_t = h Q_t - L_t \int_{t}^{t+h} W_x \, dx.$$

$$(7) \quad Q_{t-T} - w L_{t-T} = 0 \quad , \quad \text{or}$$

$$(7') \quad q_{t-T} = w.$$

Equation (7) is the obsolescence condition; while equation (7') is the same condition stated in per capita terms. The symbol T stands for the economic life of a machine of given vintage. The subscript t - T has the same meaning as the subscript . Figure 8.9 indicates that the "Golden Age" solution of the model depends upon the assumption of a well-behaved technical progress function.

The technical progress function is non-linear, showing the tendency towards diminishing returns. This is not the same as diminishing marginal productivity of capital. The non-linearity merely indicates that there is a limit to the learning process. Implicit in the technical progress function is the idea that technical progress is partly the result of a learning process on the part of the entre-preneurs. The more investment undertaken by entrepreneurs, the greater the opportunities for them to explore the existing technical knowledge. Furthermore, increased investment also provides the impetus for faster technical advance. The intercept on the vertical axis signifies that some innovation is possible, through a "learning by doing" process, even when there is zero gross investment.

The "Golden Age" growth path is indicated by the point m at which the technical progress function intersects the 45° line, where there is a unique common value:

$$(8) \quad m = \frac{1}{g_t} \frac{dg_t}{dt} = \frac{1}{i_t} \frac{di_t}{dt}.$$

Since aggregate output per man is defined as   , its "Golden Age" growth rate can be written as:

$$(9) \quad \frac{1}{y_t} \frac{dy_t}{dt} = \frac{1}{Y_t} \frac{dY_t}{dt} - n = m.$$

It follows that along the "Golden Age" growth path, aggregate output will grow at the rate of m + n.

$$(10) \quad \frac{1}{Y_t} \frac{dY_t}{dt} = m + n.$$

Figure 8.9

The Kaldor-Mirrless Model of Technical Progress

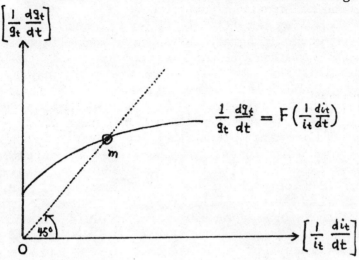

By the same reasoning, the "Golden Age" growth rates for gross investment per man and aggregate gross investment are respectively:

(11) $\frac{1}{i_t}\frac{di_t}{dt} = \frac{1}{I_t}\frac{dI_t}{dt} - n = m,$ and

(12) $\frac{1}{I_t}\frac{dI_t}{dt} = m + n.$

The real-wage rate along the "Golden Age" growth path will also grow at the same rate m. This result is derived as follows:

(13) $W = q_{t-T} = q_t e^{-mT}.$ This is the obsolescence condition.

(14) $\ln w = \ln q_t + \ln e^{-mT}.$

226

Equation (14) is obtained by taking the natural log of Equation (13). Differentiating (14) with respect to time yields:

$$(15) \quad \frac{d}{dt} \ln w = \ln q_t + \left(-\frac{d}{dt} mT\right).$$

Since m and T are constants, the time derivative of mT is zero. Therefore,

$$(16) \quad \frac{1}{w}\frac{dw}{dt} = \frac{1}{q_t}\frac{dq_t}{dt} = m.$$

We know that in the "Golden Age," q_t grows at the constant rate m. Thus,

$$(17) \quad \frac{\dot{w}}{w} = m.$$

Why does Kaldor conduct his analyses in terms of the "Golden Age" growth path? A partial answer is provided by Eichner and Kregel:

> Approaching the problem of disequilibrium in this manner gives rise to the distinction found in the post-Keynesian literature between long-period analysis, focusing on the determinants of the warranted growth rate; and the short-period analysis, focusing on cyclical deviations in the actual rate relative to the warranted rate. The methodological point is that the deviations cannot be understood except with respect to some reference growth path.[40]

Post-Keynesians and Monetary Theory

The Post-Keynesians have exposed some hidden weaknesses in orthodox monetary theory. Although a formal Post-

---

[40] Alfred S. Eichner and J.A. Kregel, op. cit., p. 1296.

Keynesian monetary theory is still in the embryonic stage, their devastating criticisms pave the way for a realistic reformulation of monetary theory in the not too distant future. This optimistic observation is substantiated by conclusions reached by some of our most distinguished theorists. For instance, Arrow and Hahn have concluded that in a "world with a past as well as a future in which contracts are made in terms of money, no equilibrium may exist."[41] Hicks confessed that "...I must say that diagram (IS-LM) is now much less popular with me than I think it still with many other people. It reduces the GENERAL THEORY to equilibrium economics; it is not really 'in' time."[42] Clower stressed: "Our first order of business is to state explicitly just what aspects of experience we should want to have 'explained' by any theory that claims to provide even a minimally adequate description of a monetary economy."[43] One of the mandatory requirements for an adequate monetary theory according to Clower is that "the theory should imply that trade is an ongoing process in time rather than a once-for-all affair that ends in the permanent elimination of incentives for further trade."[44]

---

[41] K.J. Arrow and F.H. Hahn, GENERAL COMPETITIVE ANALYSIS, op. cit., p. 357.

[42] John Hicks, "Some Questions of Time in Economics," in EVOLUTION, WELFARE AND TIME, ed. A.M. Tang, F.M. Westerfield and J.S. Worley (Lexington: Lexington Books, 1976), p. 136.

[43] Robert W. Clower, "The Anatomy of Monetary Theory" in AMERICAN ECONOMIC REVIEW, Papers and Proceedings of the 89th Annual Meeting, September 16-18, 1976 (February 1977), p. 206.

[44] Robert W. Clower, op. cit., p. 206. The other mandatory requirements are: "(2) The theory should imply that, on average over any finite time interval, each individual holds positive stocks of all goods that are regularly

A survey of the writings of these leading economists leaves us little doubt that a central thrust of the Post-Keynesian protest is the concept of historical time. The Post-Keynesian case is most forcefully stated by Paul Davidson in his MONEY AND THE REAL WORLD (1972, 1978).[45] (Davidson's main arguments are outlined in the schematic representation of Figure 8.10). Davidson stresses:

It is in a world of uncertainty and disappointment that money comes into its own as a necessary medium for deferring decisions.[46]

Money plays an essential and peculiar role only when contractual obligations span a significant interval of calendar time. If the economic system being studied permits only spot transactions, i.e., contracts that require payments at the immediate instant, then even if its members utilize a convenient medium of account and/or exchange, such a numeraire is not money in the full sense of the term. Spot transaction economies--which are equivalent to Hicks' flexprice economies--have, as

---

[44,cont.] traded. (3) The theory should imply that the bulk of all trades occur not through essentially random pairing of individuals who happen to share a double coincidence of wants, but rather through systematic pairing of specialist with nonspecialist traders in a small number of organized, continuously operating markets. (4) The theory should imply that at least one and at most a few distinctive 'money' commodities are transferred (or promised for future delivery) by one party to another in virtually all exchange transactions," pp. 206-207.

[45] Paul Davidson, MONEY AND THE REAL WORLD (New York: John Wiley and Sons, 1978), op. cit.

[46] Paul Davidson, op. cit., p. 144.

Figure 8.10

A Simplified Schematic Representation of
Paul Davidson's Arguments

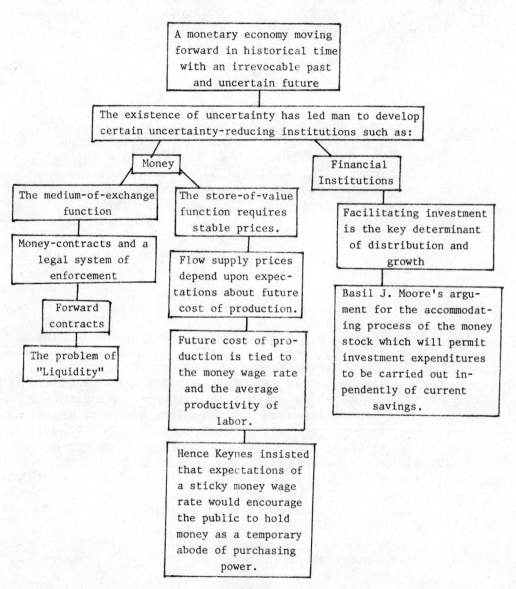

A monetary economy moving forward in historical time with an irrevocable past and uncertain future

The existence of uncertainty has led man to develop certain uncertainty-reducing institutions such as:

Money

Financial Institutions

The medium-of-exchange function

The store-of-value function requires stable prices.

Facilitating investment is the key determinant of distribution and growth

Money-contracts and a legal system of enforcement

Flow supply prices depend upon expectations about future cost of production.

Basil J. Moore's argument for the accommodating process of the money stock which will permit investment expenditures to be carried out inpendently of current savings.

Forward contracts

Future cost of production is tied to the money wage rate and the average productivity of labor.

The problem of "Liquidity"

Hence Keynes insisted that expectations of a sticky money wage rate would encourage the public to hold money as a temporary abode of purchasing power.

Keynes insisted, 'scarcely emerged from the stage of barter' (Keynes, 1930, vol. 1, p. 3).[47]

Davidson further points out that only in real world market-oriented monetary economies where production takes time does "the existence of market institutions that permit (and encourage) contracting for future payment create the need for money, and liquidity."[48] This essential feature of real world monetary economies has been overlooked by orthodox general equilibrium theory. "Since orthodox neoclassical theory neglects the fact of contracting over calendar time in organized markets for future delivery and payment, the ubiquitous liquidity provision of entrepreneurs in capitalist economies is left unattended by mainstream economists in their nonmonetized theory of the firm. Consequently, they are irresistible targets of the businessman's gibe: 'They never met a payroll!'"[49]

The store-of-value function of money, according to Davidson (who follows Keynes faithfully), depends upon the flow supply prices of producers, which, in turn, are a function of their expectations about future production costs. In the central core industrial sector of an advanced capitalist economy, future costs of production are tied to money wage rates and the average productivity of labor. "Only a contractually fixed wage and product price system permits capitalist economies to engage in the time-consuming production process; for such a system provides the sticky (meaning normal) price level of producible goods that are the basis of decisions involving future economic consequences.

---

[47] Paul Davidson, "The Dual-faceted Keynesian Revolution," JOURNAL OF POST-KEYNESIAN ECONOMICS, Vol. 11, No. 3, Spring 1980, p. 298.

[48] Paul Davidson, op. cit., p. 299.

[49] Paul Davidson, op. cit., p. 299.

This was the focal point of Keynes' view on the workings of a monetary capitalist economy."[50]

In the same vein, Sidney Weintraub emphasizes that the money wage rate is not just one of the prices in the economy. Rather, it is a parameter affecting aggregate demand and aggregate supply.[51] This assertion is demonstrated by the following simple linear model:

Aggregate Supply	Aggregate Demand
(a) $Z = kwN = Py$.	(e) $D = \alpha wN + I + G + X - M$.
(b) $P = kw\left(\frac{N}{y}\right)$.	
(c) $\frac{N}{y} = \frac{1}{\frac{y}{N}} = \frac{1}{A}$.	
(d) $P = k\left(\frac{w}{A}\right)$.	

Aggregate supply (Z) is depicted by Equation (a) above as some fixed multiple (k) of total labor cost (wN). The symbol k can be interpreted as the "mark-up" of unit labor costs or the targeted profit margin. Rearranging terms in (a), one obtains Equation (b) which defines the price level (P). The expression (N/y) denotes the reciprocal of average labor productivity (y/N). Let A represent y/N. Substituting (c) into (b) yields (d), which is an alternative way of stating the price level equation.

---

[50] Paul Davidson, op. cit., p. 300.

[51] See Sidney Weintraub, "The Missing Theory of Money Wages," JOURNAL OF POST-KEYNESIAN ECONOMICS, Vol. 1, No. 2, Winter 1978-79, pp. 59-78.

On the demand side, aggregate demand (D) is defined as:
$C + I + G + X - M$ as usual. The component C is assumed to be
some constant proportion of labor income (α wN).

"Clearly," Weintraub points out, "a shift in the wage
parameter will dislodge Z and nudge demand (with investment-
good prices being 'cost-determined', and civil servant wages
in G, the money wage also enters G)."[52] Since prices of
exportable goods are also "cost-determined" and relative
prices influence the volume of imports, a change in the
money-wage rate also affects $(X - M)$.

Thus, a sticky money wage rate is not a cause of
involuntary unemployment in contrast to views generally held
by writers of the "Neoclassical Synthesis." Davidson's work
casts "rigid wages" as a necessary stability condition for a
monetary economy. Not only does the flow supply price of
commodities require a sticky money wage rate, but the store-
of-value function of money also depends on it.

Davidson observes that "problems of liquidity and
finance are the hallmarks of everyday business decision
making in a monetary economy."[53] He writes:

> Liquidity involves being able to have the means of
> settlement to meet all one's contractual obliga-
> tions when they come due. Since money is the only
> thing that will discharge contract commitments (by
> definition), for any store of value besides money
> to be liquid, it must be easily resalable for money
> in a spot market....Liquid assets are durables
> traded in well-organized and orderly markets.
> Hence, what are liquid assets of any economy

---

[52] Sidney Weintraub, "The Missing Theory of Money Wages," op.
cit., p. 61.

[53] Paul Davidson, "Why Money Matters," JOURNAL OF POST-
KEYNESIAN ECONOMICS, Vol. 1, No. 1, Fall 1978, p. 61.

depends on the social practices and institutions that exist in that economy.[54]

Post-Keynesian monetary theorists like Paul Davidson, Hyman P. Minsky and Basil J. Moore argue that in a modern monetary economy investment decisions are intricately related to the portfolio preferences of financial managers.[55] Davidson writes:

> For accumulation to occur, two conditions must be fulfilled: (1) entrepreneurs must have the 'animal spirits' which encourage the belief in additional profit opportunities and (2) entrepreneurs must be able to command sufficient resources to put their projects into execution. Animal spirits may depend at least in part on non-monetary phenomena but the obtaining of command of resources requires the cooperation of the banking system and financial markets. If the banking system and related financial institutions acquiesce, then there will be net investment as the output of the capital goods industry increases.[56]

In the same spirit, Basil J. Moore insists on the endogenous nature of the money stock. He points out that, while the high-powered monetary base is exogenous in the control sense, it is endogenous in the real world and hence in the statistical sense. The accommodation process of the

---

[54] Paul Davidson, ibid., p. 61-62.

[55] See Basil J. Moore, "The Endogenous Money Stock," JOURNAL OF POST-KEYNESIAN ECONOMICS, Vol. II, No. 1, Fall 1979; and Hyman P. Minsky, JOHN MAYNARD KEYNES (New York: Columbia University Press, 1975).

[56] Paul Davidson, MONEY AND THE REAL WORLD, op. cit., p. 270.

money stock is demonstrated by Moore as follows:[57]

Over the long run, assuming considerations of variable velocity can be ignored, the growth rate of demand for money can be expressed tautologically as:

$$(1) \quad \frac{\dot{M}}{M} = \frac{\dot{P}}{P} + \frac{\dot{y}}{y} ,$$

where M is the demand for the nominal money stock; p is the price level; and y is real output. This equation can be rewritten as:

$$(2) \quad \frac{\dot{P}}{P} = \frac{\dot{M}}{M} - \frac{\dot{y}}{y} .$$

which represents the famous rule of Milton Friedman. In essence, the famous rule prescribes that to ensure price stability $\left(\frac{\dot{P}}{P} = 0 \right)$, the rate of growth of the nominal money stock should be increased at a rate parallel to the rate of growth of real output $\left(\frac{\dot{M}}{M} = \frac{\dot{y}}{y} \right)$.

In view of the cost-determined prices of the central core industries, the proximate determinant of inflation may be viewed as the rate at which nominal money wages rise in excess of the growth rate of average labor productivity. This relationship is depicted by the following equation:

$$(3) \quad \frac{\dot{P}}{P} = \frac{\dot{w}}{w} - \frac{\dot{A}}{A} ,$$

where $\frac{\dot{A}}{A}$ is the rate of growth of average labor productivity.

Substituting Equation (3) into (1) or (2) and rearranging terms, we have:

$$(4) \quad \frac{\dot{y}}{y} = \frac{\dot{M}}{M} - \frac{\dot{P}}{P} = \frac{\dot{M}}{M} - \left[\frac{\dot{w}}{w} - \frac{\dot{A}}{A} \right].$$

---

[57] Basil J. Moore, op. cit., pp. 132-134.

Equation (4) states that if the monetary authorities do not permit the nominal money stock to accommodate the rate of increase of money-wages (which is determined exogenously), aggregate demand will not be sufficient to maintain the secular growth of real output. Consequently there will be (a) downward pressure on the growth of real income, (b) a rise in interest rates and (c) an accompanying rise in the rate of unemployment. (Hence, it is interesting to note that the Post-Keynesian prescription is just the opposite of that of "Reaganomics.")

The endogenous nature of money stock can be seen from a different angle. According to Hyman P. Minsky, "Innovations in financial practices are a feature of our economy, especially when things go well. New institutions, such as Real Estate Investment Trusts (REITs), and new instruments, such as negotiable Certificates of Deposit, are developed; old instruments, such as commercial paper, increase in volume and find new uses. But each new instrument and expanded use of old instruments increases the amount of financing that is available and that can be used for financing activity and taking positions in inherited assets. Increased availability of finance bids up the prices of assets relative to the prices of current output and this leads to increases in investment. The quantity of relevant money in an economy in which money conforms to Keynes' definition, is endogenously determined."[58]

Minsky further distinguishes between hedge and speculative finance. "Speculative finance takes place when the cash flows from operations are not expected to be large enough to meet payment commitments, even though the present value of expected cash receipts is greater than the present

---

[58] Hyman P. Minsky, "The Financial Instability Hypothesis: An Interpretation of Keynes and an Alternative to 'Standard' Theory," CHALLENGE, Vol. 20, No. 1, March/April 1977, p. 24.

value of payment commitments. Speculating units expect to fulfill obligations by raising funds by new debt."[59]

Minsky observes that the investment boom in the mid-1960s was made possible by speculative finance.[60] However, speculating units are vulnerable to increases in the interest rates for a rise in interest rates can cause their cash payment commitments to rise relative to their cash receipts. Furthermore, a rise in long-term interest rates will lead to a fall in the market value of long-term asset holdings. These combined adverse outcomes often cause the speculating units to make a sudden revaluation of their debt structure. Thus, "a robust financial system was transformed into a fragile system during the long expansion of the 1960s. As a result of the fragility, shocks that might well have been absorbed without serious repercussions in a more robust financial structure triggered insipient financial crises in the United States in 1966 and in 1969-70."[61]

The focal point of Post-Keynesian analysis is on the credit side of bank intermediation. Their views are diametrically opposite of that of the Monetarists. The current debate is reminiscent of the "Bullionist Controversy" in the 19th century.[62] The Post-Keynesians are truly the

---

[59] Hyman P. Minsky, op. cit., p. 25.

[60] Hyman P. Minsky, JOHN MAYNARD KEYNES, op. cit., p. 162.

[61] Hyman P. Minsky, ibid., p. 162.

[62] For a lucid analysis of the debate between the Banking School and the Currency School, see Mark Blaug, ECONOMIC THEORY IN RETROSPECT, op. cit., pp. 201-204. The leaders of the Current School were Samuel Jones Loyd, Lord Overstone (1796-1883), Colonel Robert Torrens (1780-1864) and Normans. The spokesmen for the Banking School were Thomas Tooke (1774-1858) and John Fullarton (1780-1849). "Ricardo had laid down the currency principle: a mixed

heirs of the anti-Bullionists and the subsequent "Banking School."

The policy implications of the Post-Keynesian monetary theory may be viewed as variations of the original prescriptions of Keynes which are succinctly summarized by Davidson as follows:

> In both the TREATISE and GENERAL THEORY, Keynes emphasized the money wage/money supply nexus. He noted that if we have control of both the earnings of the system (incomes policy) and the monetary system (monetary policy), and if we can control the pace of investment, we can 'stabilize the purchasing power of money, its labour power, or anything else---without running the risk of setting up social and economic frictions or of causing waste' (1930, Vol. 1, p. 169).[63]

The Microfoundations of Post-Keynesian Economics

The distinguishing feature of Post-Keynesian microeconomics is that it is growth-oriented both in its long-period and short-period analyses. The long-period analysis shows a return to the Classical mode of theorizing. It should be recalled that the role of Classical "natural price" (normal price) was to assure the viability

---

[62,cont.] gold-paper currency should be made to vary in the same way as a purely metallic currency so that it responds automatically to any inflow or outflow of gold." "The Banking School denied that it was possible to overissue a convertible paper currency inasmuch as 'needs of trade' automatically controlled the volume of notes issued," op. cit., p. 201.

[63] Paul Davidson, "The Dual-faceted Keynesian Revolution," op. cit., p. 306.

(reproducibility) and surplus (growth) of the economic system. In our time, the works of Sraffa, Leontief and von Neumann clearly reflect the Classical spirit.[64]   As pointed out by Alfred S. Eichner, a short-period Post-Keynesian theory of prices is now emerging. "With its emphasis on the role of prices in assuring reproducibility and expansion of the system--rather than in allocating resources--this new theory diverges sharply from the models of pricing behavior found in economics textbooks. Since the price level depends, via the need for funds to finance investment, on the rate of economic expansion, the post-Keynesian theory of price formation is a dynamic one."[65]

While an explanation of the trend of relative prices is essential, it is the emerging short-period Post-Keynesian theory that is most relevant to the real world of oligopolies, multi-national corporations and diversified conglomerates. The pioneers of this short-period analysis are Kalecki, Steindle, Eichner and Levine.[66]   J.A. Kregel observes:

---

[64] The dynamization of Leontief's closed model resembles the von Neumann model. See Dorfman, Samuelson and Solow, LINEAR PROGRAMMING AND ECONOMIC ANALYSIS (New York: McGraw Hill, 1958), Chapter 11 and Hahn and Mattews, "The Theory of Economic Growth: A Survey," THE ECONOMIC JOURNAL, Vol. 74, No. 296, Dec. 1964. Reprinted in SURVEYS OF ECONOMIC THEORY, Vol. 2 (St. Martin's Press, 1965).

[65] Alfred S. Eichner, "Introduction to the Symposium of Price Formation," JOURNAL OF POST-KEYNESIAN ECONOMICS, Vol. IV, No. 1, Fall 1981, p. 81.

[66] See Michal Kalecki, THEORY OF ECONOMIC DYNAMICS (New York: Monthly Review Press, 1968), Alfred S. Eichner, THE MEGA-CORP AND OLIGOPOLY (Cambridge, England: Cambridge University Press, 1976), Joseph Steindle, MATURITY AND STAGNATION IN AMERICAN CAPITALISM (New York: Monthly Review Press, 1976) and David P. Levine, ECONOMIC THEORY, Vol. 2 (London: Routledge & Kegan Paul, 1981).

Kalecki's contributions, while essentially similar, are generally more concise and compact than Keynes'. Kalecki has the same views as Keynes concerning (1) the wage bargain, (2) the futility of effecting employment through reduction of the money wage, (3) the emphasis on time and (4) the concern with effective demand, etc.[67]

Kalecki made a clear distinction between "cost-determined" and "demand-determined" prices in the short run. He wrote:

Generally speaking, changes in the prices of finished goods are 'cost-determined' while changes in the prices of raw materials inclusive of primary foodstuffs are "demand-determined.' The prices of finished goods are affected, of course, by any 'demand-determined' changes in the prices of raw materials but it is through the channel of costs that this influence is transmitted.[68]

Kalecki's "cost-determined" price is given by the following formula:

(1) $p = mu + n\bar{p}$

where p is the "cost-determined" price; u is the prime cost per unit and $\bar{p}$ is the weighted average price of all firms (for the firm must make sure that the price does not become too high in relation to prices of other firms and vice versa). The coefficients m and n characterizing the price-fixing policy of the firm reflect what may be called the degree of monopoly of the firm's position.[69]

---

[67] J.A. Kregel, RATE OF PROFIT, DISTRIBUTION AND GROWTH: TWO VIEWS (Chicago: Aldine-Atherton, 1971), pp. 99-100.

[68] Michael Kalecki, op. cit., p. 11.

[69] Michael Kalecki, op. cit., pp. 12-13.

Building on the work of Kalecki, Eichner and Steindle, Levine and others have made further contributions to the formulation of Post-Keynesian short-period analysis. The institutional setting of their analyses is the dynamics of American industry structure. A simple schematic representation of this new microfoundation is shown in Figure 8.11.

According to Robert T. Averitt, the contemporary American economy is a composite of two distinct business systems: (a) the "center" firms and (b) the "periphery" firms. "The center firm is large in economic size as measured by number of employees, total assets and yearly sales. It tends toward vertical integration (through ownership or informal control), geographical dispersion (national and international), product diversification and managerial decentralization."[70] The pricing decisions of the "center" firms are growth-oriented. As aptly put by Nina Shapiro:

> Continuous and accelerating growth is the over-riding goal of the capitalist enterprise. This goal pushes the firm toward a long-run perspective in its pricing decisions. All actions must be judged in terms of their effect on the ongoing expansion of the firm. Their future, rather than immediate economic consequences, is the decisive consideration.[71]

The overriding goal of expansion is a strategy to reduce uncertainty confronting the oligopolistic "center" firm. Averitt observes that the "center" firm has to face six crises: (i) downturns in the business cycle; (ii) product growth lags, (iii) structural changes of technological

---

[70] Robert T. Averitt, THE DUAL ECONOMY (New York: W.W. Norton & Co., Inc., 1968), p. 1.

[71] Nina Shapiro, "Price and Growth of the Firm," JOURNAL OF POST-KEYNESIAN ECONOMICS, Vol. IV, No. 1, Fall 1981, p. 85.

Figure 8.11

The Microfoundations of Post-Keynesian
Economics

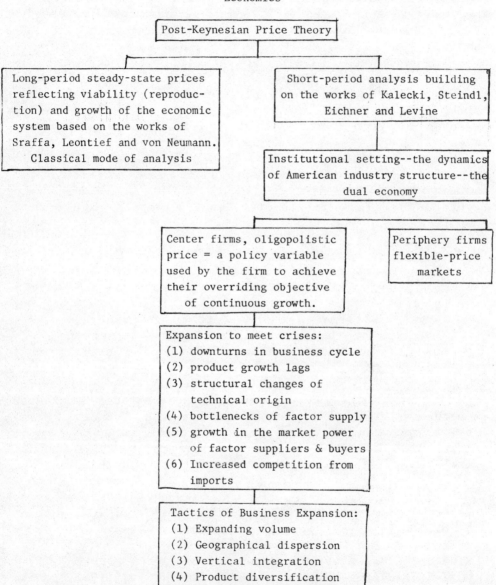

Post-Keynesian Price Theory

Long-period steady-state prices
reflecting viability (reproduc-
tion) and growth of the economic
system based on the works of
Sraffa, Leontief and von Neumann.
Classical mode of analysis

Short-period analysis building
on the works of Kalecki, Steindl,
Eichner and Levine

Institutional setting--the dynamics
of American industry structure--the
dual economy

Center firms, oligopolistic
price = a policy variable
used by the firm to achieve
their overriding objective
of continuous growth.

Periphery firms
flexible-price
markets

Expansion to meet crises:
(1) downturns in business cycle
(2) product growth lags
(3) structural changes of
    technical origin
(4) bottlenecks of factor supply
(5) growth in the market power
    of factor suppliers & buyers
(6) Increased competition from
    imports

Tactics of Business Expansion:
(1) Expanding volume
(2) Geographical dispersion
(3) Vertical integration
(4) Product diversification

origin; (iv) bottlenecks of factor supply; (v) growth in the market power of factor suppliers and buyers; (vi) increased competition from imports. "Fortunately these six crises types can be met with a single strategy: expansion. The four tactics of business expansion--expanding volume, geographical dispersion, vertical integration and product diversification- when used in correct proportions and with careful timing, guarantee initial protection."[72]

The Post-Keynesian, like Nina Shapiro and Nai-Pew Ong, revitalize the Marshallian analogy comparing business[73] survival to the maturation of young trees in a forest. With a view of maintaining viability and expansion in the long run, the dominant firms frequently employ the strategy of target pricing. As observed by Ong, there are two types of the price strategy: (a) defensive target pricing strategy, which is aimed at depriving the marginal producers of accumulation funds necessary to keep up with market growth and (b) offensive target pricing strategy, which is aimed at[74] eliminating them altogether in a destructive price war.

The mark-up pricing formula, $p = k(w/A)$, mentioned earlier is just the tip of the iceberg. We concur with Peter Kenyon's observation that "the mark-up is not only readily explained, but also the result of a complex set of economic forces operating to produce the growth and distribution observable at the macroeconomic level."[75] In other words,

_____

[72]Robert T. Averitt, op. cit., p. 12.

[73]See Alfred Marshall, PRINCIPLES OF ECONOMICS (London: The Macmillan Co.), 8th edition, p. 315.

[74]Nai-Pew Ong, "Target Pricing, Competition and Growth," JOURNAL OF POST-KEYNESIAN ECONOMICS, Vol. IV, No. 1, Fall 1981, p. 103.

[75]Peter Kenyon, "Pricing" in A GUIDE TO POST-KEYNESIAN ECONOMICS, op. cit., p. 34.

the mark-up is an important link in the chain of causal relationships of Post-Keynesian theory:

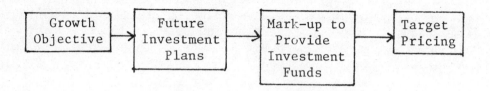

Thus, decisions about mark-ups and prices are linked directly with the firms' expectations about the future. The theory views investment as an overriding goal of the firm and is stated in the context of historical time. It is indeed an alternative of orthodox microeconomics. As aptly summarized by Shapiro:

> The notion of strategic price contains the seeds of a viable theory of capitalist exchange. The consummation of this theory requires, on the 'micro' side, the construction of a concrete treatment of the relation of pricing to technical change. On the 'macro' side it requires a theory of growth which takes in the centrality of product development to the character and pace of capital accumulation. When technical progress is systematically integrated into the conception of capitalist expansion, economics will gain its first real account of market operations in a capitalist economy.[76]

Turning now to the question of determination of factor prices, the Post-Keynesians reject the marginal productivity theory of wages and profits. Recall that both Joan Robinson and Nicholas Kaldor seek the determinants of the rate of profit outside of the sphere of exchange. In the same vein, Post-Keynesians deny that the money wage rate is determined

---

[76]Nina Shapiro, op. cit., p. 99.

by the supply and demand forces in the labor market. Eileen Applebaum emphasizes:

> The labor market is not a 'market' as that term is usually understood, for the labor market does not possess a market-clearing price mechanism. Variations in either money wages or in the real wage rate are unable to assure a zero surplus of labor, and thus eliminate unemployment. In the context of (1) an industrial structure that is largely oligopolistic, (2) fixed technical coefficients in production and (3) markup pricing, the demand for labor depends on the level of aggregate economic activity. It has little, if anything, to do with the marginal product of labor. The supply of labor, meanwhile, depends largely on demographic and other sociocultural factors, though it is somewhat responsive to changes in employment opportunities.[77]

In other words, the Post-Keynesian theory of wage determination combines the Keynesian demand analysis with the institutional approach to supply. Michael J. Piore points out that "wage rates perform certain basic social and institutional functions. They define relationships between labor and management, between one group of workers and another, among various institutional entities (the locals in a national union, the various branch plants of a national company, the major employers in a local labor market, the major international unions which compose the American labor movement) and last, the place of individuals relative to one another in the work community, in the neighborhood and in the family. The role of wages in this respect results in a series of fixed relationships among the wage rates of certain

---

[77] Eileen Applebaum, "Post-Keynesian Theory: The Labor Market," CHALLENGE, Vol. 21, No. 6, January/February 1979, 44.

groups of jobs and workers; these relationships are known as wage contours."[78]

Sidney Weintraub also argues that Keynes conceived the money wage to be an exogenous variable only vaguely resolvable by the tools of economic analysis (1978).[79] In view of the fact that the economist lacks exact details on motivation, strategic maneuvering and ideological rationalization whenever wage bargains are struck, history alone can enable us to "predict" money-wage outcomes. Thus, Weintraub calls attention to the lamentable situation that "one of our theories is missing," namely a theory of money wages. He writes:

> There is thus an imposter in the textbook literature, surviving as a disguised marginal productivity theory, dressed in (w/P) and fed by a question-begging $p = \bar{p}$; or entering in a quantity theory of money context, with $Q = \bar{Q}$, which is a curious logic for $\Delta N \gtrless 0$. Too, despite sentimental longings for 'competitive' labor markets to resolve w, the dreamers who wish away unions forego the necessary probe of the inter- actions of Δw and ΔP in that one-sided power state of unbalanced exploitative bliss.[80]

The Post-Keynesian analysis of money wages and unemployment draws heavily on "segmented labor market

---

[78]Michael J. Piore, "Unemployment and Inflation: An Alternative View," CHALLENGE, Vol. 21, No. 21, p. 25.

[79]Sidney Weintraub, CAPITALISM'S INFLATION AND UNEMPLOYMENT CRISIS (Addison-Wesley, 1978), Chapter 5. Portions of that chapter is reprinted in the author's article, "The Missing Theory of Money Wages" in JOURNAL OF POST-KEYNESIAN ECONOMICS, Vol. 1, No. 2, Winter 1978-79.

[80]Sidney Weintraub, op. cit., p. 76.

theories." The reader is referred to the excellent survey of the current literature in this area written by Glen G. Cain.[81] The Post-Keynesian literature covers the spectrum of ideologies but the common thread that ties them together is the historical process which led to dualism in the American economy. The segmentation of the labor market into primary and secondary sectors may be attributed to the coexistence of "center" firms and "periphery" firms. Cain observes that the various segmented labor market hypotheses generally invoke the following theoretical ideas--"the demand-determined allocation of jobs, the key role of on-the-job training, employer discrimination and the downgrading of observable human capital characteristics as determinants of wage levels."[82] In addition, dualists like Peter B. Doeringer, Michael Piore and others emphasize "the roles of workers' attitudes, motivations and work habits and the way these interact with community 'variables,' such as the welfare system and illegal activities."[83] The dual market idea in the hands of the radical wing is "sometimes expressed in terms of an analogy with an underdeveloped economy or even a colony that is exploited by an imperialistic primary sector."[84]

Sequential Causality in Post-Keynesian Economics

Sequential causality in which cause precedes effect is tied to historical time. In a monetary economy traveling through historical time, "the inherited stocks of durables,

---

[81] Glen G. Cain, "The Challenge of Segmented Labor Market Theories to Orthodox Theory: A Survey," Journal of Economic Literature, Vol. 14, #4, December 1976.

[82] Glen G. Cain, op. cit., p. 1222.

[83] Glen G. Cain, op. cit., p. 1222.

[84] Glen G. Cain, op. cit., p. 1223.

contractual obligations and the existing stock of money provide a continuity between irrevocable past economic behaviors and the current environment, while the existence of durable goods, contracts and money provides the essential link between an uncertain perfidious future and present activity."[85] Sequential causality is clearly conveyed by the following description of the causal links:

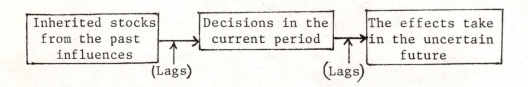

Hicks observes that "even the simplest case of sequential causation in economics has two steps in it: a prior step, from the objective cause to the decisions that are based on it, or influenced by it, and a posterior step, from the decisions to their (objective) effects."[86] Frequently, each of these steps involves time lags. "The characteristic form of a modern economy is one in which many of those who make decisions (households, firms, nations) have some reserves. They are accordingly not bound to respond to (market) signals; even if the signal persists, they have time to react. So the signal is less imperative, and therefore less dependable."[87] Thus, Arrow and Hahn draw the conclusion that in "a world with a past as well as a future in which contracts are made in terms of money, no equilibrium may exist."[88] This is also the reason why Hicks states that

[85] Paul Davidson, op. cit., p. 13. These are Davidson's words.

[86] Sir John Hicks, CAUSALITY IN ECONOMICS, op. cit., p. 88.

[87] Sir John Hicks, op. cit., p. 91.

[88] K.J. Arrow and F.H. Hahn, op. cit., p. 357.

"liquidity is freedom."[89]   In other words, the existence of
reserves gives the decision maker time to interpret market
signals and to meet their contractual commitments before they
make decisions to change courses of action.   In the words of
Paul Davidson, "Thus liquidity is essential in a world of
nonpredictable change and sequential causality."[90]

In his book, CAUSALITY IN ECONOMICS, Hicks points out:

I have tried to show that there are different kinds
of causality in economics; and that to each kind
there is, or can be, a kind of theory that
corresponds.

To static causality corresponds static theory: the
part of economic theory that is most completely
developed (neoclassical economics), but which
leaves even those most devoted to it unsatisfied,
since its field of application is so narrow.   To
contemporaneous causality corresponds the (formal)
theory of Keynes, and in 'micro' contexts that of
Marshall....It is nevertheless not surprising that
economists, even the most 'Keynesian' ones, have
become dissatisfied with it;....I have been trying
to show that the further development of theory,
which I agree is required, should begin with an
attempt to identify the questions it will have to
be concerned with.   These, I have tried to show,
are in essence questions of sequential causality.[91]

---

[89]Sir John Hicks, op. cit., p. 94.

[90]Paul Davidson, "Causality in Economics: A Review," JOURNAL
OF POST-KEYNESIAN ECONOMICS, Vol. 11, No. 4, Summer 1980,
p. 582.

[91]Sir John Hicks, op. cit., pp. 101-102.

The questions raised by Post-Keynesian writers are essentially those of sequential causality. The centerpiece of their analysis is the workings of a monetary economy progressing in historical time. Not only in their approach to the monetary factor, but in interrelated specific questions, they have continually focused on historical time and uncertainty. For instance, Post-Keynesian price theory highlights the causal links among prices, profits, investment and growth. Post-Keynesian macrodynamics emphasizes the direction of causation from rate of profit to distribution which, in turn, effects growth. In the Kaldor-Mirrlees analysis of technical progress, a sense of history is reflected in the inherited fixed-coefficients vintage machines and uncertainty about future outcomes is lurking behind the fixed-payoff-period investment decision rule. Undoubtedly, Post-Keynesian economics have answered Hicks' challenge and represent the beginning of a theory corresponding to sequential causality.

PART IV

SEARCH FOR SYNTHESIS

CHAPTER 9

THE CONTINUING SEARCH FOR A NEW SYNTHESIS

The Rejection of the Walrasian Micro-System

By the middle of the 1970s, general equilibrium
theorists had recognized the fact that any simple Walrasian
microsystem (such as the microfoundations of the standard
macro model considered in Part II of this book) could not
serve as the microfoundations for Keynesian macroeconomics.
E.R. Weintraub observed (1977):

> At a minimum, general equilibrium theorists have
> demonstrated quite convincingly that Keynesian
> macroeconomics cannot be derived from any simple
> Walrasian microsystem. This in itself is of some
> consequence. It is difficult today, for serious
> macrotheorists to argue against income policies on
> the grounds that they distort the price signals
> that enable a (Walrasian) multimarket system to
> function efficiently. That is not to say that
> incomes policies are 'good things', but rather that
> they cannot be assessed from a Walrasian
> perspective, since a Walrasian equilibrium model
> generates uninteresting macrosystems.[1]

It is rather unfortunate that, at early stages of the
search for more appropriate microfoundations of Keynesian
macroeconomics, the protagonists on both sides set up
criteria of evaluation that left them incapable of
appreciating the strong points of the opposing groups. In
the Post-Keynesian camp, Nicholas Kaldor insisted (1972):

---

[1] E. Roy Weintraub, op. cit., p. 18.

Without a major act of demolition--without destroying the basic conceptual framework--it is impossible to make any progress.[2]

The basic assumption of this theory (general equilibrium theory) is constant cost, or constant returns to scale. With Smith and Ricardo, this was implicit in the very notion of the 'natural price' determined solely by costs of production (irrespective of demand). With the neo-classical school--in any rigorous formulation of it--it was explicit in the assumption of homogenous and linear production functions which is one of the required 'axioms' necessary to make the assumptions of perfect competition and profit-maximization consistent with one another....As a result, the existence of increasing returns and its consequences for the whole framework of economic theory have been completely neglected.[3]

The same views were shared by J. Kornai and other Post-Keynesians.[4]

The general equilibrium theorists, on the other hand, clung tenaciously to traditional optimization and the choice-theoretical framework when they analyzed disequilibrium phenomena. For instance, in his well-known essay, "An Equilibrium Model of the Business Cycle," Robert E. Lucas, Jr. writes:

---

[2] Nicholas Kaldor, "The Irrelevance of Equilibrium Economics," THE ECONOMIC JOURNAL, December, 1972, 82, pp. 1240.

[3] Nicholas Kaldor, op.cit., pp. 1241-1242. The words in the first brackets are ours.

[4] J. Kornai, ANTI-EQUILIBRIUM (New York: American Elsevier, 1971).

...the model studied below has three distinguishing characteristics: prices and quantities at each point in time are determined in competitive equilibrium; the expectations of agents are rational, given the information available to them; information is imperfect, not only in the sense that the future is unknown, but also in the sense that no agent is perfectly informed as to the current state of the economy.[5]

Herschel I. Grossman in his paper, "Why Does Aggregate Employment Fluctuate?" points out:

In recent years theoretical models of macro-economic relations have been judged not only by their consistency with observed phenomena, but also by their use of convincing choice-theoretic rationalizations for the underlying behavior of individuals. Over the past decade or more, these criteria have motivated substantial research aimed at reworking the theory of macro-economic relations by using the same foundations and the same principles that have traditionally served in theorizing about micro-economic relations.[6]

This impasse has contributed to the delay of a much needed merging of strong points from each paradigm. This state of affairs reminded Robert J. Gordon (1981) of "an

---

[5] Robert E. Lucas, Jr., "An Equilibrium Model of Business Cycle, JOURNAL OF POLITICAL ECONOMY, 1975, Vol. 83, No. 6, p. 1113.

[6] Herschel I. Grossman, "Why Does Aggregate Employment Fluctuate?" THE AMERICAN ECONOMIC REVIEW, Papers and Proceedings of the 91st Annual Meeting, Vol. 69, No. 2, May, 1979, p. 64.

election between two unattractive candidates," where "the 'voters' appear to have chosen their favorite paradigm mainly on the basis of the unattractive features of the opposite approach."[7] In the same vein, Martin Shubik (1970) made the following stricture:

> I am reminded of the story of the drunk who had lost his keys at night and spent his time searching for them under a street-lamp fifty yards from where he had lost them because that was the only place he could see anything.[8]

The Harbingers of A "New Beginning"

It is encouraging to see writers of the opposing paradigms beginning to see their way clear of the initial impasse. Migration away from the dichotomy can be attributed to increasing sophistication of theoretical works on all sides. Major credit should go to the general equilibrium theorists. Their unceasing attempts to reconstruct the Arrow-Debreu value theory must be regarded as one of the great achievements of economic theory in the past two decades. Surveys of this important literature have been made

------

[7] Robert J. Gordon, "Output Fluctuations and Gradual Price Adjustment," JOURNAL OF ECONOMIC LITERATURE, Vol. XIX, No. 2, June 1981, p. 494.

[8] Martin Shubik, "A Curmudgeon's Guide to Microeconomics," JOURNAL OF ECONOMIC LITERATURE, Vol. VIII, No. 2, June 1970, p. 415.

by Jean Michel Grandmont (1977),[9] Allan Drazen (1980)[10] and John D. Hey (1981).[11] As suggested by Hey, the outburst of theoretical literature on the "new microfoundations" of involuntary unemployment may be grouped under two broad categories: (a) fixed-price models with deterministic quantity rationing and (b) fixed-price models with stochastic quantity rationing.

The label "fixed-price model" was coined by Hicks (1965).[12] In these models agents are still assumed to be price-takers. The explanation of individual decision-making is firmly based on the choice-theoretical framework. However, two innovations are introduced into the timeless Walrasian general equilibrium framework, namely, historical time and uncertainty. The economy is viewed as operating in a sequence of time periods. Owing to technical difficulties, the attention of a majority of model-builders has been restricted to just one period of the time sequence. The lack of future markets forces agents to make decisions during the current period based on the prevailing prices and expected future spot prices. Hence, an element of uncertainty is introduced into the analyses. Conceptually, the economy will exhibit a series of temporary equilibria with possible variations of economic variables in subsequent periods due to the inconsistencies of future plans on the part of decision-makers.

---

[9] Jean Michel Grandmont, "Temporary General Equilibrium Theory," ECONOMETRICA, Vol. 45, No. 3, April 1977, pp. 535-572.

[10] Allan Drazen, "Recent Developments in Macroeconomic Disequilibrium Theory," ECONOMETRICA, Vol. 48, No. 2, March 1980, pp. 283-306.

[11] John D. Hey, ECONOMICS IN DISEQUILIBRIUM (New York: New York University Press, 1981).

[12] See John Hicks, CAPITAL AND GROWTH, op. cit., Chapter 7.

In the "fixed-price" models considered in the following sections, the prevailing price-vectors are assumed to be inflexible, or not to move sufficiently to clear markets in the period under consideration. Consequently all consumers cannot complete their desired transactions. They will thus experience some kind of quantity constraint, or quantity rationing, on their trade in addition to the budget constraints. As pointed out by Lars E.O. Svensson, "a central problem in the fixed-price literature is how agents' behaviour is modified when they face these additional constraints. In particular we want to know what demand they will express to the market under these circumstances. We call that demand their effective demand."[13] It will be recalled that the initial contributions in this area were made by Patinkin (1965), Clower (1965) and Leijonhufvud (1968) (see Chapter 6 of this book). The distinction between notional and effective demand as shown by Clower suggests a definition of involuntary unemployment. The main elements of the two types of fixed price models together with Frank Hahn's flexible price model will now be considered.

Fixed-Price Models with Deterministic Quantity Rationing

Both Drazen and Hey identify two basic fixed-price models with deterministic quantity rationing: one associated with H Dreze (1975) and the other with J.P. Benassy (1977).[14] In both of these models prices are quoted by

---

[13] Lars E.O. Svensson, "Effective Demand and Stochastic Rationing," REVIEW OF ECONOMIC STUDIES, Vol. XLVII(1980), p. 339.

[14] See Dreze, "Existence of An Exchange Equilibrium Under Price Rigidity," INTERNATIONAL ECONOMIC REVIEW, 16, 1975, pp. 301-320; J.P. Benassy, "On Quantity Signals and the Foundations of Effective Demand Theory," SCANDINAVIAN JOURNAL OF ECONOMICS, 79, 1977, pp. 147-168.

sellers at the beginning of each trading period. Once prices are quoted, they cannot change during the trading period. Quoted prices may not be market-clearing prices. Equilibrium is achieved through quantitative signals perceived by agents which set upper and lower bounds to the trades they can make. These constraints represent the rationing scheme of the system. Drazen explains the structure by means of the following symbols:

$\tilde{Z}_h^a$ = the effective demand by individual a for commodity h.

Z^a = the actual trade vector of individual a.

$\overline{Z}^a$ = the perceived upper bound on purchases and sales of individual a.

$\underline{Z}^a$ = the perceived lower bound on purchases and sales of individual a.

P = the market price vector.

$\underline{Z}_h^a \leq \tilde{Z}_h^a \leq \overline{Z}_h^a$ = the perceived quantity constraints.

Drazen writes:

In Dreze's model an agent perceives a signal $S^a = (p, \overline{Z}^a, \underline{Z}^a)$. This leads him to express a constrained demand which maximizes his preferences subject to S^a. The important point is that in forming his excess demands for each commodity an agent considers constraints in all markets including the commodity in question. That is, demand functions satisfy $\underline{Z}_h^a \leq \tilde{Z}_h^a \leq \overline{Z}_h^a$ for all h. An equilibrium is defined as a set of signals S^a and actual trades such that markets clear ($\sum_a Z^a = 0$), only one side of a market is constrained, and only voluntary exchanges take place. A fixed argument is used to establish the existence of equilibrium. An auctioneer sets $\overline{Z}_a$

259

and $\underline{Z}^a$ for each trader. In response to these signals each agent sends a constrained excess demand vector $\tilde{Z}^a$ to market. If in aggregate there is excess demand for some commodity h, the auctioneer lowers the upper bounds $\bar{Z}_h^a$ imposed on agents' trades. A fixed point of this tatonnement is Dreze equilibrium.[15]

The Dreze rationing scheme resolving the quantity constraints is nonmanipulable by traders. John D. Hey criticizes the Dreze procedure as follows:

The problem with this procedure is that it envisages the individual as meekly accepting the perceived constraints--no attempt to breach any constraint (even when it would increase the utility of the individual) being considered. This would be a sensible procedure if the constraints were true, objectively determined constraints, which under no circumstances could be breached. But they are merely perceived constraints; surely individuals would, at least, try to test them?[16]

This line of reasoning led subsequently to Benassy's alternative approach. Unlike Dreze, Benassy assumes agents can send offers which may violate the perceived constraints. In the words of Drazen, "effective demand for commodity h is based on constraints perceived in other markets, but ignoring the constraints on commodity h. Therefore, $\tilde{Z}^a$ may not be feasible for a given agent. There is a rationing scheme which associates actual trades of each agent with effective demands expressed by all agents, that is, $Z_h^a = F_h^a(\bar{Z})$. The rationing scheme is assumed to satisfy certain natural

---

[15] Allan Drazen, op. cit., p. 287.

[16] John D. Hey, op. cit., p. 195.

260

conditions: actual trades balance, trade is voluntary, and the short side of the market realizes its transactions."[17]

Although Benassy's procedure is preferable to that of Dreze, it is not entirely satisfactory. Hey observes:

> There are a number of problems connected with the Benassy approach. The main problem, at an individual level, is that the vector of excess demand, derived by the procedure sketched above, may very well violate the budget constraint. In such a case, if the individual found himself successfully overcoming all the perceived constraints, he might find himself unable to meet all his commitments.[18]

Increasing sophistication in this type of non-Walrasian general equilibrium model leads inevitably to simultaneous price and quantity determination as integral to an agent's attempt to overcome his perceived quantity constraints. The leading exponent of this class of models is Frank Hahn (1977, 1978).[19] In his view:

> The economy can get stuck in a non-Walrasian equilibrium even when prices are free to vary. Price setting is now part of a story of rationally acting agents. This involves conjectures and one

---

[17] Allan Drazen, op. cit., p. 288.

[18] John D. Hey, op. cit., p. 195.

[19] See Frank Hahn, "Exercise in Conjectural Equilibria," SCANDINAVIAN JOURNAL OF ECONOMICS, 79 (1977), pp. 187-209; Frank Hahn, "On Non-Walrasian Equilibria," REVIEW OF ECONOMIC STUDIES, February 1978, 45, pp. 1-17.

must ask where they come from, or at least, whether they must be restricted in some way.[20]

These "conjectures" may be regarded as agents' estimated demand and supply curves. The Hicksian conjectural non-Walrasian equilibrium is tantamount to the situation in which the conjectural demand curve coincides with the "actual" demand curve. Unfortunately, conceptual and technical difficulties involved in the analysis of conjectural equilibrium forced Hahn to give up the criterion of "global rationality" and settle for the more realistic assumption that economic agents behave "reasonably." In doing so, Hahn is one foot in the world of the behaviorists. He writes:

> Even so the class of conjectures considered is small; but I believe sensible for a decentralized economy. By sensible I mean two things: (a) a small agent must not be expected to have 'general equilibrium theories' embodied in his conjectures. Thus he believes that the change in his budget situation consequent upon his wishing to 'break a ration' in any one market can be conjectured with reference to events in only that market. (b) an agent does not have 'perverse' conjectures.[21]

However, Hahn regrets having "nothing of a formal nature to report on reasonable conjectures."[22] In the opinion of Drazen, "the concept of local rationality advanced by Hahn looks promising but the inability to implement it may indicate that it is a dead end. My belief is that non-Walrasian models of unemployment will stand and fall on the

---

[20] Frank Hahn, op. cit., p. 10.

[21] Frank Hahn, op. cit., p. 14 (1978).

[22] Frank Hahn, op. cit., p. 15 (1978).

issue of rationality of behavior.[23] We venture to suggest that Hahn's candid rejection of "global rationality" in favor of "local rationality" is an important indicator of convergence among economic theories in the not too distant future. We concur with the following assessment of John D. Hey:

> Perhaps, most importantly, knowledge has now advanced sufficiently far for economists to be in a position to assess critically what their techniques of analysis can and cannot achieve. Ironically, therein may be the seeds of their own destruction.[24]

Fixed-Price Models with Stochastic Quantity Rationing

The leading pioneer in this area is Lars E.O. Svensson.[25] Svensson rejects deterministically based explanations of effective demand advanced by Dreze and Benassy and points out:

> The Dreze demand makes sense in a situation where there is no uncertainty and where the quantity constraints are perceived independent of the

---

[23]Allan Drazen, op. cit., p. 299.

[24]John D. Hey, op. cit., p. 201.

[25]See Lars E.O. Svensson, "Effective Demand and Stochastic Rationing," REVIEW OF ECONOMIC STUDIES, Vol. XLVII (1980), pp. 339-355. Other pioneering works include J.R. Green, "On the Theory of Effective Demand," ECONOMIC JOURNAL, Vol. 90, June, 1980, pp. 341-353 and J.R. Green and M. Majumdar, "The Nature of Stochastic Equilibrium," ECONOMETRICA, Vol. 43, 1957, pp. 647-661.

expressed demands. Such a framework is however very special, and it does not allow for a distinction between demand and trade. As for the Clower demand, the conclusion from the comparison is that its choice-theoretic foundation is very weak, or rather non-existent, in spite of it being widely used in the macroeconomic fix-price literature.[26]

Disenchantment with the choice-theoretic foundation has been shared by many writers. As observed by Hey, the central notion in fixed-price models with stochastic quantity rationing is that agents use some kind of "rule of thumb" in making decisions. One common feature of such rules is random behavior. Hence the theory of stochastic process is the natural analytical apparatus for the study of such behavior. It also implies that agents behave "reasonably" rather than "optimally." It should be recalled that Frank Hahn also questioned "optimal" decision-making in his discussion of the concept of "local rationality." Here is another significant indicator of the coming convergence of economic theories.

Svensson effective demand is defined as demand that maximizes the expected utility of actual trade "in a specific institutional setting, where there is stochastic rationing, and where the demand must be expressed to the market before it is known whether there will be rationing or not."[27] In particular, Svensson explicitly distinguished demand from trade, "the trade being random due to the stochastic rationing mechanism."[28]

---

[26] Lars E.O. Svensson, op. cit., p. 353.

[27] Lars E.O. Svensson, op. cit., p. 353.

[28] Lars E.O. Svensson, op. cit., p. 353.

The general conclusion of the Svensson model is "that the effective demand will depend on <u>the particular institutional set-up</u> that is conceived. We can hardly hope to find a specific definition of the effective demand that will make sense for a wide class of institutional environments, as the Clower demand probably was intended by some authors to do."[29] Interestingly, the arguments of the German Historical School and the American Institutionalists are vindicated by Svensson's general conclusion.[30]

The roots of the initial impasse may be traced to two factors. The first is associated with the lofty aspiration of some economists to construct a general theory "that will make sense for a wide class of institutional environments." In the history of economic analysis, many great writers have shared this impossible dream. Jeremy Bentham wanted to be the Newton of the moral world. Heinrich Gossen pictured himself as the Copernicus in the world of human discourse. The neoclassical economists after the 1870s strived to develop a unified theory of value and distribution; even Keynes could not resist the temptation of writing "The General Theory." In our time, general equilibrium theorists have endeavored to convert more and more exogenous variables

---

[29] Lars E.O. Svensson, op. cit., p. 353. The underline is ours.

[30] The most well-known writer of the German Historical School is Gustav von Schmoller (1838-1917). With the Austrian Karl Memger (1840-1921) he conducted the famous "Methodenstreit" or methodological controversies. The leading American Institutionalists are Thornstein Bunde Veblen (1857-1929) and John Rogers Commons (1862-1945). For excellent discussions of the revolt against formalism started by the German Historical School of Economics and the American Institutionalists, see Ben B. Seligman, MAIN CURRENTS IN MODERN ECONOMICS (New York: The Free Press of Glencoe, 1962), Part I.

into endogenous ones. Contemporaneous causality as discussed by Hicks is a case in point. The pioneers of Post-Keynesian economics are not free from the "occupational disease" either for they have attempted to develop a "magnificent dynamics" incorporating the strong points of Ricardo, Marx, Kalecki and Keynes. Ironically, in each case the "seeds of their own destruction" were sown by the increasing sophistication of their own analyses.

The other factor is the reluctance of the majority of writers to foresake the time-honored concept of optimization in explaining economic behavior. The disequilibrium macroeconomics considered in Chapter 6 and again in this chapter is a misnomer. It should be called "temporary general equilibrium theory" a la Jean Michel Grandmount, or "non-Walrasian Equilibria" following Frank Hahn. The basic incompatibility between optimizing and disequilibrium is forcefully stated by John D. Hey as follows:

> At an aggregate level, optimising and equilibrium
> necessarily go hand-in-hand; or, to put the same
> point another way, optimising and disequilibrium
> and incompatible. The argument is quite simple: a
> genuine   state   of   disequilibrium,   almost
> definitionally, implies that some decision-maker
> has been frustrated in his plans. But if someone
> is frustrated, then optimality has not been
> achieved. Conversely, if optimality is achieved,
> then no-one is frustrated and hence equilibrium is
> attained. The implication, of course, is that if
> one wants to model genuine disequilibrium, then an
> optimising model of individual choice must be
> abandoned.[31]

Alan Drazen also opines:
In summary, attempts to demonstrate the rationality of behavior which would support an unemployment

---

[31] John D. Hey, op. cit., p. 201. The underline is ours.

equilibrium have met limited success at best. Either some crucial aspect of the economy is exogenously specified, or certain agents are severely restricted in behavior or information sets, sometimes perversely so...[32]

Selective Approaches and Institutional Factors

Happily the profession has perceived a light at the end of the impasse tunnel. The way out has been eloquently stated by Ruth P. Mack:

> The dilemma is clear. If theoretical analysis accepts the challenge of broadly realistic assumptions, the search for grand equilibrium optimal solutions will usually need to be abandoned. If it rejects the challenge, theory will regress into ever deepening scholasticism. Possibly some revolutionary new paradigm will resolve the conflict. But in the meantime selective approaches may prove useful--approaches that utilize the rigorous methods, tools and concepts of economic analysis to explore real-world problems. Selective approaches deliberately match the method to the realities of the problem. An important aspect of the matching resorts, in effect, to a preference surface that trades generality for realism. In some connections generality can be purchased at very little sacrifice of realism. In others quite the reverse applies. It is essential to identify these situations. This is the essence.[33]

---

[32] Allan Drazen, op. cit., p. 299.

[33] Ruth P. Mack's comments on the topic, "New Ideas in Pure Theory," AMERICAN ECONOMIC REVIEW, Papers and Proceedings of the Annual Meeting, Vol. LX, No. 2, May, 1970, p. 461. The underlines are ours.

In similar vein, Martin Shubik asserts:

It may be desirable to have a theory of choice
which covers with the same neat axioms Mrs. Jones'
decision to buy an extra pound of bacon or Mr.
Jones' decision to murder Mrs. Jones or to climb an
impossible mountain peak. It would be nice: but
for almost all purposes of economic theorizing it
is not necessary. Furthermore, there is every
indication that the price paid to include these
phenomena under one unified theory is too high for
an economist to pay....With a reasonable amount of
luck, an important lesson from the false starts in
general economic theorizing can be learned.
Instead of looking for a general theory of welfare
economics, or a theory of oligopoly, etc., there
may be a greater stress upon special theories which
will be of limited scope, but with considerable
application.[34]

Indeed, the profession has begun to lay greater stress
on "selective approaches" or "special theories." On the side
of general equilibrium, no new attempt has been made to
develop a "new theory of value." Kenneth J. Arrow has given
more attention to the study of information and economic
behavior in recent years. An example of his "selective
approach" is his paper, "Vertical Integration and
Communication" (1975).[35] Joseph E. Stiglitz's research has
also centered on the economics of information and
uncertainty. His paper, "Incentives, Risks and Information:
Notes Towards A Theory of Hierarchy" (1975), is an example of

_____

[34]Martin Shubik, "A Curmudgeon's Guide to Microeconomics,"
JOURNAL OF ECONOMIC LITERATURE, Vol. VIII, No. 2, June,
1970, p. 407. The underline is ours.

[35]K.J. Arrow, "Vertical Integration and Communication," THE
BELL JOURNAL OF ECONOMICS, No. 2, Autumn, 1975.

a "selective approach."[36]   R. Radner has accepted some of the behaviorists' tenets in his paper, "A Behavioral Model of Cost Reduction" (1975).[37]   These are just a few illustrations of the resurgence of interest in selective approaches.

Increasing attention has also been given to institutional factors by general equilibrium theorists. In his John Diebold Lecture at Harvard University (1978), the Nobel Laureate K.J. Arrow questioned the legitimacy of the profit system itself. He observed that profits are not the motive that drives everything. He pointed out:

> There are many arguments along this line, but perhaps the most familiar one is that originated by Berl and Means some forty years ago: that most large corporations are run not by the people who receive profits, the stockholders, but by the managers....The managers may well want to maximize other goals, perhaps their job perquisites or their control over the corporation.
>
> There is another hypothesis which implies a divorce between profit-seeking and business decisions, one that goes back in some way to Thorstein Veblen.... This strand of argument has been developed by several writers over the past twenty years, most notably by my colleague, John Kenneth Galbraith. The motives of the firm become essentially its self-preservation, its growth, its ability to

---

[36] J.E. Stiglitz, "Incentives, Risk and Information: Notes Towards a Theory of Hierarchy," THE BELL JOURNAL OF ECONOMICS, No. 2, Autumn, 1975.

[37] R. Radner, "A Behavioral Model of Cost Reduction," THE BELL JOURNAL OF ECONOMICS, Autumn, 1975, No. 2.

innovate[38] rather than its maximization of profits.[38]

Arrow further called attention to the works of Herbert Simon and his colleagues at Carnegie-Mellon University:

(in the views of Simon) in a complicated organization it is impossible to maximize profits. It is just too hard to know what is going on. When there are so many decisions to be made, any central group will simply be overloaded with information and will not be able to handle the decision-making. Once the overload is relieved by decentralization within the firm, the actual decision-makers have many motives besides the maximization of profits.[39]

Pricing

In the camp of Post-Keynesian economics, there is now a general awareness of the limitations of the Sraffian and other Neo-Ricardian arguments about the set of "normal" prices which must prevail in the long run if the system is to be capable of maintaining steady-state growth. As pointed out by Alfred S. Eichner (1981):

Equilibrium models of this sort are not enough. Such models offer little or no insight into what happens over the cycle. They also are inadequate

---

[38] Kenneth J. Arrow, "The Limitations of the Profit Motive," CHALLENGE, September/October, 1979, p. 25. Reprinted from Benjamin M. Friedman, editor, NEW CHALLENGES TO THE ROLE OF PROFIT (Lexington Books, D.C. Heath and Co., 1978).

[39] Kenneth J. Arrow, op. cit., pp. 25-26.

for explaining the observable changes in trend over time. It is for this reason that, following Kalecki, one must also have models that are 'out of equilibrium'—whether they are of the purely short-period sort, such as those used to account for the cyclical movements of the economy, or they are of an intermediate nature and, abstracting from any cyclical movements, focus on the change in trend over time.[40]

Eichner's observations seem to have nudged Post-Keynesian microeconomics toward the line of reasoning expounded by the non-post-Keynesian, Robert J. Gordon:

Prices are neither perfectly fixed nor perfectly flexible, and variations over time and across countries with regard to the degree of flexibility require explanation as well.[41]

---

[40] Alfred S. Eichner, "Introduction to the Symposium: Price Formation Theory," JOURNAL OF POST-KEYNESIAN ECONOMICS, Vol. IV, No. 1, Fall, 1981, p. 82.

[41] Robert J. Gordon, op. cit., p. 495. Gordon points out, The phenomena the theory must explain is a long and daunting one: "(1) Some markets have prices that are set at the same level over weeks, months or years. (2) Some prices, even though they are marked on price tags, are changed every day (e.g., the price of lettuce in a supermarket), and yet other pre-set prices remain sufficiently fixed to be printed in catalogues and on product containers. (3) The division of nominal GNP changes between prices and quantities varies across countries, with evidence of a greater price response in Europe both during the Great Depression and more recently (Robert J. Gordon and James A. Wilcox, 'The Monetarist Interpretation of the Great Depression: An Evaluation and Critique' in THE GREAT DEPRESSION REVISITED, edited by Karl Brunner (Hingham, MA: Martinus Nijhoff, 1981, pp. 49-107). (4) The division of

The increasing sophistication of Post-Keynesian pricing theory has led Nina Shapiro, Josef Steindl, Nai-Pew Ong and others to study changes in the markup over time.[42] As observed by Eichner, "To develop pricing models of this intermediate sort, Shapiro and Ong relaxed two of the critical assumptions usually made in long period analysis: (1) equalized rates of return on capital investment and (2) absence of technical progress."[43]

In her paper, "Pricing and Growth of the Firm," Nina Shapiro writes:

_____

[41, cont.] nominal GNP changes between prices and quantities has varied over time in the United States, with a rapid price response during and after World War I, and after the OPEC oil shock in 1974, but virtually no price response to high unemployment in 1938-40 and 1970-71. (5) Prices, although set in advance and marked on price tags, nevertheless have the potential to move fast enough to allow hyperinflation to occur (Thomas J. Sargent, 1981)." Thus, "any adequate framework must go beyond the fixed-price paradigm which has no ingredient that would explain variations over time in the degree of price responsivenes. Similarly, the facts of price-setting and quantity-taking cannot be explained by the new classical paradigm, which simply assumes them away," pp. 494-495.

[42] See Nina Shapiro, "Pricing and Growth of the Firm," Nai-Pew Ong, "Target Pricing Competition and Growth," both in JOURNAL OF POST-KEYNESIAN ECONOMICS, VOL. IV, No. 1, Fall 1981, pp. 85-116. Josef Steindl, MATURITY AND STAGNATION IN AMERICAN CAPITALISM (New York: Monthly Review Press, 1976).

[43] Alfred S. Eichner, op. cit., p. 82.

Continuous and accelerating growth is the overriding goal of the capitalist enterprise. The goal pushes the firm toward a long-run perspective in its pricing decisions. All actions must be judged in terms of their effect on the ongoing expansion of the firm. Their future, rather than immediate economic consequences, is the decisive consideration.[44]

As a first approximation, Shapiro illustrates the pricing decision of the "capitalist firm" by means of a diagram taken from the work of Josef Steindl (1976) which we modify slightly in Figure 9.1 below:[45]

Figure 9.1

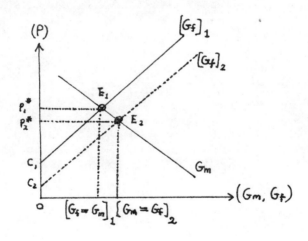

[44] Nina Shapiro, op. cit., p. 85.

[45] The diagram without modification is depicted in Figure 1 of the Shapiro paper, op. cit., p. 89.

The vertical axis measures prices while the horizontal axis measures the financially viable rate that can be funded out of profits accruing to the firm from sales of its products. The relation between the price of the firm's product and the product's "potential growth rate" is depicted by the positively sloped curve G_f. At any given price, G_f depends upon (1) the unit cost incurred at normal capacity utilization, c, (2) the capital/output ratio, (3) the firm's dividend policy and (4) the extent of its debt which must be serviced out of sales revenues. Given these factors, G_f will increase with the price.

The curve G_m indicates the expected growth rate of sales at different prices. It reflects the firm's perception of market growth opportunities. The price elasticity of G_m depends upon (1) the ability of the firm to increase its sales by undercutting its rivals and (2) the cost differentials of the industry and other factors. The greater these advantages, the greater the price elasticity of the G_m curve.

These two curves summarize the two conditions necessary to the continuation of the firm's overriding growth objective. According to Shapiro:

> First, the firm must have enough funds to fuel the growth process. Profits must be adequate to finance that part of the firm's expansion which cannot be externally funded and to 'secure' the finance for that part which is so funded. Second, the firm must hold markets sufficiently large to absorb the output potential of its productive mechanism. Sustained investment entails the expansion of markets at a rate equal to that of capacity growth. Hence, if the price of the commodity is to promote the growth of the firm, pricing has to be based on the principles of the maintenance and augmentation of (1) profit margins and (2) markets.[46]

---

[46] Nina Shapiro, op. cit., p. 87.

The equilibrium mark-up pricing of the firm, p_1^*, in Figure 9.1 is jointly determined by the intersection of the two curves. Over time, the equilibrium price could change as a result of cost-reducing technical innovation which causes unit costs to fall from c_1 to c_2 and the G_f curve to shift downward to the right. The equilibrium price will then be lowered from p_1^* to p_2^*.

Shapiro attempts to refine the theory by introducing two additional determinants of the firm's pricing decision, namely, product competition and strategic pricing. With regard to strategic pricing, Shapiro writes:

> The firm is always intent on sustaining the strategic price and does whatever is in its power to convince its customers that the strategic price is the 'real worth' of the good. Where temporary market circumstances force the firm to shave the price, it does so in a way which maintains the association of the good with the strategic price in the minds of buyers. It reduces the price by giving rebates, putting the good on sale, etc. The strategic price is, in effect, the real worth or 'intrinsic value' of the product. It is the value bound up with the commodity in that it reflects the particular place of the commodity in the growth process of the firm and its specific contribution to the firm's growth.[47]

In view of these developments, we fully agree with the following assessment made by Martin Shubik:

> Since the defeat of the institutionalists, there have been many new developments in economics that I believe are going to result in a joining together of detailed institutuional studies, advanced mathematical economic theory and political economy.

---

[47] Nina Shapiro, op. cit., p. 99.

I expect that a new microeconomics is about to emerge. It can be described (in a ponderous manner) [48] as mathematical-institutional-political economy.

Behavioral Theory

Renewed interest in the behavioral theory of the firm and the development of evolutionary models certainly bears out Shubik's prediction. The behavioral theory of the firm can be considered as another illustration of "selective approaches" to economic theorizing. Conventional theory of the firm falls under the category of "general theory" for it is designed to explain how the price system functions as a mechanism for allocating resources among markets. Behavioral theory, on the other hand, asks a different set of questions--questions designed to discover the way in which resources are allocated within the firm. The building blocks of the behavioral theory of the firm are four major sub-theories, namely, (a) organizational goals, (b) organizational expectations, (c) organizational choice and (d) organizational control. [49] The Arrow, Radner, Shapiro and Stiglitz papers mentioned earlier in this chapter are not far removed from the behaviorists' tenets.

---

[48] Martin Shubik, op. cit., pp. 406-407.

[49] See Richard M. Cyert and James G. March, A BEHAVIORAL THEORY OF THE FIRM (Englewood Cliffs, New Jersey, Prentice-Hall, Inc., 1963, Chapter 6. Kalman J. Cohen and Richard M. Cyert point out: "The behavioral theory of the firm takes the position that arguments over motivation are somewhat fruitless. The critical issue is not whether one assumes proximizing instead of satisficing behavior. Instead, it is fruitful to develop an understanding of the process of decision making within the firm. The behavioral theory is viewed as supplementing the conventional theory of the firm. The traditional theory is essentially one in

Evolutionary theory explicitly admits the possibility of disequilibrium behavior. "In not assuming the system is in equilibrium," observes Richard R. Nelson and Sidney Winter, "the evolutionary theory leaves room, for example, for considerable 'slack' and nonprofit maximizing behavior in a competitive industry which is moving toward an equilibrium but which may not be close yet, and which may not get close before the equilibrium moves away from it. This means that many of the normative implications of the neoclassical theory may not go through. But, if the system is presumed to be close to equilibrium, these differences may dissolve."[50]

The neoclassical allocative efficiency concept is also questioned by Harvey Leibenstein's X-efficiency theory of the firm.[51] Like the behavioral approach, the X-efficiency theory is concerned with inefficiencies inside the firm. As pointed out by Leibenstein, "There may be inefficiency in (1)

---

[49], cont. which certain broad questions are asked. Specifically, the conventional theory of the firm is designed to explain the way in which the price system functions as a mechanism for allocating resources among markets; relatively little is said about resource allocation within the firm. For the purpose of the classical theory, the profit maximization assumption may be perfectly adequate. It is clear, however that as one asks a different set of questions, specifically questions designed to uncover the way in which resources are allocated within the firm, the profit maximization assumption is neither necessary nor sufficient for answering these questions." See their THEORY OF THE FIRM (Englewood Cliffs, New Jersey, 1965), p. 330.

[50] See Richard R. Nelson and Sidney G. Winter, "Factor Price Changes and Factor Substitution in Evolutionary Model," THE BELL JOURNAL OF ECONOMICS, Autumn, 1975, No. 2, p. 468.

[51] See Harvey Leibenstein, "X-Efficiency: From Concept to Theory," CHALLENGE, Sept./Oct., 1979.

labor utilization, (2) capital utilization, (3) time sequence, (4) extent of employee cooperation, (5) information flow, (6) bargaining effectiveness, (7) credit availability utilization and (8) heuristic procedures."[52] The main differences between the neoclassical theory and the X-efficiency paradigm are given by Leibenstein in Table 9-1.[53]

TABLE 9-1

Components	X-Efficiency Theory	Neoclassical Theory
1. Psychology	1. Selective rationality	1. Maximization or minimization
2. Contracts	2. Incomplete	2. Complete
3. Effort	3. Discretionary variable	3. Assumed given
4. Units	4. Individuals	4. Households and firms
5. Inert areas	5. Important variable	5. None
6. Agent-principal	6. Differential	6. Identity of interests

[52] See Harvey Leibenstein, op. cit., p. 14.

[53] See Harvey Leibenstein, "The General X-Efficiency Paradigm and the Role of the Entrepreneur," in Mario J. Rizzo, ed., TIME, UNCERTAINTY AND DISEQUILIBRIUM (Lexington Books, 1979), p. 129.

Leibenstein points out that X-Efficiency theory is based on the following four major postulates:

(1)   The individual, not the firm, is the basic decision unit. This includes individuals participating in committees which make decisions.

(2)   Individuals have some discretion with respect to the nature and amount of effort put forth within certain bounds because employment contracts are generally incomplete. For instance, the payment part is known in a contract situation, but the effort part is either fuzzy or not stated. Contract incompleteness would therefore imply the existence of effort discretion.

(3)   Within certain bounds, inertia will exist. Therefore a position taken within these bounds, associated with a certain utility, will not result in a movement to another position, even if this other position is associated with a higher utility.

(4)   Individualizers do not behave as maximizers. Instead we assume that individual behavior depends on a balance of internal and external pressures. Pressure internal to the individual also depends on a balance of opposing motivating forces—on such factors as conscience, self-interest and the desire for approval, on the one hand, and on "animal spirits," including the urge to avoid responsibility, on the other.

Leibenstein further insists:

If the individual is the decision-maker with respect to effort (he has some effort discretion),

279

then he is in a position to make an effort decision that is not necessarily in the best interest of the firm. Furthermore, this is true of all firm members. Hence, there is no fixed relation between inputs and outputs....The first conclusion is that for given inputs there is a variety of outputs possible.[54]

It is interesting to note that the behaviorist postulates of Leibenstein have provided him with an important criticism of the neoclassical production function which is quite different from that of Joan Robinson.[55]

Labor

Institutional factors have also been emphasized by researchers in the area of labor economics. The outburst of literature on "segmented labor market" theory in response to human capital theory is a case in point. Through the work of Theodore Schultz, Jacob Mincer, Gary S. Becker and others, human capital theory gained a position of prominence in labor economics beginning in the 1960s.[56] It integrated labor

---

[54] Harvey Leibenstein, "X-Efficiency: From Concept to Theory," op. cit., p. 16.

[55] See Joan Robinson, "The Production Function and the Theory of Capital," in COLLECTED ECONOMICS PAPERS, Vol. 2 (Blackwell, 1965), pp. 114-131. First published in REVIEW OF ECONOMIC STUDIES, Vol. 21, 1953-54, pp. 81-106. Also see G.C. Harcourt, SOME CAMBRIDGE CONTROVERSIES IN THE THEORY OF CAPITAL, op. cit., pp. 11-46.

[56] Jacob Mincer, "Investment in Human Capital and Personal Income Distribution," JOURNAL OF POLITICAL ECONOMY, Vol. 56, August 1958; Theodore W. Schultz, "Investment in Human Capital," AMERICAN ECONOMIC REVIEW 51 (March 1961), p. 1-17; Gary S. Becker, "Investment in Human Capital: A

economics with the economics of health and education and reinforced the tie between labor economics and general economic theory through its application of capital theory and investment analysis.

Human capital theory was not without controversy, however. In the minds of some, it amounted to treating men as machines. Others complained the theory legitimized the status quo; justifying current income distribution as the natural result of differential investment in additional knowledge and skills.

Alternative explanations of the apparent link between human capital investment and labor market outcomes were advanced focusing on institutional factors. Lester Thurow's job competition model introduces certification where "the function of education is not to confer skill and therefore increase productivity and higher wages on the worker; it is rather to certify his 'trainability' and to confer upon him a certain job status by virtue of his certification. Jobs and higher income are then distributed on the basis of this certified status."[57]

Segmentation/dual labor market models "differ from the human capital model in their focus on the characteristics of jobs and job markets, rather than the characteristics of individuals.[58] The work of Michael Piore and Peter Doeringer

[56,cont.] Theoretical Analysis," JOURNAL OF POLITICAL ECONOMY, Vol. 70, Supplement #5, Oct. 1962.

[57] Lester C. Thurow, "Education and Economic Inequality," PUBLIC INTEREST 28, Summer 1972.

[58] Greg J. Duncan and Saul Hoffman, "On the Job Training and Earnings, Differences by Race and Sex," THE REVIEW OF ECONOMICS AND STATISTICS, Vol. 61, November 1979, p. 594. Segmentationists view jobs and job markets as interceding between the individual and his/her decision to invest in formal training, on-the-job training or any other form of

which borrows from multiple disciplines, incorporating sociological and political concepts with those of economics, is representative of these efforts.[59] They have been labeled "Neoinstitutionalists" as their institutionalist lineage can be traced through John Dunlop and Sumner Slichter to John R. Commons, the Father of American Institutionalism.

The interaction of human capital theory and its alternative explanations point toward synthesis. The criticism of human capital theory is not so much with its "correctness" as with its "completeness." Segmentation theories identify labor market institutions and practices that act as barriers to the unfettered market implicitly envisioned by human capital theory. The subjective nature of the hiring process, entry level discrimination confounding transition from secondary to primary labor markets, the importance of internal labor markets, are all concepts emphasizing the role of economic agents (beyond the individual) in the determination of earnings. Recognition of institutional factors adds life and realism to the discussion but does not refute the validity of the human capital approach.

[58, cont.] human capital undertaking. Organizational or sectoral characteristics are viewed as impacting on determination of individual earnings. Earnings are viewed as determined by the labor market in which the individual works. Earnings may not solely reflect human capital endowments but also the assignment of groups of individuals to specific sectors due to institutional rigidities, custom, discrimination, etc.

[59] The concepts of primary and secondary labor markets, and core and peripheral sectors are clearly reminiscent of earlier discussions of internal labor markets, balkanization, etc., found in the work of Clark Kerr, John Dunlop and others. Peter Doeringer and Michael Piore, INTERNAL LABOR MARKETS AND MANPOWER ANALYSIS (Lexington, MA: Lexington Books, 1971).

Blaug, commenting on the screening hypothesis, perceptively points out that:

> ...there is nothing about this argument that is incompatible with human capital theory....Even in the extreme version of credentialism, we are still left with an explanation of the demand for schooling that is the same as that of human capital theory: screening by employers in terms of educational credentials creates an incentive on the part of employees to produce the signal that maximizes the probability of being selected, namely, the possession of an educational qualification, and this signaling incentive is in fact conveyed by the private rate of return of educational investment.[60]

Neoinstitutional theorists have had a major impact upon human capital theory. The synthesis has been in the direction of completeness, robustness and realism rather than unanimity of opinion. Irvin Sobel succinctly expresses this vision of synthesis:

> These conclusions also imply that labor economics, while enriched and broadened by the human capital concept, and thereby joining the mainstream of economic theory both in content and methodology, will never lose its basic institutional core. In fact, that core will be even more significant heuristically. It also means that human capital and institutional theories are complements rather than rivals.[61]

---

[60] Mark Blaug, "The Empirical Status of Human Capital Theory: A Slightly Jaundiced Survey," JOURNAL OF ECONOMIC LITERATURE, Vol. 14(3), September 1976, p. 847.

[61] Irvin Sobel, "Human Capital and Institutional Theories of the Labor Market: Rivals or Complements," JOURNAL OF ECONOMIC ISSUES, Vol. 16(1), March 1982, p. 268.

Prospect of Convergence

The controversies of the past 15 years or more have paved the way for a possible general concensus in the economic profession. The strong points of the opposing groups have been accepted by economists of different persuasions. The significance of "historical time" has been emphasized by general equilibrium theorists. As early as 1971 Arrow and Hahn recognized that money is not only a link between the past and the present, but also a link between the present and the future. The Hicksian "sequential causality" has been adopted in the search for non-Walrasian equilibria mentioned earlier in this chapter. In this respect, general equilibrium theory is not too far separated from Post-Keynesian economics and the Neo-Austrian emphasis on "market process."

The strong hold of the traditional optimization and choice-theoretical framework of economic analysis has been loosened; the behaviorist tenets have gradually won general approval. This chapter clearly indicates that trend. We concur with the following observation of John D. Hey:

> Recent years have witnessed a significant increase in the complexity of the problems supposedly solved by the economic agents. This is particularly so in the branch of economics devoted to the investigation of disequilibrium.[62]

Concomitantly, the importance of institutional factors has been stressed by all sides. For years Paul Davidson has pleaded for the treatment of money in the framework of the real world, for money is essentially an institutuional phenomenon. Now Davidson's plea is no longer a voice in the wilderness. As a beginning, researchers in the area of temporary equilibrium have incorporated money into their

---

[62] John D. Hey, op. cit., p. 242.

models.[63] The earliest attempt was made by Frank H. Hahn (1965).[63] Following Hahn, J.M. Grandmont and G. Laroque made further studies with similar frameworks (1972, 1973).[64] A brief review of these developments was made by Allan Drazen in 1980.[65] The following observation of Martin Shubik may provide some guidance for future research in monetary theory:

> A complete theory of money will need at least three distinguished players. They are: some abstract form of governmental body whose preferences and powers must be stated; a distinguished player representing an abstraction of a financial intermediary. The financial intermediary, as a good first approximation in some cases (provided it is not organized as a mutual), can be regarded as maximizing its profits. The third set of players consists of everyone else. When we restrict our model to them alone we would have a general equilibrium barter model.[66]

Institutional factors have long been emphasized by researchers in the area of labor economics. The literature on "segmented labor markets" theories is a case in point.

---

[63] F.H. Hahn, "On Some Problems of Proving the Existence of an Equilibrium in a Monetary Economy," in THE THEORY OF INTEREST RATS, ed. by F.H. Hahn and Brechling (London: Macmillan, 1965).

[64] J.M. Grandmont and G. Laroque, "Money in the Pure Consumption Loan Model," JOURNAL OF ECONOMIC THEORY 6 (1973), pp. 382-395; J.M.Grandmont and G. Laroque, "On the Role of Money and the Existence of a Monetary Equilibrium," REVIEW OF ECONOMIC STUDIES, 39(1972), pp. 355-372.

[65] Allan Drazen, op. cit., pp. 299-302.

[66] Martin Shubik, op. cit., p. 429.

The strong points of their arguments can no longer be ignored by contemporary neoclassical labor economists. The return of institutions in both micro and macro theorizing has been further facilitated by the advance of computational capabilities. Continuing developments in mathematical methods and operations analysis will also help to make this aspiration a reality.

Future convergence of economic theories has been supported also by trends of development in the socialist camp. (See the introduction of this book.) Neo-Marxists are beginning to see the irrelevance of the labor theory of value in contemporary monetary economics of industrial capitalism. Fascination with Classical and Marxian theories which once dominated the Neo-Ricardians has also gradually evaporated. The "Sraffian Revolution" too has been viewed in its proper perspective (see Alfred S. Eichner's comments in the preceding section). Frank Hahn gave a balanced observation (1981) as follows:

> The theory (General Equilibrium) itself, however, is likely to recede and be superseded. There seems absolutely no reason to believe that the new theory will have been anticipated by some defunct 19th century economist or that it will be in the form of linear identities. Nor, on the other hand, does it seem likely that it will give much support to those who are now teaching politicians from vulgarizing neoclassical textbooks.[67]

In light of the afore-mentioned trend indicators, we share the optimistic views of some members of the economic profession that the emergence of a "New Synthesis" is not just an impossible dream and that the so-called "crises in economic theory" may soon be resolved.

---

[67] Frank Hahn, "General Equilibrium Theory," in THE CRISIS IN ECONOMIC THEORY, op. cit., pp. 137-138.

INDEX OF NAMES

Forman, Leonard	7
Friedman, Milton	150, 152, 153, 154, 155, 156, 157, 159, 188, 189, 235
Fullarton, John	237
Galbraith, John Kenneth	1, 269
Garegnani, P.	4, 193, 201
Gibson, William E.	151
Gordon, Robert J.	255, 256, 271
Gram, Harvey	16, 17
Grandmont, Jean Michel	119, 131, 257, 266, 285
Granger, C.W.J.	100
Green, J.R.	263
Gossen, Heinrich	265
Grossman, Herschel	5, 131, 135, 137, 139, 140, 255
Hahn, Frank H.	3, 6, 129, 130, 188, 228, 239, 248, 258, 261, 262, 263, 264, 266, 284, 285, 286
Hailstones, Thomas J.	11
Halevy, Elie	12
Harcourt, G.C.	4, 72, 93, 126, 193, 198, 199, 209
Harrod, Roy	74, 94, 182, 207, 208
Hawtrey, R.G.	158
Hayek, F.A.	158, 176, 181
Herries, J.C.	80
Hey, John D.	257, 258, 260, 261, 263, 264, 266, 284
Hicks, Sir John	1, 4, 6, 12, 20, 32, 96-102, 105, 106, 107, 121, 131, 132, 144, 145, 182, 185, 186, 187, 188, 189, 228, 229, 248, 249, 257, 266
Hindess, Barry	2
Hirst, Paul	2
Hoffman, Saul	281
Hollander, Samuel	26
Horner, Francis	80
Hsieh, Ching-Yao	90, 163, 198, 219
Huffnagle, John D.	221
Hume, David	23, 150, 165
Hussain, Athar	2
Jeans, Sir James	95

Spence, William	84
Spencer, Roger W.	158, 163
Sraffa, Piero	4, 5, 45, 59-72, 84, 193, 239, 242
Stanlis, Peter J.	22
Steindle, Joseph	75, 239, 241, 242, 272, 273
Stigler, George J.	44, 46, 58, 121, 122, 124
Stiglitz, Joseph E.	268, 269
Stuck, John	7
Suppes, P.	219
Svensson, Lars E.O.	258, 263, 264, 265
Swamy, P.A.V.B.	172
Swan, T.W.	12, 17
Tatom, John A.	11
Tawney, Ralph H.	38
Thornton, Henry	80, 150, 165
Thurow, Lester	281
Tinsley, P.A.	172
Tobin, James	76, 77, 78
Tooke, Thomas	237
Torrens, Colonel Rober	237
Trotter, Coutts	80
Vansittart, Nicholas	80
Veblen, Thornstein Bunde	265, 269
Viner, Jacob	81
von Mises, Ludwig	174, 175, 176, 178, 180
von Neumann, J.	16, 30, 75, 218, 239, 242
von Schmoller, Gustav	265
Wallace, Neil	4, 75, 164, 165, 173
Walras, Leon	109, 127, 128, 129, 137, 139, 141, 142, 144, 180, 193
Walsh, Vivian	16, 17
Weber, Max	38
Weintraub, E. Roy	106, 108, 118, 253
Weintraub, Sidney	4, 59, 193, 232, 233, 246
Whaeately, John	80
Wiggins, James W.	176
Wilcox, James A.	271
Willes, Mark H.	164
Wicksell, Knut	150, 186
Wicksteed, Philip	122

INDEX OF SUBJECTS